THE SPRINGS OF JEWISH LIFE

Chaim Raphael

Basic Books, Inc., Publishers

NEW YORK

Library of Congress Cataloging in Publication Data

Raphael, Chaim.
The springs of Jewish life.

Bibliography: p. 272
Includes index.
1. Judaism—History. 2. Jews—History. I. Title.
BM155.2.R36 1982 296'.09 82-70853
ISBN 0-465-08192-4

Printed in the United States of America
Designed by Vincent Torre
10 9 8 7 6 5 4 3 2 1

The Springs of Jewish Life

Contents

Introduction: *The Nature of Jewish Consciousness* 3
Chapter 1 *The Bible in Jewish Life* 20
Chapter 2 *The Babylonian Exile and the Return* 34
Chapter 3 *Ideas in the Hellenist Setting* 51
Chapter 4 *Dramas in the Roman Setting* 80
Chapter 5 *The Roman-Jewish War* 113
Chapter 6 *Outlook of the Rabbis* 131
Chapter 7 *Judaism and Christianity* 151
Chapter 8 *The Parting of the Ways* 170
Chapter 9 *Diaspora Judaism* 192
Chapter 10 *Patterns of Experience* 213
Chapter 11 *The Dynamics of Jewish History* 235
APPENDIX Feasts and Fasts of the Jewish Year 259
LIST OF ABBREVIATIONS 263
NOTES 264
BOOKS FOR FURTHER READING 272
INDEX 277

The Springs of Jewish Life

Introduction:

The Nature of Jewish Consciousness

A Will to Live

HIS IS NOT one more book of straight Jewish history but one which tries to deal with the central issue within it.

My English publisher, who is not Jewish, told me that the book on the Jews that she wanted to read—and publish—would pin down a question that takes many forms in her mind. Where do the Jews get their will to live, defying every attempt to destroy them and, equally, every seduction into safe anonymity? Are there some imperatives flowing into the life of Jews that instill this will to live, and if so, where do they come from? Does Jewish cohesion spring from universally held religious beliefs, or is it just defensive, a reaction to persecution?

And at the personal level, I think she was also saying to me, with Hitler's horror vivid in both our minds, how does it feel, from within, to know that one has been living out through history the words that the prophet Isaiah seems to have composed not for Jesus but for every Jew: "He is despised and rejected of men, a man of sorrows, and acquainted with grief."

This last point is so remote from what I feel about being born into the Jewish people that I felt tempted, for a moment, to write a book that would be unbalanced in the opposite direction. In this mood, I conceived the idea that I would call the book *A Cheerful Look at the Jews,* hoping to dissipate, with one unexpected word, the woe and self-pity that fill so much Jewish writing. To set out Jewish history as a story of suffering, intensified beyond all measure in our own day, can easily be justified by the facts; yet by itself it is surely an arrid presentation of what Jews have meant to themselves and to the world in these long centuries. If I introduced the word *cheerful,* no one would think that I had done this casually, still less, jokingly. Surely, it would bring out instantly the spirit that animated those who survived the blackest of horrors and kept their courage high.

I still feel that there is a quality in this word that says something about the Jews. But it does not define the deeper question: What is the source of this courage? How was the spirit that comes out in the Jewish will to live forged in antiquity and kept alive until today.

What I examine here, therefore, are the springs of Jewish life, flowing powerfully in ancient times and, by a miracle, still life-giving today. Of those Jews who survived all the various forms of persecution, many bowed their heads in despair and even self-hatred. But Jewish life flowed on, as if with a secret energy. Where does this spirit come from? I have been intimately aware of it in my own lifetime, as surely every Jew has who, by the merest accident —almost the throw of a dice—escaped the fate that overwhelmed the millions. One feels impelled almost in piety to look in a book of history for the elements that gave Jews a unique kind of fulfillment. To look solely at the tragedies is to turn one's back on a living and sustaining miracle.

This is not a miracle which rests solely on the ancient marvel of the Bible, though this heritage alone fills the mind with enduring wonder. Jewish history can indeed be interpreted, in one approach, as a continuous exploration of the holiness and poetry of the Bible; but in the same breath it is an entirely human story, a secular story, a celebration of kinship by the people who first created the Bible and were then themselves re-created by the book they had brought into being.

One has to say *celebration* of kinship to offset the pallid idea, often heard, that Jewish survival has meant merely lingering on against all odds, century after century. The Jews would never have survived if this had been what Jewish life was like from within. The opposite was, in fact, true. There is a dynamic in Jewish consciousness which, in every age, has infused Jewish existence with a new transforming experience. This is not to say that the result has always been positive and attractive. Jews are not necessarily loveable, even to the unprejudiced. As human beings, they have their fair share of sinners and no extra endowment of saints.

What does seem extra to them is the quality first shown in the Bible—an eagerness to put some meaning into life. Even in the eras of overwhelming sadness, there is a vitalizing principle at work. Jewish life has not been merely resilient but creative. The form of this creativity has never been predictable. One knows only that it will be tuned, in decisive and original ways, to the varieties of background in which Jews find themselves. The hallmark is a sense of urgency which is inspiriting, intellectually and emotionally—an exploration of life that seeks and generates fulfillment.

It is uplifting, looking back, to feel that one is part of this everflowing vitality; yet one needs to be cautious. The idea is to take in Jewish history in a way that can be sad without self-pity, involved without megalomania, proud —this is the hardest part—without vainglory.

This last word—pleasantly archaic—is brought in from the beginning to counter another misleading tendency in much historical writing which seeks to offset suffering by elevating the Jews—"source of three of the great religions of mankind"—into an almost cosmic role, as a unique embodiment of God's purpose and man's discernment. Perhaps there is only a thin line between self-confidence and "we're the greatest," but it is something to watch out for. The pride that Jews are entitled to feel reflects not superiority but self-respect. The identifiable heritage into which Jews are born offers a base of endless interest; but if we are assessing their creativity, this is only part of the story. In some ways, certainly, the Jews have established their character through the exploration of their own heritage; in other ways, the sense of fulfillment is a mark of Jewish absorption in the world outside—giving and receiving, and in this dual process enlarging man's vision.

The story is too long, too full of contradictions, too varied in tone to be summarized as expressing some set purpose either of God or man. The Jews have embodied, equally, narrowness and broadness of vision. They have turned their backs on the world and responded to it with fertile imagination. They have produced good men and scoundrels, quiet citizens asking to be left alone and activists obsessed with change. There is unity in the story for a Jew because he identifies with all aspects of this experience. The affection and fellowship which are at the core of Jewish life turn kinship into an open-ended exploration. In this search, all of us are drawing on the same heritage, which had already taken shape two thousand years ago. One looks back, then, for the sources of this heritage.

To put ourselves, the Jews of today, at the heart of this inquiry immediately brings to light a quality that separates Jewish history from the usual pattern.

Because of the stories of persecution which are all too familiar, Jewish history often seems simply to present Jews as being disposed of by other peoples. The Jews are taken as a datum, and we are then told what happened to them. But this leaves out of account the essential generative power in Jewish life itself. To have one's eyes fixed predominantly on what happened to the Jews turns them, as the great historian Salo Baron said in a pregnant phrase, from subject to object. It opens up one's concept of being a Jew to consider the meaning of this cryptic remark.

To look on the Jews as an object of history is to see them always as operated on by others—a familiar enough notion in which a helpless people is buffeted at every turn by contempt and persecution. Jewish history can certainly be told this way; and a Jew today, fed with this idea, can find it filling his consciousness.

In the opposite approach, the Jew is his own subject. The events of his life are woven into the history of his time and place; but the character of the Jew is his own creation, and it is in this independent, self-sustaining form that he must be seen in history. The values by which Jews live will never be uniform, nor will the way they operate on individual Jews be easy to determine. It is as if there is a reservoir of thought and motivation on which a Jew draws, consciously and unconsciously, to give substance to feelings which would otherwise be fragmentary and sterile. For some, there are unshakable absolutes at stake; for others, the connection develops new meanings, not as dogma but as illumination, with ideas of different ages striking the mind with personal relevance. But if there is no uniformity, there is a continuum; and it is the character of this continuum and the springs which filled it in pre-Diaspora days that I talk about in this book, not to surrender to the past but to assert our place in it as living Jews today.

If I emphasize *today,* it is because our self-evaluation now reflects something more than ordinary change. In no period of history have inborn Jewish feelings been injected with more content and drama. Most obviously, this has been an era in which alternating tragedy and pride have filled Jewish minds with an intensity never before imaginable. But there are also other factors at work. For one thing, historical discovery has, in our time, offered Jews a new enrichment of intellectual and emotional delight. But beyond this, the Jews today are in a totally different world setting. The independence of their interior life, which Jews have always carried with them, is matched now by social independence, a startling change from the position two hundred years ago. In a double sense, it may be said, a Jew is now born free.

To say this is not some glib way of ignoring the unexampled horror of Nazi Germany or of pretending that hatred, prejudice, and exclusion in the old forms do not exist and surface everywhere. History has left a baleful mark, perhaps forever. Yet to interpret this into some generalization that nothing changes is to turn one's back to the realities of Jewish experience in the world we now live in. The Jew of today who, in a great variety of ways, still meets age-old prejudice is not the Jew who was bowed down by this in years gone by. There are new factors in the equation, not universal but dominant enough to have introduced a sea change in Jewish personality. The visible marks of a new self-confidence reflect the political and economic position of the Jews and the manifold expressions of their creativity. To this must be added the intense desire of the world at large to come to terms, after centuries of hostility or indifference, with the mainsprings of Jewish feeling. In all these ways, the Jew has become, more than ever, his own subject. What he makes of his Jewish heritage is now, in a quite new way, his own choice.

But if Jews today are, in this sense, born free, the story never comes to them without trailing ancient clouds of affection and memory. Even before we begin, we know that there are two elements in Jewish consciousness which are in the scene to stay, as if they were lighthouses to our feelings. The first is our sense of kinship or loyalty, where the beacon is always visible. The second, a more flickering light, is a sense of aspiration—a reverence for life, for nature, for the unseen, the unreachable, the power that transmutes daily existence with a recognition of holiness. There is a mystery in both feelings which history must illuminate, but with our anchor still in the present. Throughout the centuries, millions abandoned the ties of kinship and were lost to Jewish life; and of those who never ceased to consider themselves Jews, adherence to a formal religious faith has ranged between total belief and indifference. Yet one is always aware of these two forces in the background.

In our own time they might seem to have moved, paradoxically, in opposite directions. Kinship has intensified in the focus of the Holocaust and the emergence of the State of Israel. Religious faith, in contrast, has unquestionably weakened in line with a similar decline among other religions. Taking this by itself, one would conclude, as many do, that the Jewish attachment today has become dominantly secular in tone.

In fact, however, a summation of this kind is far too superficial. It leaves out of account a unique aspect of Jewish consciousness, in which the sense of kinship is never reducible to social loyalty and always carries with it memories or echoes of the stirring issues in which kinship first took shape. The more strongly that Jewish secular loyalty expresses itself, as it does today, the more insistent becomes the desire to recapture something of the elemental power that has harnessed Jewish thought, from earliest times, to the deep questions of man's fate on earth—the awareness of moral absolutes, the sense of duty and responsibility, the dedication to truth, the opening up of the mind to powers beyond oneself. Against the background of a secularist age, this drive to bring out what lies buried in Jewish kinship makes itself felt all the more clearly, however diverse are the forms of its expression. For some the new impetus expresses itself in a revival of interest in Jewish theology. For others it takes shape in art forms—in the novel, music, painting, or poetry. Others again, sometimes unconsciously, have testified to the content of their Jewish past in a passion for sociological or psychological study or in revolutionary politics.

In every century of the long Diaspora, those Jews who stayed within the fold or hovered on the edge or rebelled against it were reflecting in different ways the passions that had gone into forging Jewish identity in the dim past, which is the subject of this book.

The Nature of Jewish Identity

That Jews give expression to many aspects of their heritage even without a formal knowledge of Jewish history is a reflection of two complementary forces operating on their consciousness.

The first, predictably, is a carryover from familiar elements in the Jewish background, expressed not as abstract creed but as an amalgam compounded of ritual, prayers, stories, myths, legends, and a moral code—indefinable—that emerges from fellowship. Anyone born a Jew is aware of this as a hovering tradition, to be absorbed, explored, enjoyed—or resisted.

The complementary force, immensely formative to Jewish character, stems from the inescapable fact of Jewish distinctiveness. A Jew does not merely live out the implications of his own tradition, vaguely or deeply understood; he is always in tension—mostly a creative tension—with the world outside. A knowledge of history documents this; but a Jew feels it as a stimulus even without an informed awareness of how this tension has expressed itself in the past.

To be different has posed unending problems, material and psychological. The situation of which this is a part has sometimes exploded into tragedies beyond words. But this is not the enduring picture. Hard as it is to say this in the shadow of the greatest tragedy of all, the distinctiveness of the Jew has not been, throughout history, a formula for fear and negativism. The sorrow that stands so starkly in the foreground is not the abiding picture. One sees this easily enough merely by considering what this small, "helpless" people has achieved during its existence. We shall find, indeed, that the distinctive status of the Jews is precisely what has given their identity a unique cutting edge of meaning.

Jews have been "different," until our own time, in two ways. First, their religion and the social practices it enjoined have, from the most ancient times, set them apart. Second, they were for many centuries, following the destruction by the Romans of what remained of their state, a people without a land of their own, the eternal stranger. Yet when we examine what happened to the Jews in the act of becoming homeless, we see the beginning of a change in their life that was to make them, ultimately, an extraordinary carrying force for the adventure of living. History opened up for them in a new way. The grip on them of their ancient homeland was transmuted into the vitalizing challenge of existence as a world people.

Until that time, Jewish kinship had been expressed in the passion which Jews felt for their national-religious cult, centering on the Temple at Jerusalem. There was a pattern of worship for every Jew, in which the Temple was the focus. Behind this—explaining it, justifying it—there was folk memory, expressed in history, ceremony, law, and literature, going back a thousand years. But the Temple was the anchor of what was otherwise a wildly chaotic and certainly amorphous political and social existence.

The Temple was burned down by the Romans in A.D. 70 and never rebuilt. This is when the decisive mutation in Jewish history took place, destroying all preconceived ideas of how fate and doom work themselves out. The Jews had lost their anchor; the kinship which fused them might have been expected, in time, to lose its power. Instead, Jewish loyalty, far from being weakened, was invigorated. A people whose traditions had been, until then, internal and almost parochial in range emerged, in the centuries which followed, reinforced with a faith in themselves that became a vibrant element in world history. It was not that they now saw the need, in adapting themselves to constantly changing surroundings, to play down what was special in their own traditions. On the contrary, it was Jewish distinctiveness that now acquired new satisfaction and strength. Jerusalem was still the anchor of Jewish identity; but where before it was attached to a political setting which had no chance of survival, it was now transformed with infinitely greater power into a dream.

To understand the generative power of this dream, one has to see it lighting up the dark places, strengthening the Jews, uniting them, giving them a long and steady view of life, so that wherever they were and in whatever circumstances, there was something to draw on that spelled hope and cheerfulness. The dream of Jerusalem, with all its overtones of kinship and faith, brought enlargement, growing century after century in the power it had to add magic to the routine of living. To let it evaporate—to give up one's historic involvement in the adventure of Jewish existence—was betrayal, not of the Jewish people but of oneself.

The transformation of the Jews into a world people did not begin with the destruction of the Temple but took on a form, in that period, that would give Jewish existence its unique character. Jews were already living in great numbers throughout all the countries of the Mediterranean and the Middle East; and in some of these lands, notably in Babylonia, a long settled existence away from the ancestral home had already shaped the characteristic mixed pattern of distinctiveness and absorption. Yet until Jerusalem fell, there was no full acceptance of Diaspora (which means *dispersal*) as a norm. The vestiges of self-government in the Holy Land still conveyed authority. The Temple, calling for thrice-yearly pilgrimages at festival times, was the lodestar. When the news came of its destruction, the Jews of the existing Diaspora were too scattered to unite in a fight to restore it. The despair they felt was expressed, instead, in fierce local revolts in various parts of the Roman Empire, mainly in protest against edicts forbidding Jewish religious practice. For a time there were stories current that the Romans were relenting and would allow the Temple to be rebuilt. The end of all such hopes came with the crushing of the Bar Kokhba rebellion in Palestine itself, in A.D. 135.

With hindsight, one can see how the ending of these pitiable struggles began to set the scene for a flowering of Jewish life in forms that would no longer be determined by the economic, social, and cultural conditions of a small, rocky, and distracted homeland. With the loss of Jerusalem, an unutterable sadness had spread over the Jews; but mixed with the vivid feeling of tragedy there was, potentially, a sense of liberation. Henceforth, as we can now see, the Jews, as a people of the world, would follow their fortune wherever the opportunity arose, different from their neighbors but open to every kind of influence from the varied environments in which they were to live. Like the majority of mankind they would mostly be poor and harassed, and in a particular sense they would be looked on with suspicion and dislike. Yet this separateness—both imposed and self-sustained—would be a spur. As conscious "outsiders," they would be alert and adventurous, gaining experience and building connections in many countries, in one sense homeless, in another, carrying their home with them. Politically, they would be imposed on wherever they lived; but offsetting this they would be uniquely independent—inviolate—in the security of faith and the memory of Jerusalem. Daily life would be a struggle for economic existence; and at times hatred, danger, expulsion, and murder—rising to hideous proportions—would threaten the ultimate base for survival; but the kinship they carried with them would be a living force, indestructible, growing in power as the passage of time saw it exemplified in a thousand forms and with enduring satisfaction.

History is full of examples of the adventures of emigrants in new lands, settling, adapting themselves to new ways, but always keeping alive, in varying degrees, a vestigial attachment to their lands and peoples of origin. This was the story of the Jews but with the attachment infinitely greater in scale and intensity. Looking for the reason, one sees first the fateful emergence of an opposing force, Christianity, which, as it swept through Europe and took on much of the secular power of the Roman Empire, gave the Jew, willy-nilly, a lasting identifiable role—a dual role, in effect. In the deepest sense, the Jew, by virtue of the traditions and faith of the Bible, was essential to Christianity; in the same breath—by the same token—he was the eternal enemy, the unbeliever, the outsider. In a Christian world, the Jew could never be irrelevant; there would be a lasting battle, from both sides, taking many forms. One obvious effect would be a constant seepage by Jews into assimilation with the dominant civilization; but the tension would also intensify the sense of identity among those Jews who clung obstinately to their own faith and pride. Sometimes their obstinacy would express itself in obscurity, a low profile; but for the most part it was an open dialectic, with vibrant power. There was not much tolerance in the air from either side; but the Jew found a way to live, both cut off and involved, fearful yet proud, inward-looking but alert to the world outside, rooted yet ready to move. It was a hostile world, but he had a place in it. Everything in his tradition, going back to the days of Abraham, made it seem natural that he would be in some sort of tension with his neighbors; but this tradition provided its own sustainment, the comforts of kin and ritual, a moral and intellectual stance which came with the inheritance, and behind it all the escape into a dream, the dream of Jerusalem.

If Jewish identity reinforced itself through the centuries in its oppositional stance to Christianity, it flowered in a different way through taking root in the rich civilization which Christianity gave birth to in Europe; and the same process was evident in the Muslim world in its periods of high culture. So much is usually written, rather bombastically, about "the Jewish contribution" to the Christian and Muslim worlds that the other equally important point tends to get overlooked: what about the contribution of these worlds to the Jews? It is not a question of weighing one against the other but rather of recognizing what being part of a wider society has meant for the substantiation of Jewish identity.

To emphasize the Jewish contributions might seem at first more comforting to amour propre, and if this is one's approach, there is certainly no difficulty in making a list. In producing the Bible, the Jews gave the world an inexhaustible treasure. In later centuries, scattered among the nations, the roll call of Jewish service to mankind is endless: in the arts, science, philosophy, government, industry, and trade. The climax of this kind of exposition is usually reached with a recital of the astonishing number of Jewish (and ex-Jewish) Nobel prizewinners. What one needs to understand, however, is the nature of the drive within Jews that could release such fertile originality.

This drive always seems to carry forward, to some extent, the passion generated in early times by a feeling among Jews that Providence has made them "special." It finds new form when they discover that there are things in the world undreamed of in their Jewish background. Emerging, they are captivated by what they see, reach out for points of contact, and gradually, as they find their feet, become an active part of the scene, often with originality and distinction, but always—inevitably—within the context of the host culture. If the record of achievement by Jews, in these terms, is extraordinarily high in many fields, the debt is owed, paradoxically, by the Jews. Without the stimulus of their unique sense of identity, the story would have been thin and poor; yet the ultimate enrichment is not Jewish but a mark of civilization itself.

The cultural process is a continuum. The circumstances of Jewish existence—the separateness which was its hallmark—deprived the Jews, for long periods, of routine participation in the general unfolding of what we call civilization. In every situation in which they finally established contact, they found a world bursting with interest, arousing talent and enthusiasm too long dormant. Some writers, astonished by the scale of Jewish achievement that followed, have looked for genetically developed qualities in the Jewish mind, notably the refinement of intellect through centuries of training in talmudic reasoning. More plausibly, the mystery explains itself in social terms: the dynamic generated at the point of contact between exclusiveness and liberation.

It was here that the long-established sense of identity was powerful and stimulating. It was disturbing, too; but its most obvious quality was that it haunted the imagination. For emergent Jews, destined to fulfill themselves in new ways, the driving force for change always included a desire—conscious or unconscious—to come to terms with the old inbred attachments. This could be satisfying or frustrating, but it was always in evidence.

Entering the world, these emergent Jews were governed by the need to explore issues still close to them, drawing now on new sources of knowledge, new weapons of analysis to deepen their understanding of themselves as Jews. For Maimonides, living in the twelfth-century Muslim world, the ideas of Aristotle and the Arab philosophers would be reformulated to find a new synthesis for the underlying struggle in Judaism between reason and faith. For Freud, in the twentieth century, the penetrating ideas to which he gave expression still related him firmly to his personal problems in Jewish bourgeois (and anti-Semitic) Vienna. In this broad sense, Jewish identity has been a potent involvement for every writer, artist, scientist, or businessman born with some residual awareness of Jewish roots. Sometimes the Jew took flight from it in timidity or self hatred; the roots died; and where this happened the world lost something precious—an angle of vision, a special concentration, a stimulus for exploration, a sense of concern. Where the roots are still alive, the Jew living in a free society draws on a cultural heritage far wider than the Judaic past, is enriched by this broader heritage, and yet expresses it with a tone or mood that takes in unfailingly his dream of Jerusalem.

The Diaspora and Israel

If Jewish identity reached its full characteristic expression in the context of the Diaspora, how is this affected by the most heartening episode of our time: the emergence of the State of Israel?

In one sense, Israel appears as a reversal of the Diaspora, taking Jewish identity back at a bound to its original source. The Jews, restored to their ancient home, have come into their own, free once again to create their own civilization as they did in Bible times. But if one tells the story this way—leaping, as David Ben-Gurion liked to do, from the battles of Joshua to his own triumphs in 1948—one is leaving out the essence of Jewish history. In building Israel, the Jews have not made the Diaspora redundant; they have, on the contrary, given new expression to its creativeness, its vitality.

The Jews have been, and will remain, citizens of the world. Israel has not diminished this but reinforced it. What the founders and settlers of Israel have done is to create in the biblical land a marvelous evocation of the highest ideals and culture which they absorbed in their own distinctive way as wanderers, aliens, settlers, and participants in Western civilization. It is an assertion of Jewish identity, not as a return to an archaic past but as a living expression of the response Jews have always made—or tried to make—to the constantly evolving pattern of human existence. Its freshness and power in Israel are marks, once again, of the dynamism that is always generated at a new point of contact. In the shadow of an unexampled tragedy, the people of Israel were called upon to create institutions and a way of life that would embrace and satisfy a situation of extraordinary complexity, molding into one nation individuals of bewildering differences of origin and character. The moral inspiration which met this challenge flowed from an ancient, deeply embedded faith; but the forms in which the rebirth was achieved reflected at every point the creative power of the long Diaspora.

The founders of modern Zionism all drew on biblical words to express their vision; and for some of them, the notion of a "return" was always to be seen as a literal fulfillment of the specific promise made by God to His people. For the great majority of the leading pioneers, however, Zionism was an expression of modernity. They were men and women who were already deeply involved in the liberal world, committed to its ideas, enjoying what it might offer, and determined that the masses of Jewry still cut off from this emancipation should be free to create a form of it in their own right. If the idea of return was almost holy in its potency, its intent was to express in the ancestral land a higher—holier—form of the European idea. Life itself was to be revolutionized. For some, the revolutionary concept would call on Jews to ennoble the whole idea of nationalism, so powerful a force in nineteenth-century Europe. For others, the heart of the concept lay in a socialist brotherhood built on the dignity of labor. There were many among these pioneers from Europe who also saw life in the Holy Land as an absolute of holiness, clothing a Jew's life with the sanctity expressed in the words of the Bible. But speaking broadly, Zionism was linked to Diaspora concepts—political independence and social modernity. The astonishing range of achievement in Israel is an expression of the cultural identity shaped in Diaspora experience.

To say this is in no sense to diminish the remarkable originality of Israel's settlers in devising and carrying out the programs through which the new life has been built. The massive ingathering of Jews, accomplished against a background of war and sacrifice, is Israel's own triumph. Yet the Diaspora is ever present, not merely as a legacy but in a revitalized role that offers a new understanding of what their history has meant to the Jews.

The issue is brought to a head in considering the huge support for Israel by Jews outside. At one level, this is an act of identification with kinsmen; more deeply, it is an amazing distillation of everything that the Jews of the Diaspora have achieved during their living fulfillment in their countries of settlement. A people who, once they were free, learned and gave so much everywhere, have caught up Israel in their zest and excitement. It is as if Jewish identity, enriched through the centuries, found its ultimate meaning in the opportunity to produce an uninhibited demonstration of its cumulative debt to exile. A land of poverty and desert has been lifted to the highest standards of culture and is aglow with enterprise, social experiment, science, literature, and music. Nothing ever showed more clearly the positive aspect of the paradox that Jews express: that their inward-looking concern, the will to survive distinctively, goes hand-in-hand with a passion to enhance the potential and grace of all mankind.

In these terms, Israel and the Diaspora, working close together, are a joint expression of Jewish identity; yet there is a sense in which the ethos of the new country runs counter to Jewish history almost by definition. Something different has been created which almost makes the word *Jewish* inapposite. It is not just that in political action the people of this country are not Jewish but Israeli, independent of their devoted kinsmen elsewhere. In a deep sense they can also be separate in feeling, especially the younger generation; and when one thinks of it, it is not too hard to understand why many of them have felt impelled into a clear remoteness from the Diaspora. Naturally, it is not very comforting for deeply concerned Jews overseas to find the simple Jewish bond not always operative in the traditional way, but it is a tangible fact. On the big issues, of course, the Israelis rely on them, and at the personal level, kinship can smile through; but they are resentful, with a mixture of jealousy, as well as dislike. The jealousy is understandable: they are a beleaguered state, on their own, ground down by taxes, and exposed to danger, while their sympathizers worry from their safety afar. One is reminded of the letter which Bar Kokhba wrote at the height of his battle for freedom to the men of En-Gedi: "In comfort you sit, eat and drink . . . and care nothing for your brothers."[1]

But there is a deeper quality than resentment, something which impinges on the whole question of Jewish identity. Until Israel emerged, being a Jew was ultimately a matter of choice. Born into a Jewish family, one made of it what one wanted. Where Jewish sentiment was fluid, one could drift away; but if one opted to stay in, impelled by an amalgam of unanalyzable emotions, it could become a vibrant element in an open-ended existence. In Israel today, the Jewish basis, which might have been thought to be self-evident, has been overlaid with a binding, inescapable statehood. An Israeli can be interested in the Jewish past as history; but identification with this past, as an anchor of existence, is no longer the critical issue. Survival as a state is what matters now.

Interpreted in public terms, the values to be preserved are not the tradition and sentiment of being a Jew, but life, liberty, and the pursuit of happiness. In private terms—in the area in which novelists and poets struggle to evaluate their consciousness—the subjects of their concern can be strange, almost out of key, to the Diaspora Jew. The novelist may sit writing in a kibbutz—a setting which has woven itself into Jewish myth—yet be carried off in imagination to issues that break all the comfortable molds. As a writer, he may want to express the desire to break out of what he feels is the trap of Israeli existence; he may see himself as a victim of blind authority; he may sense within him a strong empathy for "the enemy"—all very disturbing to sympathizers overseas for whom Zion has to be a satisfying dream. The poet can be even more remote. The verse he writes may translate itself fairly easily into a lyric of simple, accessible sentiment, but the Hebrew words—and poetry draws all its meaning from the character of its words—reflect a distancing evolution, a vocabulary which has been shaped by the intimacy and subtlety of an entirely new experience, a polyglot source, both ancient and everyday, which delivers itself with a spontaneity that marks out new forms of feeling and expression.

Has there been a sea change, then, in the whole concept of Jewish identity? Expounding this logically, one would be pushed into an ironic position. For the great mass of Jews—those of the Diaspora—concern and pride in being a Jew have been immeasurably strengthened by the emergence of Israel. In Israel itself, the unifying bond with these same Diaspora Jews has lost its automatic assurance. Fortunately for our peace of mind, nothing in Jewish existence lends itself to such a logical dichotomy. Without soft-pedaling in the least the break implicit in Israeli self-centeredness, one knows how heavily it is offset by living contact with the Diaspora, not only on practical questions of cooperation but in the bonds which carry this contact to the traditions of the past. A symbol ready to hand is the new affection for the Diaspora language, Yiddish. Israel is strong enough now to let its roots come to life, just as this strong ethnic base has been invigorated also in recent years among the hitherto timid elements in the Diaspora. Even more significantly, logic is upset constantly by the reality of cross-fertilization. If the stream of Jewish visitors to Israel inevitably dramatizes the gap between the life of a Jew in Israel and the Diaspora, the flow in the opposite direction—partly on business but more particularly in ever-increasing cultural safaris—opens the windows of Israeli life to blow away the cobwebs of self-absorption.

In courage and military prowess, this small people has created something unique to themselves at which the rest of us can only gaze in wonder. The springs of feeling which they draw on have a flavor equally independent. But when we stand back from the immediacy of events, the common feeling is paramount. If the Israelis are turning a fresh page of history through the new circumstances of their existence, it is ultimately in concert with their fellow Jews everywhere, ready for every fresh exploration of the meaning of Jewish identity.

"When the morning stars sang together"

In what I have said so far by way of prelude, I have talked freely about some of the elements in my own consciousness as a Jew. In the book itself, I try to give this more solid form but still in a way that flows from my own approach to the heritage.

Inevitably, I had to begin with the Bible, not as straight history but for the constant place it has had in Jewish life. The nature of its appeal and how this was sustained in the social life of the Jews are major factors in understanding the feelings of Jews in the long centuries of the Diaspora.

But the spirit of Jewish life in these centuries drew on more than the Bible. If one mentions the hold that the rabbis had on their followers in this period, it can sound arid and forbidding. In reality, the practice of what may be called rabbinic Judaism was uniquely creative. How it all emerged always seemed a mystery to me until I began to explore that long dark period after the exile in Babylon in which the Jews felt their way into a new kind of existence and ultimately emerged with a religious faith and a social purpose all their own. Now that I understand how much the Jews drew on their own resources and how much they absorbed from the people among whom they lived—Babylonians, Greeks, and Romans—I see the independence and originality of the Jews in an even stronger light.

A major part of the book covers this period (from the fifth century B.C. to the Roman times), rarely explored in nonspecialist works because it is so mysterious. And when it opens up and becomes more familiar in talk of political and religious struggles under the Romans—the last line of Jewish kings, the wars with the Romans, the interplay between Jesus and the authorities—it is all the more rewarding to dwell at some length on topics that one has usually seen discussed only briefly.

The same is true of that momentous period in which Judaism and Christianity began to go their separate ways. The shadow of this period lies over all that ensued in Christian Europe. I confess that I had never fully understood it and am glad to had have an opportunity to explore it naw.

It was in these early centuries that the Jews forged a common faith and purpose even though they lived for nearly two thousand years afterward in conditions of great disparity. What have been the religious beliefs of Jews in the Diaspora, and how have these beliefs received expression in religious and folk ritual? The chapter (and appendix) or Diaspora Judaism form a natural postscript to the long creative period which produced rabbinic Judaism; yet here again the spirit has to be distinguished from the letter. If beliefs and rituals can be catalogued briefly without too much trouble, the spirit behind them and the sense of fulfillment they offered take us into an area central to the aim which provoked this book: to set out what it is that kept the Jews going against all odds, surfacing from tragedy with an inextinguishable sense of courage.

This was the legacy the Jews carried with them in their wanderings and settlings, which are discussed in the two final chapters. At one level, these chapters offer a bird's eye view of the physical disposition of Jews throughout the twenty centuries of the Diasporn, but at another level they show the jews in their unique dialogue with the rest of the world, both in the religious and the economic fields. One says "the Jews" as if there was a fixed pattern, but well aware that we are talking ultimately of millions of individuals, drawing on a common legacy but fulfilling it in endlessly different ways. The author is just one of those individuals, who wants to say something from his own time and place.

The title of the book echoes a verse from Job (38:16) which is both a reproof and a challenge. In one mood, Jewish experience seems so unfathomable that it is presumptious to add a word of one's own: "Hast thou entered in the springs of the sea? Hast thou walked in search of the depth?" Yet in another mood, one wants more than anything else to join in the celebration of Jewish existence, to recapture from verse 7 of the same chapter that magic time "when the morning stars sang together, and all the sons of God shouted for joy."

1

The Bible in Jewish Life

The Intimacy of Its Appeal

EWISH CONSCIOUSNESS is linked to the Bible—by which Jews mean the Old Testament—in two specific, if overlapping, ways.

First, the Bible offers Jews a story of their origin as a people from the days of the patriarch Abraham (c. 1800–1600 B.C.) to the conquest of the kingdom of Judah by Nebuchadnezzar (586 B.C.), which led to a large part of the Hebrew people being carried off to exile in Babylon. The historical story covers a stretch, therefore, of over a thousand years. For good measure, the first eleven chapters of the Bible (dealing with Creation, the Flood, et cetera) provide a prologue to the Jewish story, while the books Ezra and Nehemiah, describing briefly the return from exile in Babylon, constitute a kind of epilogue.

Important as the historical story is to Jews, it constitutes, of course, only part of the Old Testament. Side by side with thirteen books recounting the adventures of the patriarchs and their descendants in settling in Canaan, escaping from slavery in Egypt, and then founding a kingdom in the Holy Land, there are twenty-six other books of rhetoric, storytelling, poetry, exhortation, and argument (including, Psalms, Prophets, Proverbs, Job, Esther) which emerged from the second half of the Bible period and fill out the background with variety, intensity, and delight. But though the Jews absorbed these books deeply, the heart of the Bible message lay for them in one great historical event, the Revelation on Mount Sinai. At this holy spot, God had selected this people, shown them His favor and given them, through Moses, teaching—moral laws—by which they were to live. This was the Covenant that God had made with His "chosen" people. If they obeyed His laws, He would protect them; if they disobeyed, they would be punished.

This, then, was the first way in which the Bible dominated Jewish consciousness: the Bible as history and the moral imperatives enshrined in the story. There was a vivid sense—which still exists—that this ancient story has been part of the personal life history of every individual Jew and Jewess since time began. When Moses leads the Israelites out of slavery in Egypt, he is leading *us* to freedom. When we turn to God in prayer in synagogue, we are as much in awe of Him as the Israelites were in the wilderness tabernacle. The Bible lies at hand to express everything we feel today. When we are exultant at some triumph, we are reliving the victories of King David. When disaster strikes, it is expressed in the bitterness of Jeremiah's Lamentations. As the living document of the Jewish past and present, the Bible is awesome in its authority.

The second way the Bible has sustained Jewish life is more lighthearted. The intense familiarity of Jews with the Bible allowed them to turn to it not quite as entertainment, but certainly to fill life with pleasure. In the present century, of course, the Bible text no longer plays this role universally, but it still does for many. Certainly, before the horizons of Jewish life were widened through emancipation, the Bible was the cement of Jewish culture in a uniquely intimate and familiar way, spelling satisfaction and happiness.

It is impossible to understand how Jewish life sustained itself through poverty and persecution unless one sees how enlivening the knowledge of the Bible was for Jews. Not that the Jews, en masse, were scholars. They could always read Hebrew, of course; but apart from the rabbis and learned laymen who knew the whole Bible by heart (this is not an exaggeration), ordinary Jews absorbed it through routine and love rather than through learning. The miracle of Jewish history is how these two elements—routine and love—created an undying spirit of instinctive understanding.

The ordinary Jew had no idea—certainly, no precise idea—how and when the Bible as a whole came into being. The text was read for the immediate story it offered. There were no dates to hang on to; the setting was merely ancient. What did emerge, however, was a sense of direct communication. In some cases, a Bible book seemed clearly to establish its own author, in the form of the central character; but even without this, the personal element was dominant. The Bible appealed through the contact it offered with an endlessly varied gallery of individuals who never appeared as plaster saints but were always recognizably human—brave and fallible, venal or inspired.

The pivotal character of the whole Bible was Moses, and here the authorship communicated itself very clearly. The Five Books of Moses (the Pentateuch) was basic to everything, taking the story from the first days of Creation to the moment the Children of Israel were poised to enter the Promised Land. There was a deep acceptance that Moses had written these five books—the Torah—himself, except for the last sentences of the fifth book, Deuteronomy, a brief epilogue describing his death.

The holiness of the Torah was always taken to be of a different order from everything else in the Bible. Moses, writing it, was only a human being, but every single word that he put down was accepted as divinely inspired. Later in the Bible there were other leaders to whom God spoke, but never in the same way. The epilogue in Deuteronomy, expressing this, is riveting in its authority: "There arose not a prophet since in Israel like unto Moses, whom the Lord knew face to face" (34:10).

The visible symbol of the Torah's uniqueness is the physical form in which it has been presented to every Jew for more than two thousand years. The five books are inscribed on parchment in one unbroken scroll—the Sefer Torah, or Torah Scroll—with one or more copies nestling in the Ark, or sanctuary, of every synagogue. Each scroll is garlanded in a sumptuously decorated costume, fronted by a breastplate of gold or silver and with a gay pomegranate of tinkling bells on the wooden handles around which the scroll is rolled. In every major religious service, the Sefer Torah is taken out of the Ark with great ceremony to be read from with minute care and in an old solemn chant. The entire scroll is read through each year on a weekly rota. Before and after the reading of the day, the scroll is raised and displayed, open at the passage, for the veneration of the congregation.

The Range of Involvement

If there is nothing comparable in Jewish experience with this concentration on the Books of Moses, there is always plenty of excitement in the other historical books—Joshua, Judges, Samuel, Kings, and Chronicles—even though the story is more diffuse. The ordinary Jew probably never got a coherent picture of the story as a whole, but the great characters seized the imagination—Saul and David, Deborah, Jezebel, Samson and Delilah, Elijah and the prophets of Baal.

A Jew could identify with the dramas surrounding these characters but would feel something of a different order with other books—Prophets, Psalms, and individual storybooks like Ruth, Esther, or Job.

With the Prophets, there was a communication of power, doom, and hope in a rhetoric that burst through the ordinary canons of language. Even for those who only heard the words in translation, there was urgency and dynamism, reaching back through vehemence and archaism into the very roots of life's meaning. No one asked where and how these great orations had been spoken or recorded. They carried their own truth; and the prophet who spoke —Isaiah, Jeremiah, or any of them—was addressing each generation of Jews with the same authority, intimacy, and love. There was one way, particularly apt, in which the Jews through the centuries heard these words repeated year after year. From earliest times, it had become the practice to follow the weekly Torah reading in the synagogue with a short reading from later books, particularly from Prophets. This additional reading—the haftarah—would be read by individual members of the congregation rather than by the synagogue official entrusted with the Torah reading. It became a custom, indeed, for the haftarah of the week to be read by a boy on reaching his majority, becoming a bar mitzvah. For this reason alone, the prophetical reading became an intense focus of attention. It was also likely to be expounded in any d'rashah, or sermon, which the rabbi might give. But above all, the prophets were fed into Jewish consciousness through the force that a single verse could convey, evoking the picture of a man of God who drew fire from an inner faith which transcended everything mundane and transitory in life.

The impact of Psalms was of a totally different order. Here was David singing to his people, sometimes with vehemence but more often with tenderness and joy. Every Jew knew at least some of the psalms because they had been fed into the liturgy, to be chanted with love—or to be gabbled through if one was in a hurry. Apart from the pious who worked their way through the whole book over and over again in a daily rota (often by heart), there were psalms for everybody to recite, in addition to the synagogue liturgy, on all kinds of occasions, at weddings and funerals, or whenever a festive mood called for the great 150th Psalm of Hallelujah. Most known and beloved of all, perhaps, was Psalm 126, sung quietly and happily before the Grace at the close of every Sabbath meal and beginning: "When the Lord turned again the captivity of Zion, we were like them that dream: then was our mouth filled with laughter and our tongue with singing."

There was a similar personal involvement in five of the books of the Bible known as the Five Scrolls. All five—Ruth, Esther, Ecclesiastes, Lamentations, and Song of Songs—became books to be read on regular annual occasions, often from individual scrolls. In this way they drew to themselves the excitement of the occasions, enhancing the attraction they carried in their own right for Jewish feeling.

The Book of Ruth, a novella written in the purest Hebrew, was read every year during the spring harvest festival of Pentecost, the Feast of Weeks, conveying with nostalgic charm the simple trustfulness of pastoral life. There is no more beloved character in Jewish literature than this warm-hearted Moabite girl—the marvelous non-Jew that all of us have met at one time or another.

The Book of Esther, by contrast, is a thriller, read with fear and delight at the Feast of Purim, whose origin it purports to explain. The fear it projects lies in its extraordinary evocation of Jew-hatred in classic form; the delight is in the defeat of the villainous Haman, which provides the reason for the Purim carnival. Unlike Ruth, who is a simple country girl, a character out of a Thomas Hardy novel, Esther is big-town, "Miss Persia," with the mixed motivations that this implies. But there they are, twin heroines of Jewish feeling, at one in their loyalty.

With Ecclesiastes—"vanity of vanities, all is vanity"—we are in a very different mood. Ascribed to the philosopher King Solomon, it was read regularly during the Feast of Tabernacles, though no one really knows why. Here, with its endless epigrams, irony, and skepticism, the Jewish reader saw a projection of himself which was very satisfying to one side of his character. The early rabbis were none too sure whether to admit the book to the Bible canon. But with the decision taken, it soon became a happy outlet for speculative minds, a sophisticated relief from both romance and tragedy.

Tragedy, deep and unrelieved, surfaced in Lamentations, a dirge of rhythmic beauty which was read annually on the fast day Tisha B'Av commemorating the destruction of the First Temple. Here, nothing would be held back. Seated on a low stool, the head sprinkled with ashes, a Jew surrendered to the inextinguishable sorrow that the loss of Jerusalem evoked. The prophet Jeremiah was thought to be the book's author. The simple words—a catalogue of grief sung in an ancient chant of mourning—burned deep into Jewish memory.

But once again there was another side in Song of Songs, its annual recital assigned to Passover Eve, the Feast of Freedom. Surrounded by family and friends for the Seder celebration—an evening of ecstatic delight—the master of the house would turn, when the party was over, to a quiet reading of this poem, followed, I rather guess, by a marital experience of love. Given the frank eroticism of the song, which was thought to have been written by Solomon in his role as master of the largest harem known to man, one is rather surprised to find it nestling so firmly in the Holy Book. The puritans among the rabbis had justified this by claiming that the book was really a religious allegory—God's boundless love for his people Israel. Maybe. But to the Jewish husband, flown with the four cups of wine that the Seder calls for, the happiness of love poetry was one more testimony to the endlessly varied joy that the Bible offered. Solomon, the skeptic of Ecclesiastes, had moved over to Solomon, the lover.

Even with the Five Scrolls, we have not exhausted the sustenance of the Bible for the Jews whose lives it framed. Two works in particular made a very individual impact, running the gamut from self-satisfaction to the most profound perplexity.

The first was the book known as Proverbs. It, too, was ascribed to Solomon; but it offered this time the assurances of common sense, the homely sentiments that puncture skeptical argument with reminders of the solid virtues of life, the underlying verities that we fall back on with a sigh of relief. Throughout, the text was infinitely quotable; but there was one section—the second half of chapter 31—which became, over the centuries, a unique expression of the deepest happiness in Jewish life, an abiding rock of family joy. On Friday evening, the Jew welcomed the Sabbath in a synagogue service as dusk fell and then returned home for its more personal celebration. The house would shine with welcome. The drudgery of the workaday week had disappeared as by magic. The tablecloth was snowy white. A bottle of wine glittered with the sparkle of the Sabbath candles. The family stood waiting for the simple ritual preceding the meal—the blessing on wine, the Kiddush, and the blessing on bread as the splendidly twisted loaf, the challah, was cut and distributed. But before this, the family itself had to be greeted. There was a brief benediction for the children, and then the husband recited aloud the rapturous passage in Proverbs (31:1–31) extoling the mother of the house, the supreme architect of this hour of joy. In the King James Version it opens famously: "A woman of worth who can find, for her price is above rubies . . . the heart of her husband trusteth in her . . . her children rise up and call her blessed." In the original Hebrew, the two first words, *eshet hayyil,* ring with even stronger feelings. The word *hayyil* means *army.* The wife is not so much "a woman of worth" as "a valiant woman" who soldiers on with infinite courage keeping the home together. Who can doubt that a key to Jewish experience lies here, as always, in the words of the Bible?

At the other extreme, the Book of Job floated above the head of the Jews —threatening, disturbing, almost beyond reach. For most Jews, it was never a book they were at home with. Job's suffering became proverbial; but the setting of the story, the argument with his friends, and Job's own vehement bitterness with his fate, was curiously alien—un-Jewish. The rabbis were, of course, more receptive to the many-faceted power of the story; but even for them it never slotted into the structure of the Bible as history and theology, which was otherwise absorbed so directly. They could never decide when Job had lived—in the time of Abraham or Moses or later. Legends multiplied to spell out the hints of the text but never with assurance. Some thought he was the most saintly Jew who had ever lived; others that he was not a Jew at all but one of the trio of outstanding non-Jews—with Balaam and Jethro—who had become witnesses, willingly or not, to Jewish truth. There were some who even questioned daringly if he had ever existed at all, seeing the story as an allegory or myth. It was as if Job was powerful enough to absorb any question, offering ideas that transcended ordinary reason or comfort.

New Forms of Enthusiasm

This, then, was how the Bible secured and expressed its hold on Jewish life in all the centuries of the Diaspora. Until relatively modern times, most Jews were content to see the Bible story as the whole of their official history, with only a few exceptions for events that came later. One of these exceptions was the story of the Maccabees, which was not included in the Jewish Bible but became fully known (and loved) through the festival of Hanukkah.* It is true that Jews, migrating to new lands, would carry with them tales of their former homes, and they would be familiar through the work of popular preachers with endless stories or fables of heroic figures of the past whose adventures, wisdom, and wit enriched the received Jewish tradition. But the Bible, factually and mythically, was the true basis of historical feeling, and it is by a quite astonishing revolution that this has all been changed in the present century.

There are two distinct ways in which this has happened. First and most obviously, Jewish postbiblical history began to be written up coherently in the nineteenth century, and it has now reached a wide audience through countless scholarly or popular books. If the Bible story, culminating in the exile to Babylon, is still the rock, most Jews have some idea now of subsequent themes: the return from Babylon under Ezra, the war with the Romans (which includes Masada), the golden age of Spain, the massacres of the Crusades, the horrors of the Inquisition, the messianic episode of Sabbatai Zevi, the social and cultural pattern of life in East Europe (including Hasidism), the pogroms, and the great migrations to the West. The story of the Holocaust and the emergence of Israel rests now, therefore, on a broad appreciation of Jewish history after Bible times.

The second fillip to Bible enthusiasm has come through a revolution during the last fifty years in the ways Jews now understand the Bible. Two factors have operated here: the return to the land of the Bible and the development of archaeology.

On the first, it has been overwhelmingly important to Jews to see the Bible coming to life everywhere in modern Israel through place names and scenes and what one might call the atmosphere of the land, so completely in tune with the stories and poetry of the Bible.

On the second, Jews have been mesmerized by the digging up from ancient times of what lay beneath the soil of the Holy Land. The archaeology of the Near and Middle East—the Bible setting stretching from Egypt to Iran—had

*The Festival of Dedication, when the Temple was recovered by the victorious Maccabees from Antiochus of Syria and cleansed of the "abominations" he had introduced. The Books of the Maccabees, telling this story, were preserved in Greek and included by Christians in the Apocrypha (books in addition to the Bible). Hanukkah is known popularly as the Festival of Lights because of the candles lit every night (see appendix).

been richly developed in the nineteenth and early twentieth centuries; but the pace of discovery began to quicken decisively from the late 1920s and has achieved a momentum all its own, since the foundation of Israel, through the marvelously productive work of Jewish archaeologists. Much of their work (for example, on Masada and Bar Kokhba) covers postbiblical times; but when archaeology illuminates Bible times—as it does, say, on Hazor, Jericho, Megiddo, Arad, or Jerusalem itself—it adds a new dimension to the unique hold that the Bible has on Jewish feeling. An illustration of how this all comes together at the popular level can be seen in the immense excitement generated in Israel by the annual Bible Quiz, which holds the entire population glued to their television sets.

Every time an archaeological discovery is shown to fit in with the Bible story, the feeling mounts that archaeology has proved the Bible to be true. In some ways, this is a misleading approach. No one needs the truth of the Bible to be proved if it is accepted in the traditional way as quite literally the word of God. And even for those who do not phrase things this way, the truth of the Bible makes itself felt, without need or benefit of proof, through its artistic power and moral appeal. It might be different if some ancient text emerged substantiating Abraham or Moses in reality; but archaeologists don't expect this. All they claim is that their discoveries illustrate the background of the Bible, both in physical objects found and in the demonstration of how social, ritual, and legal elements of the Bible are in tune with what we know increasingly from archaeology of the conditions in those very ancient times. Yet there is no denying that this, in a sense, is establishing the truth of the Bible. The transmission of the Bible story in such authentic detail over a stretch of three or four thousand years testifies to its inner power. This is what Jews felt and feel about their involvement with the Bible. It is very satisfying to the Jewish ego.

The authenticity of the Bible in this sense comes through particularly in what has happened to the modern understanding of the Bible text. Scholars have always had to cope with difficulties of the Hebrew text, the many gaps and repetitions, the contradictions, and above all the baffling passages in which the real meaning of the words seem to have been lost. In the nineteenth century, German Bible scholars began to develop critical ways of explaining these difficulties. Jewish scholars had long met some of these difficulties by proposing some gentle emendations for obscure words. The new scholars were prepared to be infinitely more ruthless in verbal criticism, dropping passages or moving them around on the assumption of endless corruptions; but even more seriously, they ascribed difficulties (such as varying names for God) to the existence of different sources, out of which they constructed revolutionary ideas on how the Bible had come into being. This new approach came to be called Higher Criticism.

A major element in Higher Criticism was the view that many stories of really ancient times in the Bible (for example, on the Patriarchs and Moses) were not genuinely historical but inventions of the priestly class in relatively late times to claim ancient authority for the existing system, in which the priests enjoyed unique wealth and privilege. To these Higher Critics (led by the scholar Julius Wellhausen), monotheism and the moral teachings ascribed to Moses were too advanced to have come from such a primitive stage of history; they must have evolved much later, during and after the Babylonian exile (from the sixth to fifth centuries B.C.). All in all, these critical ideas seemed to destroy the integrity of the Bible text as accepted for countless generations by the world at large and, particularly, of course, by the Jews.

One of the bounties of archaeological discovery is that it has tempered many of the cruder conclusions of the Higher Critics. Far from the patriarchal stories or the psalms all being late, we see through archaeology that the setting and language offered by the Bible are authentic to the periods described. And it is good for Jewish feeling to know that though the Hebrews were, in a real sense, part of the Canaanite background now revealed, they were already stressing the differences—long before the Babylonian exile—that were to establish the broadest and most advanced religious ideas.

A striking illustration of this flows from the unearthing, since 1928, of the literature and civilization of Ugarit, a coastal town in Syria which was a great metropolis in the early twelfth century B.C., the period of Israelite settlement in Canaan. The magnificent epics of Ugarit tell of the powers of the Canaanite god Baal in a language very close to that used in the psalms to describe the powers of the Hebrew god. Some of the imagery of these psalms is more understandable now. It goes back to the Canaanite stories of battles between the gods, most particularly in fighting for survival each year against the destructive gods of Storm and Sea. But the differences are even more striking. In the Baal epics, the gods die and are revived each spring; in the Hebrew poems, the deity is always the One God, sustainer of the universe. The Canaanite gods win victories over the enemy as adventures in the annual fertility struggle; the victories of the Hebrew god are adduced as an expression of His moral purpose, which is to crush evildoers and support the poor and helpless.*

This is just one example of the way in which modern Bible scholarship seems often to start by puncturing traditional ideas but ends up by reinforcing the feeling that has always made the Bible the pivot of Jewish life.

Does this remain true if we accept the view of some scholars that the Bible description of how the ancient Hebrews conquered and settled in the Holy Land cannot be taken literally? This might be particularly disturbing to Jewish sentiment because until modern times no one questioned the secular side of the ancient story, even if one left open the question whether God actually spoke to Abraham or physically gave the Torah to Moses. The secular story seemed clear of these questions. The Hebrew people, it was accepted, were all descended from the patriarchs, whose descendants moved to Egypt, were enslaved, and then led to freedom by Moses. Joshua then took over, leading the entire people into the conquest of their ancestral land, which was then divided among the twelve tribes, all descendants of the twelve sons of Jacob. For a time, the Hebrews were governed by Judges, but ultimately they became a kingdom, under Saul and David.

It is a good story, but the Bible itself stimulates a few questions on how literally to take it. When Jacob and his family settled in Egypt, we are told that they numbered seventy in all (Gen. 46:27). In the Exodus, a census of the people following Moses in the wilderness showed more than six hundred thousand men of military age (Num. 1:46), yielding a total population, one might say, of two or three million. Can one really believe that a population of this number followed Moses from Egypt? One commentator observes drily: "A host of this size, even in close marching order, would have more than extended from Egypt to Sinai and back. It would have had no need to fear the Egyptian army."[1]

But even assuming a considerable exodus, including, as we are told, a "mixed multitude" of non-Israelites (Exod. 12:38), the story of a unified

*Here is a telling example. Professor W. A. Albright quotes the following biblical-sounding passage from the Baal epic in his book *Yahweh and the Gods of Canaan* ([New York: Doubleday, 1968], p. 5):

> "Behold, thine enemies, O Baal,
> Behold, thine enemies thou shalt crush,
> Behold, thou shalt crush thy foes."

It is very like Psalm 92:9; but note the difference in the last line:

> "Behold, thy enemies, O Yahweh,
> Behold, thy enemies shall perish,
> The workers of iniquity shall be scattered."

approach under Moses to the borders of the Promised Land, followed by a unified conquest by Joshua, still raises problems. Much of the argument focuses on one apparently direct conflict of evidence. The account in Joshua is of a series of lightning campaigns which brought all (or almost all) the land under Israelite control, after which it was divided among the tribes. On the other hand, the picture in the following book, Judges, is of a struggle of individual clans winning sporadic victories here and there, sometimes capturing cities (for example, Hebron) already supposed to have been captured by Joshua, and with nothing suggesting the national spirit expressed in Joshua.

If, in fact, only a relatively small group of patriarchal descendants escaped from Egypt, how and when did they grow into a nation? Scholars believe that the names of people appearing in the Bible story reflect accretions from non-Hebrew peoples during the wanderings or in early settlement. One hears, for example, of the Midianites (into whom Moses married) or the important Kennizites, Caleb and Othniel, who were of Edomite extraction but became part of Judah. Extending these hints, it is thought that the Israelites found allies during their long march with many who were kin in stock, or escapees in a similar way from Egyptian slavery. In addition, once the settlement had begun, residents in the cities or areas taken over would have been likely to amalgamate with the new conquerors.

All this runs counter to the Bible notion of a mass descent of the Hebrew people on the Promised Land. It is suggested, therefore, that the story of a straight conquest under Joshua is only a heroic chronicle created later under the monarchy. A more likely original picture, scholars think, is a gradual infiltration into Palestine during the wanderings so that when a conquest (of modest proportions) was undertaken by Joshua, it was successful because of many kinsmen willing, in various places, to make common cause. Some, putting tribal references under a microscope, have gone so far as to build up a picture of two conquests, the first by the tribe of Judah in the south, followed by various tribal settlements east of Jordan, and only then by the campaign of Joshua. He was of the tribe of Ephraim, and this led to Ephraim's acquisition of a particularly choice area in the rich highlands of central Palestine.

In much of the argument about the conquest, the fall of Jericho—so graphic in the Bible—becomes the key criterion. At first, archaeology seemed to show that massive walls had indeed fallen in the thirteenth century B.C., the time of the Exodus; but later excavations of the mound there proved decisively that while Jericho as a town had been very old, nothing had survived that could be dated to this period. A similar problem arises over Ai (the name means *ruins*), nearby, described in the Bible as having been destroyed by Joshua, but now known from archaeology to have been destroyed in the middle of the third millenium B.C. and not reoccupied until after the Israelite settlement. On the other hand, towns have been found in parts of Palestine which clearly suffered intense conflagration and destruction in the thirteenth century, followed by poor, rather scrappy settlement in the twelfth century of a type which the struggling Israelites could well have carried out. This is illustrated strikingly at Hazor in Galilee, excavated brilliantly by Yigael Yadin over a period of years from 1955 to 1968.

That archaeology offers evidence pointing in different directions is a salutary reminder that there is no way of using it to prove, in some simple fashion, that the Bible is true. The truth of the Bible lies in the power that it has exercised; but the historical story itself has a way of asserting its validity out of the web of argument. On Israel's origins in Palestine, for example, the dismissal of the idea of a mass invasion by hundreds of thousands of men under Joshua still leaves a feeling that the settlement must have been more than an undramatic infiltration. What is certainly undeniable is that a drive for national expression must have unified the Israelites at some very early stage after the settlement, both those who had been in the presumed mainstream under Joshua and all who might have entered or joined up from different sources. The record that rings true in this sense is the account (Josh. 24) of a great gathering at Shechem of "all the tribes of Israel . . . the elders, their judges and their officers" to celebrate the fact that they were now in the Promised Land as a people, renewing the covenant with the God who had come to them through the patriarchs and Moses. The undying theme of Israelite history is thus expressed, allowing one to see the story in the focus of a national will that ultimately transcends the fascinating analyses of scholarship.

In any case, none of the scholarly question marks about origins affect the Bible's account of the later period, in which the drama of the rise and fall of the Hebrew monarchy burned itself into Jewish consciousness for all time. Here, the Bible story was both realistic and myth making. The power of the monarchy under David and Solomon fed Jewish pride and remained in permanent contrast to the split up and corruption that followed, with most of the successive kings of Israel and Judah "walking in evil ways" and turning their backs on the religious traditions expressed in the Torah.

A reader of the Bible always felt a growing despair in the historical books which told this story, and the approach of doom was intensified by the rhetoric of the prophets. Yet nothing of this matched the sense of tragedy expressed in the final story in which Jerusalem and its Temple were destroyed by Nebuchadnezzar and the Jews were carried off to captivity in Babylon.

Even though a Jew, reading this story, knew that it was not to be the end, it gave a shape to Jewish feeling that was never to change. What followed the Bible story would amplify it beyond all imagination; yet this would never change the unique role of the Bible in Jewish life.

Holiness was at the center of this role, and it was the genius of the rabbis to create a pattern of faith around it that was satisfying in an entirely different way. In the centuries which followed the exile, the common heritage that Jews were to live with drew in law and culture from the world around them. In this sense the heritage emerged as a secular and humanistic force in Jewish life, dealing with the legal and social questions of everyday life. But it still carried with it the holiness and authority of the Bible. This, in a word, is how the Jews survived as a people, proud and fulfilled through the reassurance of this heritage.

2

The Babylonian Exile and the Return

The Flow of Empires

IN SHARP CONTRAST to the Bible period, where a firm account of Jewish history is recorded voluminously even if the texts present many problems to the reader, the centuries which followed are disastrously bare of documentation. For about five hundred years, until the rabbis and their ideas began to be visible, nothing emerged with a contemporary flavor dealing comprehensively with Jewish history and the development of Jewish consciousness.

Scholars have found this an immense challenge. The material that does exist has been scoured for detail to help us understand what was going on in a period that was obviously crucial for the Jewish future. One way is to try and envisage how Bible study developed in this period, germinating the power it was due to have in the times of the rabbis (and Jesus). Another approach is to look for clues in books—moralistic or visionary—that have been discovered and assigned to this obscure period, even though they made little mark on the official tradition. Another important Jewish source—though unknown to the rabbis—is the historical writing of Josephus which he produced in the first century A.D. for his Roman patrons and which he must have based to some extent on records now lost to us.

But there is a limit to what can be learned about this period through concentration solely on Jewish sources. Throughout this period, as indeed throughout all Jewish history, we need to know what Jews may have been deriving from external sources. In this and the next chapters, therefore, we consider the impact, successively, of the Babylonian, the Hellenistic, and the Roman settings. It should help us to understand not just how Jews developed their own outlook but what elements from the world outside furthered the development of Judaism's daughter-religion Christianity. In turn, when Christianity became fully independent and authoritative, the rabbinical authorities had to find ways of adjusting to this now external—and challenging—force.

A table of dates is offered here (see page 36) to help in charting the main historical developments over this five hundred-year stretch, from the destruction of Jerusalem by Nebuchadnezzar (586 B.C.) to its destruction by the Romans (A.D. 70). Viewed in outline in this way, it is hardly a very cheerful picture, since the Jews start and end in *galuth,* exile, with only a brief period of political independence in between under the Hasmonean dynasty. In a bird's-eye view of this kind, the Jews and their ancient homeland seem insignificant pawns for the most part in a mighty game of empires. The Babylonians who take the Jews captive in 586 B.C. are conquered by the Persians, whose empire—first under Cyrus (539 B.C.) and then Darius (from 522 B.C.)—becomes dominant over the whole of the Near and Middle East. Greece alone sets a limit to Persian expansion, following a number of famous battles which bolster its proud resistance for nearly two hundred years. In due course, the Greek-Macedonians become the dominant power. By the time of Alexander the Great (336–323 B.C.), they have absorbed the territories ruled by the Persians into an even mightier empire, whose cultural style—Hellenism—is to affect the political, social, and intellectual life of the Mediterranean for centuries.

Turning specifically to the Jews, Palestine in this period is exposed to a succession of Hellenist rulers who take over after Alexander's death. The Ptolemy dynasty of Egypt is the first, keeping control of Palestine for more

TABLE 1

From the Bible to the Rabbis: Main Dates

B.C.	586		BABYLON Ascendant: Nebuchadnezzar conquers Jerusalem; Jews exiled to Babylonia
	539		PERSIA Ascendant: Cyrus takes Babylon
		538	Edict allowing Jews to return to the Holy Land
		522	Darius
		520–515	Temple at Jerusalem re-established
		445	Nehemiah, governor of Jerusalem
	458? 428?		EZRA LEADS RETURN
	336–323		GREECE Dominant
			Alexander the Great
	323		EGYPT Dominant: Ptolemy I overlord of Palestine
		323–200	Successive Ptolemys
	200		SYRIA Dominant: Seleucid dynasty begins to rule Palestine
		175–163	Antiochus IV
		167	Profanation of Jerusalem Temple
	166		MACCABEE REVOLT: Hasmonean dynasty
		166–160	Judah Maccabee
	164		TEMPLE rededicated
		160–	Jonathan
		152	Jonathan becomes high priest
		142–135	Simon
		135–104	Johanan Hyrcanus
		104–103	Judah Aristobulus
		103–76	Alexander Jannai
		76–67	Salome Alexandra; friendly with Pharisee leaders
		67	Aristobulus/Hyrcanus; civil war
	63		ROME PRESENCE BEGINS: Pompey enters Jerusalem
		63–40	Hasmonean dynasty continues. Hyrcanus II leans on Idumean Antipater for support
		48	Antipater virtual ruler
		39	Antipater appoints sons provincial governors: Phazael in Jerusalem, Herod in Galilee
			Herod king
	37–4		HEROD THE GREAT (Hillel, founding rabbi, lived at this time)
		4–A.D.6	Sons: Archelaus "king"
		4–A.D.34	Philip tetrarch of northeast area
		4–A.D.39	Antipas, tetrarch of Galilee (John the Baptist)
A.D.			PALESTINE UNDER PROCURATORS of Judea, Samariah, and Idumea
	26–36		PONTIUS PILATE procurator
	30		Jesus crucified
		41–44	Herodian-Jewish rulers: Agrippa I
		50–100	Agrippa II
		44–66	Procurators
	66–70		WAR WITH ROME
		70	Jerusalem destroyed
		73	Masada
	132–35		BAR KOKHBA rebellion (Akiba and other rabbis martyred)

than a hundred years—from 323 to 200 B.C. The Seleucid dynasty of Syria then becomes dominant in Palestine for a few decades, but in less assured fashion, for Rome is now on the horizon. The Seleucid dynasty begins to falter, faced with Roman hostility and provincial rebellion to the east. In this context, the Jews themselves win a form of political autonomy, starting with the triumph of the Maccabees in 166 B.C. As an ally of Rome, the Jewish state —growing into the Hasmonean kingdom—becomes expansionist over a period of 130 years; but its Jewish character, as well as its power, ultimately becomes diluted. The turning point comes when the Roman general Pompey sets out to bring the whole of Syria-Palestine under direct Roman rule, besieging and capturing Jerusalem in 63 B.C.

For a hundred years, the Jews in Palestine live uneasily under Roman suzerainty. In A.D. 66 they rebel, in a bitter fight which lasts four years. In A.D. 70 the Roman armies under Titus capture and destroy Jerusalem. The Jews have lost their fulcrum and are poised for another dispersion, this time for nearly two thousand years.

But if one accepts this familiar presentation, with Jews merely buffeted by outsiders as an object of history, the nature of their survival becomes inexplicable. Instead, we must look into this relatively empty stretch of five hundred years to see what forces were germinating that would mark the Jews out distinctively, as subject rather than object. Creating their own character did not, of course, mean living in a vacuum. The fascination of this formative period lies in the demonstration it offers of the way the Jews wrestled with a host of different environments, absorbing at one level, resisting at another, timid and militant in turn, but ending, as they experienced the second loss of Jerusalem, with a fully formed unifying outlook that was to guide and inspire them through nearly two thousand years of the new *galuth*.

The fulcrum of this long-term outlook was their faith in the Torah. It ultimately took the form of an imperishable sense of kinship expressed in ritual and moral teachings and linked to minute interpretation of every word of the Bible; but it is impossible to define exactly how this happened. The exiles to Babylon had taken with them poignant memories of a different order: a Temple at Jerusalem which was the abode of their God, a line of kings to whom God had entrusted His worship, a place in God's favor which had been shown in history. These memories were already woven into a rich tapestry of tradition. There were stories, ceremonies, and customs, oracles of the prophets expressing reproof as well as hope, songs, and psalms which were known and recited. Even without a completed Bible to live by as yet, the Jews in exile could maintain their distinctiveness with no great temptation or pressure to assimilate with the world around them.

It was more difficult later, when the center of Jewish life had shifted back to the Holy Land. By this time, Hellenism was beginning to exert its influence over the whole of the Near East. The Jews responded, too; yet in this setting they still continued to forge their distinctive outlook. The literary evidence on this is scanty, with only a few major works to illustrate what was happening. But unless we envisage a steady creative force taking shape in this period, the strength of independence that was to characterize Jewish history remains inexplicable.

Character of the Return

The ordinary Jew in later centuries never saw any problem in the apparent paucity of historical documentation over the vast period of time we are considering. His datum by then was the timeless authority of rabbinic Judaism, harnessed at one end to the revelation of the Torah to Moses, and at the other to the future arrival, one day, of the Messiah. The expression of this Judaism was a code of faith and ceremony which had no particular time stamp in its current experience and could, therefore, cheerfully absorb any hiatus in the historical record. The few books of the Bible which told of the days of exile and return were seen as exemplifying perfectly the Judaism that Jews had come to accept as natural. On life in the Babylonian exile, there was the Book of Daniel, taken to have originated in the background it described—the story of a Jew who was ready to die for his faith and who testified to the power of the Jewish God through his adventures, dreams, and prophecies. On the return to the Holy Land, there were the Books of Ezra and Nehemiah, in which the graphic detail seemed absolutely consistent with the Judaism they now took for granted. The teaching of these two books was total obedience to the Torah; and it seemed to later generations that Ezra, in proclaiming this message, had almost the same authority as Moses on Sinai.

This mythic role dwarfs anything else we know. He is described as a priest, "a ready scribe in the Torah of Moses," who decides to return to the ancestral land "to teach in Israel statutes and judgments." We are told that permission for Jews to return had been given earlier by Cyrus and confirmed by Darius, in whose reign the Temple had been rebuilt (520–15 B.C.) and refurbished with spoil looted by Nebuchadnezzar. Now again, nearly a century later, a Persian king shows his favor (and respect for the Jewish God) by furnishing Ezra and his companions whose names are given in great detail, not only with cash and goods but also with royal authority. Ezra, on arrival, finds the Jews neglectful of Torah law, most particularly in having intermarried with the local population. Summoning the Jews to a great assembly, he denounces their failings; obediently, they resolve to put away their alien wives and obey "the commandment of our God."

The Book of Nehemiah rounds out the story from another angle. It is a chronicle written in the first person, which is unusual for the Bible. Nehemiah, a high official of the Persian court, grieves for the fate of his people and is given permission to return to the Holy Land. His main task, once he is in Jerusalem, is to harness the energies of the Jews to rebuild the walls of the city. With this achieved, the emphasis in his story shifts to the role of Ezra in securing obedience to the Torah, a campaign described in greater detail than in the Book of Ezra itself. We hear in Nehemiah how the people call on Ezra to bring before the congregation—"both men and women"—the book of the Torah of Moses. He stands on a pulpit, opens the book "in the sight of all the people," and reads. The ears of all the people "are attentive to the book of the Torah." The officials standing with him "give the sense, and cause the people to understand the meaning." They hear the wonderful story of the Exodus and of God's protection and learn of the ceremonies and practices which are part of the Torah—the Sabbath, the sacrifices, the festivals. Hearing the words of the Torah, they recognize their past wickedness and dedicate themselves to future obedience.

For the Jewish tradition, therefore, the Books of Ezra and Nehemiah are enough by themselves to establish the needed link between the classical period of the Torah's emergence in Bible times and its equally authoritative elaboration under the rabbis, hundreds of years later, in the Talmud. Historical memories in the background were lively but unsystematic; the profusion of anecdotes and sayings in the Talmud referring to this earlier period never emerges as a consistent picture of events or ideas. Modern scholarship has tried to establish a more documented approach; for though the period as a whole is full of the most perplexing question marks, we do, at least, have much more raw material to draw on for speculation then the rabbis were aware of or allowed to come through.

With books largely ignored or only recently discovered, it begins to add up, in fact, to a rich Jewish literature by the time we reach the second century B.C. In the foreground, there are stories, histories, and religious works which never found a place in the official Bible and became available because the Church preserved them in Greek translations to form what became known as the Apocrypha, or hidden writings. Increasingly, we are aware now, also, of a considerable range of sectarian writings, fierce projections of apocalypses to come or imaginative retellings of Bible stories (in the name of Bible characters) in a form which makes these books vivid, if indirect, commentaries on current events. All of this was in the background as the rabbinical tradition began to take shape in the second century B.C. There are endless echoes of it all later in the Talmud; but in formal historical terms it was downgraded and drawn on only for argumentative, moralistic, or purely anecdotal illustration of the main themes of the rabbis—the study of the Torah. In the orthodox Jewish tradition, therefore, this mysterious period—from Ezra to the rabbis—never yielded up its original character as a period of light and shade but was always tailored in retrospect to the rigid certainties of the ensuing talmudic age.

These carefully nurtured certainties were a positive influence in creating the devotion with which Jews came to regard the common heritage, but it would be wrong to ignore or play down a certain loss which is its obverse. Surely it was a limiting factor that generations of rabbis were unaware for centuries of the full historical background in which their tradition had taken shape. A striking example was the exclusion of *The Wisdom of Ben Sira* from the official Bible, which meant that this majestic book of philosophical maxims (completed c. 200–170 B.C.) ultimately disappeared in its original Hebrew version and was only known, until recent times, in the Church's Greek translation, automatically alien to traditional Jewish study. Yet it is a work which expresses the struggle between Greek and Jewish thought at a crucial time, and though many of its sayings are quoted approvingly by the early Talmud rabbis, its role on the Jewish-Greek issue was never explored until modern Jewish scholarship broadened its range.

From the same angle, one has to recognize how quickly straight historical books became evanescent, even when dealing with dramas of the time. A major account of the heroic revolt of the Maccabees (166 B.C.) was written originally in Hebrew by an eyewitness but soon disappeared in this form and was preserved only in a Greek translation which was included, like *Ben Sira*, in the Apocrypha. Many graphic stories of the Maccabean rebellion surfaced later, it is true, in the rabbinic literature, mostly in relation to the observance of the Festival of Hanukkah which was instituted to celebrate the triumph. But the full historical picture was lost to Jews until such time as they were willing—very much later—to read the non-Jewish Apocrypha.

Dwarfing this particular gap in self-knowledge, there is the startling fact that the fascinating account (in Greek) of the politics of the post-Ezra period in the books of Josephus was completely unknown to the Jews of his time, the first century A.D., in Palestine; it became available to Jews in general only ten centuries later in a derivative work called *The Book of Jossipon.* Today, all Jews know about Josephus if only because it was he who told the story of Masada and thus prompted its unearthing in our time. Only through Josephus, who joined the Romans during the war of A.D. 66–70 and subsequently wrote his books are we aware in detail of the cultural range of an upper-class Palestinian Jew of the time. The dominant Jewish tradition that came down to us via the rabbis seems to have done its best to shut this all out and to concentrate instead on issues arising from the Torah. In examining the sources of this all-important attitude, we shall not overlook the extraneous forces that found some expression in Jewish life; but it is clear that we must identify, first, how the Torah established itself among the Jews independently of all that was happening in the world around it.

In folk memory, everything went back to Ezra producing "the book of the Torah of Moses" and getting it fully accepted by the Jews whom he and Nehemiah found in Jerusalem. As far as the rabbis—and later generations—were concerned, that moment said everything.

But without denying the historic importance of the story that came down, one wants to know more. What was the book, or scroll, that Ezra produced? Was it the Torah as we now have it? It would be pleasant to think so, but we cannot be sure. The exiles had certainly carried Jewish writings with them, due at some point to be brought together into the Bible. It is enough to understand the drama of the occasion if we regard the book Ezra produced as one of the Bible's constituent elements. As a "ready scribe," Ezra knew his way around all this literature. To arrive from exile with a message for those dwelling in the Holy Land was in itself a phenomenon of great symbolism for Jewish history. Later it happened repeatedly that Jews in the Diaspora developed an attachment of peculiar intensity and carrying power to Jewish tradition, but this was its first illustration.

However, there was a more practical side to the occasion, which needs examining. If the audience in Judea listened to the reading with rapt attention, it was not because they knew little of the issues Ezra was talking about. The Jewish tradition due to be canonized in the Bible had long been familiar in early forms of written and oral literature—narratives, folk poetry, Temple hymns, court chronicles, and prophetic oracles. Much of this must have been vivid in the minds of the remnant of Jews in Judea, reinforced, as they were, by the first waves of returnees at the time of Cyrus and Darius. But if one wants to understand the true character of Ezra's meeting with them, one has to see it in a very practical context. In religious terms, he was expounding a book of the Torah of Moses. In practical terms, the high point of his drive was for something we might think less spiritual: the full restoration of animal sacrifices at the Temple.* Yet this aim, when realized, became crucial to the survival of the Jews, for it reestablished for all time the centrality of Jerusalem in the Jewish faith.

Under David and Solomon, this had never been in question; but under the split kingdoms of Judah and Israel which followed, the principle had been submerged for a time with worship taking place anywhere—"in every high place and under every green tree." Jerusalem had become central again when an ancient scroll—usually thought to have been the Book of Deuteronomy—was discovered in the Temple precincts in the days of the young king Josiah (640–609 B.C.).

It is a central theme of Deuteronomy that the elaborate ritual of festivals and sacrifices was to be centered exclusively in God's holy city. The young king Josiah had launched a campaign to bring this about, making Jerusalem once again the focus of national pride. In the aftermath of the Destruction, the remnant in Judea had the same motivation, and Ezra was there to support it.

Jerusalem was the place where God had "caused His name to dwell." To offer sacrifices there was a greater demonstration of Jewish survival than even the existence of the monarchy had been. Kings had come and gone, leaving memories of glory overshadowed by wickedness and tyranny. By contrast, the holiness of Jerusalem was absolute. To sacrifice there was to express again the unity which had brought the tribes of Israel together in the first place in a sacred federation.[1]

It was, then, the restoration of sacrifices which gave Ezra his authority. Though he is remembered as a scribe, conveying the idea of a rabbi expound-

*Some scholars think that a partial ritual of sacrifices had always been maintained or at least restored with the pre-Ezra returnees.

ing the law, it is his role as a priest, skilled in carrying out the sacrificial rituals, which is given pride of place, to begin with. His book opens with a genealogy which establishes that he was in true line of descent from Aaron and Zadok. Immense detail is given of the Levites and other Temple officials who were part of his company. Central to the story are the many sacrifices he carried out on returning.

Josephus, taking a broad historical view, refers to him as "high priest," a title which links him to the central structure of Judea's political life in the ensuing four centuries as a temple-state. It is a role which also helps to explain how the Jews managed to lay the basis in these centuries for enduring social and religious independence. When the Persian king (Artaxerxes I or II) encouraged Ezra's mission to Jerusalem, the decree armed him with financial power and legal authority to set up a largely self-governing society, conducted under Jewish law and built around "the house of your God which is in Jerusalem." It was part of Persian policy that vassal communities should have a large measure of independence and the backing of Persian law to enforce absolute control over their members. This pattern of socioreligious autonomy was fully maintained under the empires which followed, and this explains the fanatical faith which the Jews came to attach to the Temple and its rituals as the mainspring of their life. It was only when the Temple was desecrated —as by the Syrian Antiochus IV and later by the Romans—that the Jews moved into rebellion.

The clues are clear enough in the Ezra story if one turns to the detail (as given in Nehemiah 9) to amplify the broad picture. The main thrust of Ezra's argument to the Jews assembled before him is that they must maintain their distinctiveness as a people, which was explicit in God's Covenant first with Abraham and then with Moses. God had maintained the Covenant by providing them with their own land. The Jews had broken the Covenant in turning aside from "the right judgments, true laws, good statutes and commandments" which had been made known to them by Moses on Sinai. Listening to Ezra, they all agree that they will henceforth keep the Sabbath with the greatest strictness and put away their non-Jewish wives. But it is the Temple which is to dominate the pattern of their lives. They resolve on a new covenant, "sealed by Levites and priests," under which they undertake the most meticulous forms of subservience to Temple law, including the provision of sacrifices for the daily, Sabbath, and festival rituals, the surrender of the first fruits of cattle and produce, "the fruit of all manner of trees, of wine, and of oil," the tithes of all produce to the Levites, and the annual payment of a third of a shekel "for the service of the house of our God."

It is necessary to acknowledge to the full the dominance of the Temple in Ezra's message as a prelude to examining the other strands in the exposition of Judaism that was now being generated. In one sense, Jewish history in the ensuing five centuries seems to have been constructed almost entirely on this newly invigorated Temple base. A priestly class entrenched itself in the seat of power, first with deputized authority from the current overlord empire and later, after the emergence of the Hasmoneans, with periods of direct identification with the newly created monarchy. Certainly, the office of high priest, with its many political, sacerdotal, and financial aspects, was of unique importance to Jews everywhere until the destruction of the Second Temple in A.D. 70, five hundred years after Ezra.

One accepts this, yet one knows in the same breath, that it is only part of the story. A force of a very different order, centered on biblical teaching in what we would consider its more spiritual aspects, was gathering momentum in the same period and far more significantly for the future of the Jews. Once again there is little documentation. All one can be sure of is that by the second century B.C.—that is, two hundred years after Ezra—the Bible, in all its varied forms, had taken hold of Jewish life. Schools and meeting places for Bible exposition were universal; the statutes that Ezra had pleaded for were part of a deeply embedded pattern of social life; crowning all, for the future, leaders of a new type had emerged—sages (the future rabbis) who were totally involved in giving precision to the written and oral traditions of Jewish life.

These traditions came to be respected with the holiness of Revelation and from two linked aspects. First, the exact observance of Bible regulations, based on written and oral sources, was felt to generate holiness in every act that a Jew did, including his participation in the rituals of Temple sacrifice. Linked to this was the holiness ascribed to study. The Bible had to be studied in order to arrive at the right laws, but there was holiness in the act of study itself. To study the Torah was not merely pleasant and praiseworthy, it was a form of worship, as directly as prayer.

One can never exaggerate the importance that devotion to study was to have on Jewish life. But because it surfaces first in this undocumented period, one is left wondering how far it sprang from specifically Jewish circumstances and how far from influences in the world outside. On this, we have, first, to consider the experience in Babylon.

Echoes of Babylon

The first clear sign that we have of Bible study is Ezra reading the book of the Torah to the assembly in Jerusalem, assisted by Levites "who gave the sense and caused [the people] to understand." Was this a new approach, arising from the special conditions of the exile?

Let us recall that Ezra appeared on the scene some one hundred fifty years after the beginning of the exile in 586 B.C. We know almost nothing of the social life of the Jews in Babylon up to this time but can reconstruct some elements in their ideas from scattered references to the period in Haggai, Zechariah, Ezekiel, some of Psalms, and through the passage in Isaiah which sees Cyrus, in giving the Jews permission to return, as the agent of God—the Lord's annointed, or messiah.

In everything we read, it is clear that the experience of those in exile gave a new dimension to their feelings as Jews. Living closely as one settlement, in a wasted area near Nippur, they tried, to begin with, to see their lot as temporary, a punishment for sin that God would reverse. Bereft of the Temple, they undoubtedly gave added weight to institutions that expressed the sense of continuity with the past, notably the Sabbath and circumcision. With equal intensity, they must have assembled to listen to readings and tales from their history.

Some think that here lies the origin of the synagogue, with its ritual of prayers and Bible readings. Nothing so formal—and certainly no routine of prayers—emerges, in fact, from this early time. All one can predicate for this period is an involvement with stories of the past through close attention to readings by priests and scribes and to oracles by prophets.

But though the exiles must be envisaged as wrapped up in their Jewish background—their history, ceremony, and fate—one soon becomes aware also of influences from outside. If some of their leaders moved into official roles at the Babylonian court (which Nehemiah did as cupbearer), it is safe to assume that Jews were affected equally by intellectual contact. Babylonian wisdom became legendary in Jewish folk memory, as one sees in the opening sentences of the Book of Daniel, composed in the second century B.C. at the time of the Maccabean revolt but purporting to describe events in Babylon four hundred years earlier. We are told that to qualify for selection for service at the court, Daniel and his fellows had to be judged sufficiently intelligent ("skillful in wisdom . . . and understanding in science") to be developed by "the learning of the Chaldeans."

It is a classic Diaspora picture, with Jews learning avidly from the outside world. There is evidence that many Jews in exile took Babylonian names. They adopted the Babylonian names for the months (Nisan, Iyyar, et cetera) and also became more responsive to Aramaic, the lingua franca of the whole western empire as far as the Mediterranean.*

More important is the effect which the exile had in producing the Bible. Some scholars think that a very large part of our present Bible, including the Pentateuch, must have been brought together and edited in Babylon, where scribes had an immense interest in furnishing their nostalgic fellow Jews with an authentic guide to conduct and faith. Other scholars, it must be said, place the editing later and in the Holy Land when the office of high priest had assumed a central administrative power that it had not had under the monarchy. In this view, the priestly class would have had a strong motivation in ensuring that the holy writings always established the antiquity of their authority as proof of its validity. To make this possible, they worked into the final Bible an angled narrative of the past,† setting the story in a heavily chronicled context going back to Creation.‡ But even if the final editing was in the Holy Land, the exile furnished a setting for intense preoccupation with the Bible in ways that may even have affected its content.

The Books of Kings, for example, may well have been written in the exile, influenced by the style of Babylonian chronicles. The authors would have used the primary Jewish chronicles which are mentioned as sources in our present

*Aramaic cursive replaced the ancient Hebrew script. See H. H. Ben-Sasson, ed., *A History of the Jewish People* (Cambridge: Harvard University Press, 1976) p. 164.

†In critical Bible studies, this source is referred to as P, the Priestly source.

‡M. Noth, (see *The History of Israel* [New York: Harper and Row, 1960], pp. 295–97) arguing for an editing in Palestine believes that the religious significance of Sabbath and circumcision in the Priestly narrative was a late feature of Jewish life. Before the exile these had been merely old social customs but had been built up during the exile for nostalgic reasons. The editing had to be done in Palestine, in his view, because "this was and remained the central arena of Israel's history," while Babylon was a "mere outpost." John Bright (in his book, also titled, *A History of Israel*, 2nd ed. [Philadelphia: Westminster Press, 1972], p. 350) disagrees. In his view, the historical corpus (Joshua to Kings) was probably composed before the fall of the state but reedited and expanded in exile, to meet the new situation. The oracles of the Prophets were likewise preserved and expanded. The same applies to the cultic laws which comprise the bulk of the so-called Priestly Code and which reflect the practices of the Jerusalem Temple. The Priestly narrative was probably composed in the sixth century B.C. in exile, setting out a theological history of the world beginning at Creation, "an eternally valid model not only for the past but for all time to come." This still leaves it uncertain, in Bright's view, whether the exilic edition was produced in Babylon or in Palestine; but the source material was so voluminous as to indicate that the original historical work was composed in Jerusalem before the Destruction in 587 B.C.

Kings, but reworked the story as a whole to establish a consistent chronological framework for both the northern and southern kingdoms.

At the other end of the story, it is quite possible that some of the archaic passages in Genesis, which have a Babylonian setting, were picked up there at this time and merged into the ancient Jewish traditions. As one scholar puts it:

> By means of the wisdom of the Chaldeans, the Jews had become familiar with many of the old Babylonian myths—the creation, the deluge, the early generations of man, etc.—and they sought to harmonize the myths with the Biblical reports of these events.[2]

Some stories may have come in entirely from the Babylonian setting, such as that of the Tower of Babel, linked so clearly to the visible ziggurats. More surely, perhaps, one sees mysterious passages in Genesis—notably the brief references to the almost supernatural character of Enoch (Gen. 5:21–4)—becoming clearer in a Babylonian context. All we know from Genesis is the suggestion that Enoch never died—"for God took him." In apocalyptic and rabbinic literature (also in Christian literature), Enoch is a powerful and clearly defined individual—the bearer and creator of human culture and the transmitter to man of heavenly experience drawn from his regular communication with angels. All this, especially the angelology, reflects Babylonian concepts which must have entered the Jewish oral tradition even if they had only cryptic expression in the Bible.

Going beyond this, some scholars have seen the Babylonian exile as the locus in which the Jews, in direct contact with the highly spiritual and deeply entrenched Persian religion of Zoroaster, must surely have been interested in, and even influenced by, the worship of Ahura Mazda, seen by the Persians as the great god who created heaven, earth and mankind. Expressed baldly this way, it might indeed seem as if the growing conception in the following period of a more philosophic Jewish monotheism might have echoed in some ways the dominating worship around them of a Supreme—and nonimaged—Being. On closer examination, there is an influence but not in this form. The worship of Mazda did not envisage an absolute monotheism in the Jewish sense but a struggle between a Supreme Being and the forces of evil. It was even, in some ways, an equal struggle, with Mazda's supporting gods (Devotion, Holiness, Immortality, et cetera) always matched by subsidiary creations of the evil power Ahriman. Another basic distinction was in the role of the priests. The approach of the Jews, as it emerged later, linked the priestly rituals to open, clearly defined moral purposes, while with the Magi the emphasis was on magic, astrology, and Orphic mysteries.

Yet the Persian religion did leave a most pronounced mark on the exiled Jews, identifiable mostly in stories of celestial beings who were involved in dramas that linked Heaven and earth and lent themselves to the expectation of supernatural intervention in the affairs of man. Ideas of this kind must have been absorbed by Jews and carried orally from Babylon to surface later in sectarian thought. One aspect of this is the increasing power given in Jewish thought and writing to God's opposer Satan, who is, to begin with, merely a plotter, the leader of angels who have fallen from high estate. Starting with him as an ingenious participant in the judging of men, as in Job, this grew (for example, in the pseudepigraphical Book of Jubilees) into the notion of a directly opposing power, and finally in The Testaments of the Twelve Patriarchs into a fully fashioned dualism, with seven evil spirits arrayed against the seven good spirits, an exact echo in number of the set battle between the respective supporters of Mazda and Angra Mainyu.

Dualism of this kind became too much for the rabbis, but a subsidiary aspect certainly survived effectively in the concept of angels, protective and dangerous. In the earlier books of the Bible, messengers of God *(malakh* is *messenger* or *angel)* appear in various stories, with their status somewhat blurred. Are they in fact disguised versions of God, or supernaturalized men? There are also vague accounts of a host of celestial beings, seraphim, flying around God and praising him. From exile times, however, angels begin to be seen with explicit roles, in particular as guardians of specific peoples. In Ezekiel and Zechariah they dominate apocalyptic visions. In Daniel, leading angels (that is, archangels) appear for the first time with personal names—Michael and Gabriel—and distinct personalities. In a book ascribed to the Genesis hero Enoch, the archangels with special missions are increased to four by the addition of Uriel and Raphael, and the number sometimes rises to seven. In various other books from late Temple times (some of which have survived as fragments among the newly discovered Dead Sea Scrolls), the seven angels have distinct protective roles in world history. In one of these scrolls, the future apocalyptic conflict is set out in terms of a fight between the Prince of Light and the Angel of Darkness, highly suggestive of Iranian origin.

In general, the idea of apocalypse—the Last Judgment, the End of Days—undoubtedly received a strong build up from this source, dwarfing the more restrained expression of the idea among earlier prophets. Yet the outpouring of writings and oracles of this kind in the centuries immediately before the Christian era was very much played down later by the rabbis, who felt that apocalypse and the arrival of the Messiah were subjects full of danger. Not that they themselves were uninfluenced by forces from outside the Jewish world, but what appealed to them much more than angelology, apocalypse, and magic in Persian style was the rational pursuit of truth as implicit in the words of the Torah. Study and a stoic mind were virtues that drove them forward. There was a strong element in this approach of the learned standards of the Greek world around them.

Yet the Babylonian influence survived, and most particularly in having projected for the first time a paradigm of Diaspora existence in a form that was infinitely adaptable for the future. The uniqueness of the Jewish Diaspora lies in its being anchored firmly at two ends—the ancient homeland and the land of settlement. The double connection was organic, in this case, for it was the land of new settlement, Babylon, that made it possible for the ancient base to be sustained.* The remnant left in Judea might well have disappeared before constant attacks from surrounding nomads if the Persian Empire, which reigned with paramount authority all the way to the Mediterranean, had not permitted—indeed encouraged—the Jews in the Holy Land to develop intense loyalty to their tradition, an amalgam of what emerged from their own folk history and what they had picked up in Babylon. As Elias Bickerman, an outstanding scholar on this period, puts it:

> Imperial protection shielded the Palestinian Jewry from the Arabs and the Philistines, Edom and Moab. . . . If Jerusalem had not been part of a Gentile empire, the nomads would have driven the Jews into the sea or swallowed up Palestine, and the rock of Zion would have been the foundation of an Arabian sanctuary a thousand years before Omar's mosque.[3]

The base in the Holy Land was affected by the Diaspora in another sense, too. The enlargement of experience in drawing on Jews living "outside" prevented what Bickerman calls "spiritual inbreeding." Dispersed Jews everywhere always felt a living connection with the Holy Land, but this was never rigid in drawing only on the formal structure of the tradition in Judea. There was, as there still is, a symbiotic relationship between the Diaspora and the homeland, in which Diaspora developments find their way back.

*One inevitably thinks of the parallel today with the new settlement of the United States sustaining the ancient homeland of Israel.

There were special reasons why the Babylonian Diaspora was uniquely influential in this sense. The Jews transported by Nebuchadnezzar's soldiers had settled down as a community which kept the old traditions alive, established its own characteristic institutions, and for the next thousand years was to be incomparably more influential than any other Diaspora settlement. It was in close relation to them that the Jews of Palestine developed new ideas, incorporated permanently in the Jewish outlook. But this was only part of what Jews drew from outside. The new background of Hellenism had its own effect on the Jews when it became pervasive over the whole of the Near East after the conquests of Alexander the Great.

3

Ideas in the Hellenist Setting

The Greek Background

EWS used to grow up believing that in ancient times the Greeks were the enemy. This was partly because of the fight waged in Maccabean days (from 166 B.C.) against the Syrian-Greek oppressor Antiochus. More generally, it reflected a distaste among the rabbis, whom we begin to hear of a century later, for the pagan outlook and all that they thought went with it—worship of idols, sport and sexual freedom, irreverent philosophising.

Given this strong anti-Greek feeling, it might be natural to think that when Hellenism—the social, religious, and intellectual ideas of the Greeks—swept over the whole of the Mediterranean world in the fourth century B.C., the Jews stood out against it, holding on to a fundamentally distinctive religion and culture. But though this does highlight a divergence of historical importance, it conveys a thin and misleading picture of the texture of Jewish life in this formative pre-Talmud (and pre-Christian) period.

It is true that this was the period in which the traditions of the Jewish past grew organically into a most distinctive outlook on life, carrying immense and lasting authority. The ancient writings, long known in various forms, were now lived with as a single, integrated work—the Bible—conveying sanctity not only in what it said but in its very existence. Hearing it read and expounded regularly in meeting places (ultimately synagogues), the Jew saw it as an inexhaustible source sanctifying all that had come to him in tradition and folk memory—ritual, law, and legend. Everything in this tradition emphasized that the Jew stood alone; but from within, this was not a narrowing experience. The literature which was the rock of his faith spoke with grandeur and conviction; the intensity of feeling which it conveyed gave Jewish existence depth and satisfaction.

Yet this same distinctive Jew was also responding freely to many features of the Hellenist background. Jews had been aware of the Greeks as part of the world close to them long before the arrival of the Macedonians under Alexander. As far back as the second millenium B.C.—the patriarchal age—Greek pottery was being brought regularly into Palestine and Syria. In the days of the Jewish monarchy, Greek traders were familiar from the early seventh century B.C. with coastal sites everywhere, particularly with important harbors in Egypt. Greek mercenaries were in Egyptian and Babylonian armies, including that of Nebuchadnezzar. Athens, from the time of its great fifth century B.C., poured a profusion of explorers, adventurers, and scholars into the Near East. Their craftsmen were carving in marble for the Phoenicians. Attic coins set a pattern everywhere, including Judea during the Persian period where the inscription *Yehud* appears on coins side by side (perhaps surprisingly) with "graven images"—the owl of Minerva or a god on a winged chariot.

It is a widespread error, Elias Bickerman points out, to think that from the time of Ezra the Jews were so much "under the yoke of the Law" that they were "immune to foreign contagion." Palestine, in fact, "belonged to the belt of an eclectic Greco-Egyptian-Asian culture, which extended from the Nile Delta to Cilicia. Greek painted pottery, Phoenician amulets and Egyptian idols are equally typical of Palestine in the fourth century."[1] Indeed, the Jews of this period were in one important sense less exclusive in the application of their religion than was common among other peoples. In the non-Jewish ancient world, it was basic that all nations had their own gods from whose worship aliens were excluded. For the Jews, the stranger was free to share everything. Biblical texts specified that he was to keep the Passover with the congregation of Israel (Ezra 6:21), that the same law applied "to the home-born and the stranger who sojourns among you" (Exod. 12:49), and even more remarkably that "thou shalt love the stranger as thyself" (Lev. 19:34). As part of the same approach, the Jews were the first, it seems, to open the gates to proselytes. There was nothing particularly tolerant in this. If anything, it was a natural corollary of their confidence that theirs was the One True God, who would be worshipped ultimately by all peoples. Isaiah had presented God as saying: "My house shall be called a house of prayer for all peoples" (Isa. 56:7). The far-reaching religious implications of this had strong social echoes in a time of change.

In the early restoration of the Temple, the remnant of Jews in the Holy Land had undoubtedly grown in number by intermarriage and by direct affiliation to the worship at Jerusalem. However inadequately, these new Jews were at home in the tradition. Later, through the military conquests of the Hasmonean dynasty, conversion of whole peoples (for example, Edom and Moab) to Judaism raised no problems for the authorities. Throughout the whole period, in fact, proselytism of non-Jews was familiar over a very wide area, a demonstration of how false it is to think of the Jews as exclusive in a racist sense. The ultimate effect of this religious expansionism was, it is true, a mixed blessing for the Jews. To some extent, emigration and proselytism hugely enlarged the base of Jewish loyalty, especially during the later struggles with Rome. In another sense, it diluted the faith and in this way provided a base, especially in Asia Minor, for the fateful transition to Christianity. For the moment, however, it can be seen as clear evidence of social and doctrinal flexibility in this formative period, side by side, paradoxically, with a move at the center of Jewish life toward an increasingly rigorous definition of how being a Jew was to be expressed.

The Social Effects

In working out their religious ideas, the Jews drew on or paralleled Greek thinking much more than is usually realized; but the most immediate influence of Hellenism was in the secular field.

In the division of Alexander's empire among his generals after his death in 323 B.C., Palestine was first under Egypt, the dynasty founded by his general Ptolemy, and subsequently, from 200 B.C., under Syria, the dynasty founded by Seleucus. The governmental pattern was set by Egypt in a tight administrative control for a hundred years. It brought Palestine into a military and economic system which deeply affected the history of the community there.

Martin Hengel, a profound student of this subject, has expressed this very bluntly:

> The Greek spirit first revealed its superiority to the people of the East in an inexorable, highly secular way: in a perfected, superior technique of war and —particularly in the Egyptian sphere of influence—in a no less perfect and inexorable state administration, whose aim was the optimal exploitation of its subject territories.[2]

For the military aspect, the startling victories of the Macedonian war machine under Alexander were followed by the establishment of an elaborate system of citadels and fortifications all over Palestine by the Ptolemaic armies trained in the same advanced techniques and enjoying personal attachment to the ruler almost as a military caste. With other inhabitants of the area, Jews were drawn in as mercenaries, serving in Palestine and also settling in large numbers as veterans in Egypt itself, where they were proud, in some cases, to adopt the designation "Macedonians." There is evidence that Jewish mercenaries were also heavily employed by the equally Greek Seleucid dynasty of Syria. Incessant battles between Egypt and Syria for the control of Palestine meant that the terrors and skills of warfare became a powerful feature of Jewish life. Echoes were to be heard later in the fiercely military language and symbolism of the apocalyptic literature, highlighted in the Dead Sea War Scroll. It has indeed been suggested[3] that this may explain how Jewish soldiers acquired the skills that enabled them to defeat the Syrian armies in the war of the Maccabees. Many of the Jews would have had a good military training as mercenaries, which they then put to good effect in their own cause.*

In these terms, Jewish military experience under Hellenist guidance may have been to the benefit of the Jews. The picture is less certain when one considers the mixed benefits that the Jews of Palestine absorbed in the eco-

*There is a parallel in our own time. Many Jews of Palestine who fought in Allied armies in World War II drew on the skills they had learned when they came to fight in Israel's war of independence in 1948.

nomic and administrative fields under the stimulus of Hellenist Egypt. As an entity, Palestine, it might be said, prospered. Agricultural production expanded with new methods and markets. Side by side with Phoenicians, the Jews of Palestine and the adjacent Diaspora countries grew increasingly active in international trade. The other side of the coin was less attractive. The country undoubtedly grew richer, but the form this took most notably was the accumulation of wealth by the rich, leaving the ordinary people poor and hungry. If the administrative system was more efficient, it meant that the overlord government (first Egypt and then Syria) had found more efficient ways of raising taxes. These two evidences of economic progress came together in the emergence of a few rich Jewish families who bolstered their wealth through acting as tax-farmers for the Egyptian, and later the Syrian, authorities. The most famous of these families mentioned as great landowners in Transjordan as far back as Nehemiah (fifth century B.C.) had the name Tobiah. In the third to second centuries B.C. they are known for their huge wealth as tax-farmers and for the application of their power to maneuver the Temple leadership, itself a focus of great wealth.

But if the riches of the Tobiahs were legendary, it was more significant that the disparity between rich and poor was also widespread socially below this peak, making its impact visible in much of the literature which ultimately emerged to reflect the moral dilemmas projected by the contrast of wealth and poverty. We see it explicitly in the rabbinic writings, where care for the poor is a constant concern. As Hengel notes, the Gospels establish the same point:

> The milieu of the parables of Jesus, with its great landowners, tax-farmers, administrators, moneylenders, day-labourers and custom officials, with speculation in grain, slavery for debt and the leasing of land, can only be understood on the basis of economic conditions brought about by Hellenism in Palestine.[4]

This change was taking place over a five hundred-year period—poorly documented—from the time of the return of Ezra to the Holy Land in the fifth century B.C. In itself, the economic picture would have been paralleled in other lands of the area. But there is a crucial difference for Palestine arising from the existence there of one institution, the Temple of Jerusalem, which, at one level, unified Jewish feeling in a unique way and at another, became the focus of a fundamental struggle between tradition and assimilation. Even the internal Jewish tradition which survived this struggle was permeated with ideas drawn from the surrounding Hellenist world; but without this there was still a dilemma for Jews in what the Temple stood for.

There is no difficulty in documenting the overwhelming importance of the Temple as a unifying factor in Jewish life during these obscure centuries. The rituals had come down as the word of God, conveyed by Moses and described by him with immense precision as the way in which the Jews could identify with God's holy purpose for mankind. The Temple was, thus, the visible symbol of Jewish history and its meaning. The priests might be greedy and treacherous, but a Jew was still fulfilled by being present at the rituals for which they were responsible. The sacrifices he brought to them enlarged his own life.

But the Temple was also the focus of wealth and power. Its leaders were a social elite who felt, as many emancipated Jews were to feel with equal force in the nineteenth century, that tradition was overdue for reform and that the Jews should assimilate more intensively with the world outside. Temple leaders pressed this hard on their Hellenist overlords, and when it was adopted as policy, to the disgust of loyal Jews, revolt broke out.

Antiochus IV had been encouraged by an avaricious and strongly Hellenist high priest to issue decrees for the reformation of the Jewish religion by abolishing its social and religious distinctiveness. Jewish rituals were to be harmonized with practices elsewhere, and as part of this program the Temple was deliberately defiled through the introduction of unclean animals as sacrifices. To ordinary Jews, the insult was unbearable. A family of obscure country priests—later to be known as the Maccabees or Hasmoneans—broke into revolt and were joined by all who were determined to restore the Temple's ritual purity. Contrary to what might have been expected, the revolt was successful and ultimately led to the establishment of a new Jewish state, very large and independent. If this new dynasty lost touch with the masses later, at least the Temple had been saved and remained for Jews a celebration of holiness.

But the split between the priestly upper class and the mass of ordinary Jews persisted and had indeed shown its force soon after the national uprising. Among those who had rallied to the support of the rebels was a group, or movement, known as Hasidim, pious ones, who must have been stern traditionalists. They soon lost their enthusiasm for the Maccabeans when this new dynasty, under increasingly powerful leaders, expressed its character in diplomacy and military expansion. We have to envisage that the Hasidim, and others like them, had no interest in this and turned, instead, to the traditionalism of Torah study and practice. We see this laying the foundation in that century for the Pharisaic Judaism of strict observance which is such a strong feature of the Gospels and is fully fashioned later in the rabbinic writings.

Ideas in Common

If many generations of Jews saw the Torah Judaism they knew as emerging, in this way, exclusively from internal Jewish traditions, scholars of our time ask us to note the wider sources of the common heritage. Even in familiar Bible books, like Ecclesiastes or Proverbs, we see now reflections of the Hellenist background, and there are other sources or links to Greek ideas which can widen our understanding of the living flow of the Jewish faith.

There is never any problem in accepting that Jews living in the Hellenist world outside Palestine drew heavily on this background and indeed became highly assimilated. The supreme symbol of this was the translation, beginning in the third century B.C., of the Bible into Greek—the Septuagint, as it is called. The Jewish community of Egypt, which was already very large (it is said to have grown to a million by the first century A.D.), needed to have the Bible in Greek because this was their first language. Egyptian Jews went to Greek schools, and even the fragmentary writings that have survived indicate a strong effort to develop some cross-fertilization. We know of a popular account of the kings of the Jews in Greek from the end of the third century B.C.; in the second century we hear of romances and poems on Jewish themes, including a drama on the Exodus (with some echoes of Euripides) by a poet called Ezekiel. More solidly there are different kinds of historical writing in Greek, notably the *Letter of Aristeas* (an imaginary account of how the Septuagint was composed), and the factual story of the Maccabean revolt by Jason of Cyrene, the kernel of *Maccabees 2*, composed specifically for Egyptian Jews. In philosophy, fragments survive of the writings of Aristobulus of Paneas, offering an allegorical interpretation of the Bible, an approach which was seen later in full majestic flow in the work of the great Philo Judaeus of Alexandria (c. 20 B.C.–A.D. 50).

This assimilation pattern in the Diaspora was to be expected. But within the Holy Land itself contacts were closer than used to be believed. The merchant and aristocratic classes were, of course, fully at home with the Greek language, but even the masses had the kind of smattering of Greek that, many centuries later, the Yiddish-speaking Jews of the Pale had of Russian and Polish. The Jews were aware of Greek art; the Greek cities offered them a lively picture of Greek culture in all its forms; and even in religion and methods of study much was absorbed.

The strong Greek influence had been felt, as Elias Bickerman points out, long before Alexander came on the scene. In the fifth and fourth centuries B.C., Greek dominance in social and commercial life was just as marked in Palestine as in the other countries of the Mediterranean. Athenian coins were the principal currency for trade in the fifth century and were imitated in Palestine in the fourth century by Jewish coins bearing Greek symbols. A democratic assembly of the Jews, known as the *gerousia,* existed independently of the Temple hierarchy. The Jews whom Greeks met in coastal towns or in other Diaspora countries at this time seem to have earned some respect for their religion as one free of crude imagery and calling for reflection ("a nation of philosophers"); the Jews in turn acknowledged, as the whole world did, the Greek absorption in wisdom.*

When we consider those writings by Jews of Palestine which bear a strong echo of the Greek world of ideas, we are dealing not so much with assimilationists of the priestly elite as with Jews who were involved intelligently with their own tradition but still wanted to assess it in terms of ideas around them. Language was a limiting factor, since Hebrew and Aramaic, in which they wrote, had not developed, as Greek had, to accommodate philosophic ideas; but they managed to express a good deal all the same.

Another problem in assessing how far the more sophisticated Jews of Palestine were in tune with the Greek background is that the surviving Jewish written material cannot be assumed to be representative. Much was lost, either by accident or deliberately when Jewish leaders from early rabbinic times repudiated Greek influences. What survived, or has been discovered in our own time (like the Dead Sea Scrolls), is by its nature narrowly sectarian.

But if much from these pre-Christian centuries has been lost, there is still a wide range of material that brings out the Greek links. We are lucky, of course, that some late books of the Bible which the rabbis saw as somehow alien to the basic tradition were nevertheless finally admitted into the canon.

*In light-hearted stories told in the Midrash, Jews showed that they could always get the better of Athenians, who thought they were so clever. For stories of this kind, see C. Raphael, *The Walls of Jerusalem* (New York: Knopf, 1968), pp. 114–22.

We have benefited also from the fact that some rejected books of the time were preserved in Greek translation by the Church. These books of the Apocypha help us to build a picture, with the late Bible books, of the argument in progress between Jewish and Greek ideas.

Two books—Ecclesiastes and *The Wisdom of Ben Sira*—are particularly helpful in this regard. Ecclesiastes is a late biblical book with the title in Hebrew *Koheleth,* "the lecturer"; and its tone is set by its well-known opening: "Vanity of vanities . . . all is vanity" (Eccles. 1:2). The author announces that he is "the son of David, king in Jerusalem," which has always ascribed the book in popular terms to King Solomon, though this is not taken seriously by scholars, as the book clearly comes from the Hellenist period. In brilliantly tailored epigrammatic style, the author, writing in the first person, tells how every experience he has had has ended in emptiness. He has built great estates and accumulated treasures but without any lasting satisfaction; he has given himself to sensual passion, food and wine—all vanity. A man is better unborn—"an untimely birth is better than he"—who suffers disillusion on this scale.

But there is more to Ecclesiastes than this fin de siècle negativism. The author is establishing a positive position but has to go round a little to reach it. First, he shows that he is not interested in glib answers about human happiness. Nor is he going to deal with specifically Jewish answers. He is applying his experience and reason to all existence—"everything under the sun." Having cleared the deck, so to speak, he is ready to open his mind to what might ultimately have value in human existence, and here he deals with Jewish themes though without identifying them as such. As in Greek thought, the supreme virtue is taken as Wisdom, which Jewish thought linked with the Torah and hailed—particularly in the Book of Proverbs—as the plan on which God has created the Universe. Wisdom calls for the moral life, and traditionally the Jews put themselves at the center of this ideology. They saw the Torah as God's plan because it is built around a clear principle affecting conduct: God will reward those who obey His commandments and punish those who disobey. The author of Ecclesiastes is ready to consider this. Is there any way in which this principle of the Torah can be seen to work? There is not, he decides. The righteous suffer, the wicked prosper. More deeply still, man is not free to choose, since his life is governed by what comes to him as chance, though in fact God has already worked it all out. In this sense, the pattern of life is preordained. If one looks for ultimate satisfaction, one has to find it within these limits, before "the dust returns to the earth as it was, and the spirit returns to God who gave it" (Eccles. 12:7).

It is a view that communicates not pessimism and certainly not frivolity but a cool skepticism with Greek overtones. No refuge is sought in mystical ideas; nothing is said of any reward in an afterlife. It is in earthly terms that one makes the best of things by pursuing wisdom. One enjoys the pleasures that come along. One behaves decently to one's fellow men. One delights in the astringency of rational debate—as the author shows by writing his book.

Ecclesiastes—probably written, to judge by its style, in the third century B.C.—is a good clue to what many educated Palestine Jews might have thought in those times. The author would have come from a family—perhaps tax-farmers—that had done well under the Ptolemaic control of Palestine and was thoroughly at home in the Greek style of argument. At one time it was customary to think of this book, like all the other late wisdom books, as having a direct Greek source; today it is emphasized that parallels can indicate common sources. The Jews themselves had a long tradition of wisdom schools, drawing on ideas common in the Near East or even further afield in the oriental world. Ecclesiastes certainly echoes the mood of Stoic philosophy, but this, too, had an oriental source. Zeno, the founder of the Stoics at the end of the fourth century B.C., reflected the interaction between Western and Eastern ideas which followed the conquests of Alexander, when many important thinkers came to Athens from oriental cities.

But if the author of Ecclesiastes was not necessarily drawing on Greek sources, he was certainly expressing himself in Greek style and perhaps reflecting some distaste among educated Jews for the exclusiveness of their inherited tradition. Carried to excess, this attitude ultimately led the high priest elite toward self-destructive forms of assimilation, as seen in the causes of the Maccabean revolt. By this time, however, many thinking people among the Jews had recovered their nerve. They could respect Greek wisdom yet see Jewish faith justifying itself in equally satisfying terms.

A perfect expression of this approach appears in the second book, *The Wisdom of Ben Sira,* which was written around 170 B.C. For centuries later, its maxims were widely quoted by the rabbis, even though the book was not included in the Bible and has come down through the Apocrypha. The original Hebrew text disappeared until fragments of it began to be found in the Cairo Genizah (synagogue storehouse) at the beginning of this century. Since then, more of the original has surfaced, including pieces among the Dead Sea Scrolls and at Masada, as if to dramatize once again the extraordinary links between our own time and the fateful era two thousand years ago when Judaism took shape.

In contrast to Ecclesiastes, whose author leaves the Torah on one side to consider man's fate in universal, philosophic terms, *Ben Sira* sets out deliberately to guide Jews on how to lead good lives in Jewish terms. The author is identified as a scribe, and the style has biblical echoes both in the maxims it offers for sensible conduct, which are reminiscent often of Proverbs, and in the richly written poems and prayers that surface repeatedly. Yet the book has a distinctly Greek tone in its organization and imagery; and the underlying argument is implicitly philosophical in coming to grips, however quietly, with the skepticism that a book like Ecclesiastes reflected.

In *Ben Sira,* the wisdom that a Jew must pursue flows from God and is enshrined in the Torah. Obedience to the Torah is the way in which a Jew identifies with God's purpose, and this finds its expression in ethical conduct, which the author spells out in patient detail. Love of the family is at the heart of the good life. Side by side with this are the rules for being a good citizen, based like everything else on "maxims of prudence and self-discipline," as the New English Bible version puts it. But the book is not dull; its rhetoric rises repeatedly above the pragmatic level, notably in its last section, chapters 44 through 50, which looks to the great men of Jewish history as exemplifying the noblest urges within our life. It was fitting that the famous opening of this section, "Let us now praise famous men . . . ," was among the manuscripts in the original Hebrew that Yigael Yadin discovered at Masada in 1964.

In its love of the Torah and its moral guidance, *Ben Sira* expresses perfectly the attitude that was to develop later among the rabbis. It is highly significant that the book was written—c.170 B.C.—just at the point when the Jews who clung to their tradition rose, under Maccabean leadership, to reject the ordinances of Antiochus IV proscribing their ancient practices. One cannot think of Ben Sira as a member of the group called Hasidim who took to arms, since this implies a certain extremism in faith and action. Ben Sira is obviously observant of the Law, but his tone is too poetical and also too urbane for sectarian aggressiveness. He gets by, as did many of the rabbis later on, with a cheerful nature, a sense of optimism, and a readiness to hedge on sharp philosophical issues for the greater good of the cause.

The optimism comes through all the time, as in the opening verses of Chapter 33:

> Disaster never comes the way of the man who fears the Lord:
> in times of trial he will be rescued again and again.

A wise man never hates the Law,
but the man who is insincere about it is like a boat in a squall.*

As for the philosophical issue, it emerges in a firm exposition of free will, in sharp contrast to the tone of Ecclesiastes, which had pushed logic to its extreme in showing that man was deceiving himself in thinking he was a free agent. In general, Ben Sira is constantly warning against pushing logic too far:

Do not pry into things too hard for you
or examine what is beyond your reach.
Meditate on the commandments you have been given;
what the Lord keeps secret is no concern of yours
[Ch.3: 21–22].

The dilemma of free will is one such issue. It may well have been, as Martin Hengel suggests, that "in the Jerusalem of Ben Sira—whether as a continuation of the thought of *Ecclesiastes* or under the influence of determinist astrology—the freedom of man, and thus the foundation of obedience to the Law, was denied."[5] Ben Sira finds the solution through a kind of robust common sense:

Do not say "the Lord is to blame for my failure":
it is for you to avoid doing what he hates. . . .
When he made man in the beginning, he left him free to take
his own decisions:
If you choose, you can keep the commandments;
whether or not you keep faith is yours to decide [Ch.15: 11–15].

In the same spirit he refutes the idea, Epicurean in style, that God is not concerned with the fate of the individual, one of the strands of thought in Ecclesiastes which makes man a shuttlecock of fate. Certainly, Ben Sira says, man seems nothing "compared with the measureless creation," but that is precisely why it is wrong for man to think he can comprehend God's purpose. God's works "are done in secret." We cannot discover the canons of reward and punishment but must simply have faith that "God judges man by what he has done." In this way, we can hold on to our sense of being able to choose between what is right and wrong, even though God knows what we are going

*The New English Bible version is particularly successful on *Ben Sira* and is therefore used here.

to choose. These basic ideas of Ben Sira on free will were reexpressed by Akiba, the outstanding rabbi of the early second century A.D. in a famous paradox: "All is foreseen [by God] but freedom of choice is given" (Mishnah, Aboth 3:16), which is echoed in another rabbinical paradox: "All is in the hands of Heaven, except the fear of Heaven" (Ber. 33b).

We cannot tell how many other traditionally inclined Jews might have been writing in the same vein; but even *Ben Sira* alone helps us to understand the major shift in thought among Jews at this time that would, within two hundred years, stabilize Torah Judaism within a permanent carapace of rabbinic teaching. Until the Maccabean revolt, Hellenist and Jewish ideas rubbed shoulders within Palestine, as well as in the Diaspora. From then on, Palestine Judaism turned inward, whereas abroad, especially in Alexandria, the full development of the Hellenist framework meant that by the time of the great Alexandrian philosopher Philo Jewish thought in the Diaspora and the thought of the early rabbis in Palestine were out of communication. It was a bifurcation that would be momentous later, when early Christianity developed its ideas and support among Jews in the Diaspora; but it is interesting enough as a pointer even when all the Jews considered themselves in one camp.

As always, there were losses and gains when different ideas were being developed. In the Diaspora, the philosophic exposition of Jewish ideas in Greek terms created an aura of such respect as to encourage the thought that the source of Greek wisdom might lie in the Jewish Bible. In fragments that have reached us of the writings of the Jewish philosopher Aristobulus of Paneas, Moses is credited with a form of divine inspiration that was at the same time based on reasoning powers fully adequate by Greek standards. The ideas of Moses, he said, reached Pythagoras, Socrates, and Plato in an early Greek version of the Torah through which they understood and accepted how the world was created and sustained by God. As a Greek philosopher, however, Aristobulus still felt obliged to offer allegorical explanations for aspects of the Bible (for example, anthropomorphism or the oddity of the Sabbath) that were not otherwise acceptable to Greeks.* Ben Sira, who was his contemporary,

*There was nothing offensive to Greek philosophy in suggesting that their ideas might have originated among wise men elsewhere, in Egypt or Phoenicia. In presenting Bible ideas in Greek terms, one had, of course, to get rid of crudities like anthropomorphism. One could explain the Bible example of this allegorically. One could also draw on oriental ideas to help the exposition, as was done, for example, in explaining God's order in the Bible to rest on the seventh day. Orientals, it was said, assigned a special role to the number *seven* in the control of the universe.

There is no need to think that a writer like Aristobulus was trying to soften his attachment to his Jewish background. On the contrary, he was engaged, like Philo later, in showing how attractive Jewish ideas were when "properly" understood. On the Sabbath, for example, the never apologized for the Bible this way. If his reasoning was cool and his attitude stoic, he still expounded wisdom in Torah terms and with an emphasis that could lie easily with the faith of the Palestine teachers—the rabbis—who were to emerge two centuries after him.

Rationalism of the Jewish Teachers

Our main interest must obviously lie in the process that produced these teachers, the rabbis, since it was they who formulated the traditions with which Jews lived for the next two thousand years. As already noted there is little documentation for the whole period from Ezra to the rabbis. A crucial point on this is how far we can regard the rabbinical writings, which began to emerge from the second century A.D., as a reliable guide to the formative period of Torah teaching at least three hundred years earlier.

The dominant feature of this formative period must certainly have been the increasing attention being given to the study and practice of the Torah. From what appears in Josephus and other sources, we know that at the time of the Maccabean revolt there were many sects offering different approaches to Torah observance and the Hasidim, that strictly observant group of Jews, had contributed a powerful visionary, apocalyptic element.

In contrast to this, the Pharisees, whom we hear about—and not pleasantly—in the Gospels as strictly observant Jews, seem closer to an establishment group. It has always been assumed that the Pharisees were the forerunners of the rabbis, but with an important distinction. The Pharisees, who, according to Josephus in the first century B.C., had some political weight, were known for strict observance of the Law. The rabbis were observant, too, but their dominant characteristic was the attention they gave to study.

The scarcity of contemporary documentation on all this raises questions on one very important issue. The rabbinical writings are heavily concerned with what one might call rational activity—legal and social questions, moral homilies, et cetera—and give little attention to visionary ideas. Yet we know that in the pre-Christian centuries there was a whirlwind of mystical and apocalyptic notions in the air, soon to make their presence felt in sectarian—and ultimately in Christian—beliefs. The editors of the Talmud, which began to be committed to writing in the fourth century A.D., certainly played this down. They may well have wanted to discourage talk of redemption and messiahs among ordinary Jews, since this had had disastrous results in promoting the war against the Romans and in the emergence of Christianity. At the same time, they may have expressed a genuine tradition about the prerabbis—the Pharisees—in showing them as practical and moralistic rather than visionary and mystical.

The picture given of the Pharisees in the Gospels would fit in with this but is inadequate in a different respect by painting them as hypocrites because of their concern with observance of the letter of the Law rather than its spirit. We get a very different picture from the rather few references to the Pharisees that appear in the Talmud. Putting the two together, we begin to understand that the legacy of the Pharisees to the rabbis lay precisely in the spiritual quality that distinguished their preoccupation with observance of the Law. Dominating their lives was their concern for ritual holiness. In this they went far beyond routine observance of the Law; their devotion to ritual purity had an almost cosmic significance. God was the Creator of the universe: the Torah was the plan which He had followed. The Temple at Jerusalem was God's home and therefore the epitome of purity. The priests who carried out the rituals had a holy function; but the Jews were a nation of priests, so that every Jew had an obligation to aim at this high level of ritual purity, expressed in personal life, in human relations, in food, in tithes, and in any way—the more extreme the better—which established that the Jew existed for identification with the holiness of God.

It was this devotion to ritual purity which led them to organize themselves in brotherhoods, *haburoth.* Purity involved not being "contaminated" accidentally by the activities of people of less rigorous standards. In the brotherhood, they could count on their fellow members having gone through all the ritual ordinances, for example, on personal hygiene, on food, and on tithing.

To the Pharisees—as later to the rabbis—Torah Judaism achieved its spiritual aims by being practiced with the greatest strictness in the daily conditions of ordinary life. In this respect, it was very different from the faith of sectarians, some of whom felt that the standards demanded by the Torah could be realized only in desert conditions, remote from the materialism of the cities and the hypocrisy of priestly politics. We have long known from Josephus that a sect called Essenes went off this way to live a totally ascetic life in the desert. In our own day, amazing new light has been shed on this by the discovery, starting in 1947, of the books, or scrolls, of a sect who lived in the desert near the Dead Sea and are identified by most scholars with the Essenes. The scrolls tell us—mostly in deliberately secret language—of their origin as a sect in the last century B.C. and of their rules of conduct as a community. In origin, they clearly sprang from the same historic movement in Jewish life that had inspired the Hasidim, but their sectarian ideas, under a charismatic Teacher of Righteousness, had taken them out of the mainstream that was to produce the rabbis. Without Josephus and the Dead Sea Scrolls we would have known very little about them. The piety of the rabbis, as expressed in the Talmud and Midrash, is of a different order—learned, socially oriented, and full of robust common sense.

We have, perhaps, to see this rational outlook as a deliberate turning away from the wild visionary beliefs that had risen to a peak in the period before the destruction of Jerusalem by the Romans in A.D. 70. What the rabbis seem to have felt and passed on into the tradition Jews have inherited was a certain distaste in looking to salvation through some magic intervention by God in the affairs of the world. It is ironic that these ideas, which assumed Jewish form in talk of a messiah, had originally had strong parallels with Greek mystical ideas; but this is understandable since both Jews and Greeks drew, in this regard, on ideas in the air in oriental religions.

Jews had, it is true, always liked dreaming about a golden age, and these thoughts were manifest in the later books of the Bible. What had emerged in the second century B.C. however—during and after the Maccabean wars—was a visionary faith of a different kind. We see the outcome in the programs spelled out in wild detail in the scrolls found in the Dead Sea area. These discoveries have completely transformed the picture we had of this period, which had been based for Jews on the rabbinical tradition.

Until recently, the only really visionary book that ordinary Jews knew for this period was in the Bible—the Book of Daniel. The early Christians had preserved other visionary books of the time in Greek, or Ethiopic, translation, but there was a feeling, even when Jewish scholars began to draw on them in relatively modern times, that they were somehow un-Jewish in content. The discovery of the Dead Sea Scrolls has been a major factor in removing this notion. The "library" of the Dead Sea sect includes a great number of texts, some almost complete, others only fragments, duplicating and adding to the visionary writings preserved by the Church. These books are mostly written in the name of an ancient character—Enoch, Abraham, Moses, et cetera—and are therefore known as Pseudepigrapha. Taken together with the other writings preserved in Greek translation and now found in the Apocrypha, they furnish scholars today with a solid amount of original source material unknown, or virtually unknown, to generations of rabbis all through the Middle Ages and, indeed, to our own day.

The Visionary Movements

We can linger on this for a moment since it projects an interesting paradox on what Jews of today are to make of the tradition they have absorbed through the ages. Existentially, Judaism must be whatever was handed down, generation by generation, over a period of the last two thousand years. This was a composite faith, expressed in the theology and morality of the Bible, the traditional ordinances of the rabbis, and the prayer book, the Siddur, which enshrined this. This Diaspora religion included a vague idea, never spelled out in detail, that one day the Messiah would come to rescue the Jews and transform the world. But in other respects it excluded supernatural ideas of the kind expressed in the visionary books and even more, of course, those that had surfaced in the Christian faith, such as Virgin Birth, the Resurrection, the Second Coming. It is true that mysterious teachings of a supernatural type did develop during the Middle Ages in the mysticism of the Zohar and the Kabbalah, but the ordinary Jew was led to feel this was a secret lore open only to scholars of special quality and to be kept apart from the straight Jewish tradition, which emphasized rationality and common sense.

On the basis of the new material now available, Gershom Scholem, the outstanding scholar of Jewish mysticism, has shown that we must revise our ideas of what constituted normative Judaism. There was in the pre-Christian centuries an intense preoccupation with the visionary realm. The rabbis tried to stifle this but were unable to do so completely. It survived, therefore, linked to two particular themes which opened the mind to the wildest cosmic speculation—*ma'asei bereshit,* Creation, and *ma'asei merkabah* the Chariot of God's throne, as described in Ezekiel's vision (Ch. 1). The persistence with which these mystical themes were pursued, despite official discouragement, and the huge development of eschatological ideas in the books and fragments that are now available indicate, in Scholem's view, that apocalyptic and theosophical beliefs must have been very powerful. Against the view that this energy found its way solely into Christianity, he sees these ideas (especially on *merkabah* themes) as persisting and fertilizing Jewish thought powerfully and consistently throughout the centuries—which leaves a Jew of today with a difficult problem. Is this new light on Jewish ideas in the crucial prerabbinic period merely interesting historically, or does it call on us to reconsider the character of the faith we thought we had inherited?

Under Scholem's influence, we certainly have to look with a fresh mind not only at material newly discovered but even at writing which we thought we understood. Two books in particular are illuminating in this regard. The first, long familiar to us, is the Bible book Daniel; the second, unknown to Jews until relatively modern times, is a book of roughly the same period called *Enoch.*

Daniel, as everybody knows, purports to describe the adventures and visions of a Jew whom Nebuchadnezzar took back with him to Babylon after conquering Jerusalem (586 B.C.). The first half of the book describes the rise of Daniel and three companions to top rank at the court. When imprisoned through jealous rivals, the firmness of their Jewish faith saves the companions "in the fiery furnace" and Daniel "in the lion's den." In this part of the book, Daniel is shown as a sage who interprets the king's dreams brilliantly. He continues to serve successive kings, Darius and Cyrus.

In the second half of the book Daniel rises from being merely a sage to a visionary, predicting, with the help of angels, the dramatic course of history, leading to a supernatural transformation of mankind. The basic idea is that there is to be a succession of four monarchies—all due to perish—followed by a fifth ruled by "the saints of the Most High," that is, the Jews. In some passages, the transient kingdoms are named and also identified with animal symbolism, the last one being a half-comic "horn" (Antiochus IV) who abolishes the sacrifices of the Temple. In another vision, the angel Gabriel leads Daniel on to see that the ruins of Jerusalem would persist for "seventy weeks of years," followed, first, by the cutting down of the "annointed one" (probably the high priest) and then by the Temple turning into "an abomination of desolation." The final visions bring these wild "prophecies" to the time of the Roman intervention, with the Syrian king Antiochus instituting direct measures against Judaism—the exact conditions preceding the Maccabean revolt.

Daniel was accepted and enjoyed for centuries as emerging from its imagined Babylonian setting; but it is clearly linked in fact to the time of its villain, Antiochus IV, around 170 B.C. The "prophecies" are a good historical account of the broad dynastic struggles of the previous four hundred years; the theme is the immediate situation—the need to resist attacks on the faith. But above this practical message, it offers a graphic picture of the apocalyptic ideas that had invaded the Jewish mind by the beginning of the second century B.C. The previous picture that had held the field was the biblical covenant with God, in which, broadly speaking, obedience by the Jews to God's Commandments would ensure reward in earthly terms—long life, good crops, good rulers, justice, and a happy family life. But now, a sensible promise of this kind was no longer credible or adequate in the atmosphere of persecution and distress that had permeated Jewish life. Responding to this, a believer tried first to give some rational meaning to God's purpose in bringing about the Destruction and the ensuing persecution of the Jews for this endless stretch of time—"seventy weeks of years." One couldn't count on any sudden end being in sight; but one day, as defined in the visions, God would reorder the world He had created. His messengers—the angels—were communicating the good news in dreams to those selected (like Daniel), gifted by great understanding to penetrate the secret knowledge of God's purpose—the visions of the End of Days. Armed with the knowledge that the world would be turned over one day at God's will, one could survive in hope and, indeed, in happiness.

Enoch has a very different coverage of the same subject—and a very different history as a book. The visions described are built around the biblical Enoch because of the mysterious verse in Genesis (5:24) which says that "Enoch walked with God, and then was no more, for God took him," which was understood to mean that he ascended to Heaven during his lifetime. In its original form, *Enoch* was written in Hebrew or Aramaic or a mixture of both, like its rough contemporary Daniel;* but it is mainly known in translation. It was translated into Greek around 135 B.C., and later by the Church into Ethiopic, which is the only full version to survive. Though it is of supreme importance as a guide to apocalyptic thought in the second century B.C., it was not known in the West after the fourth century A.D. and only began to emerge

**Daniel* has come down in the Bible version as more Hebrew than Aramaic, though it was probably written originally in Aramaic. See H. L. Ginzburg in *Encyclopedia Judaica* vol. 5, col. 1289, and references there.

again in the eighteenth century. Parts of the Greek translation were subsequently found; and for Jews it is of great interest that fragments of the book in Aramaic—the original version, perhaps—were found among the scrolls of the Dead Sea sect. This Dead Sea library contained many texts or fragments of apocalyptic works. *Enoch* is, however, the most important in range.*

The main theme of the book is that Enoch, having ascended to Heaven, is taken on a tour by the angels for an inside view of stories in the Bible—seeing the coupling of the *nephilim*, giants, with the daughters of men (Gen. 6:4), watching an angel being sent to warn Noah of the flood, and acting as a neutral scribe in dealings between God and the giants (compare the Titans story). He travels through the whole universe, seeing all the elements of Creation, and also "the seat of glory," upon which sits "the great glory" (God)—which brings to mind *ma'ase merkabah*, the mystic ideas centered on God's throne.

Many passages of the book deal with The Last Day. The Messiah, waiting to judge all humanity on that day, was born with Creation and has been waiting since then for this purpose. The timing of these great events is envisaged, as in Daniel, by dividing history into periods, ending with the rebuilding of the Temple and the Day of the Last Judgment.

If this broad idea of salvation at the End of Days is the major issue of *Enoch* and the many other pseudepigraphical writings found at the Dead Sea sites,† the detail of their presentation is particularly relevant to a consideration of how significant these visionary ideas were for the later emergence of rabbinic Judaism. Certainly much of the myth and legend in these books reappears later; but the style of the books is in sharp contrast with that of normative Judaism. One issue in the visionary books is their insistence on a solar, as distinct from the normal lunar, calendar. One is struck also by the vehemence of their ideology, stemming, in the case of the Dead Sea sect itself, from a decision to reject the whole Temple institution as it existed at the time of their

*It is usually known as the *Ethiopic Book of Enoch,* for obvious reasons, or as *Enoch 1,* to distinguish it from another apocalyptic work on the same subject, written in Greek and translated into Slavonic in the tenth or eleventh century, and known as the *Slavonic Book of Enoch,* or *Enoch 2.*

†The book most similar to it is *Jubilees,* which is in the form of a conversation between the Angel of the Presence and Moses on Mount Sinai and includes an exact timetable of "heavenly dates" going back almost to Creation. Other works are the *Ascension of Isaiah,* the *Assumption of Moses* (history from Moses to the death of Herod), the *Book of Adam and Eve* (myths and legends), the *Testament of the Twelve Patriarchs* (an ethical work in which each son of Jacob offers advice based on his own experience), and numerous other books ascribed to Abraham, Joseph, Moses, Solomon, Zechariah, Ezra, and many other Bible characters.

founder, the Teacher of Righteousness, and wait for the days when mighty battles would overthrow both the Jewish establishment and the wicked nations. The pattern of life of this sect is dry and rigorous, as revealed in their *Manual of Discipline,* which conveys nothing of the warm humanity that is revealed in the sayings for normative Judaism going back to the great Rabbi Hillel (born at the end of the first century B.C.); on the other hand, there is a wealth of poetry and aspiration in their prayers, drawing heavily, of course, on the language of Prophets and Psalms.

Linked, as we now know, to the Dead Sea experience is the story of a particular sect that was so overcome by the sense of sin and impending disaster —perhaps after the Maccabean wars—that they decided to flee as a group to Damascus, recording the whole drama in a document now available to us—the Damascus Document. The history of the document's discovery is in itself a sign of the confusion of the times, only now becoming clear to us.

Scholars first found fragments of the Damascus Document in the Cairo Genizah at the beginning of the twentieth century and were uncertain what to make of it.* Today, we know from copies of the whole document found among the Dead Sea Scrolls that the sect had seen their life of piety attacked by "a man of mockery" who misled the people, as a result of which Israel was "delivered to the avenging sword of the covenant."[6] The leader of those who "turned back from impiety in Israel, went out of the land of Judah to sojourn in the land of Damascus." The life they led in exile is set out in immense detail, showing rigorous ascetism. The fact that this document was found at Qumran (Dead Sea) suggests that the sect lived there, perhaps after Damascus, but more probably from the beginning, with Damascus as only a symbol of their destination. Their scathing references to politics in Jerusalem identifies them as a splinter movement of protest against all authority, whether that of the ruling priestly class, or the establishment Pharisees.

It is ironic that the picture we now have, through discoveries, of the visionary sectarians, clearly a minority, is in some ways fuller than that of the ordinary Jews. One would like to know how far the visionary ideas permeated Jewish life, and for a particularly practical reason. Central to all the visions is the idea of a messiah. Can we determine now what was thought about this among ordinary Jews before Christianity gave it a form of its own?

*Solomon Schechter (1847–1915) was the first to work on the manuscripts, ascribing them to the tenth or eleventh centuries A.D. But fragments began to be found among the Dead Sea Scrolls from 1947, and built up to original copies of the document, written in biblical Hebrew (without Aramaisms) and going back to the first century B.C.

Ideas of the Messiah

The way into this is to try and reconstruct, from later rabbinic writings, what the prerabbis talked about when they met in their conventicles, which we must regard as proto-synagogues. They certainly read and discussed the Torah: The picture in *Ben Sira* and in the Gospels on this is very authentic. What is harder to establish is how far they were absorbed at the time in the ideas of the sectarian literature.

Ezekiel's vision of the Chariot was certainly a ready subject for much of this kind of speculation, which must have included ideas about the *hayoth*, living creatures, and other beings in Ezekiel, forming what Scholem calls "an angelogical hierarchy at the Celestial Court." But Scholem adds that because of the fragmentary nature of the material "we shall probably be unable to say how much of this was mystical and theosophical speculation in the strict sense."[7]

Are we on surer ground in reconstructing what must have been said about the advent of a messiah, so powerful an image in the visionary books and certainly a major Jewish concept for all time to come? The prerabbis undoubtedly talked of a Messiah; and we know from Josephus of men who arose from time to time (especially in Galilee) claiming to be one. All one can say, looking back from the later rabbinic writings, is that the idea of a messiah actually arriving seems always to have been kept deliberately vague, in the realm of myth and rumor rather than with the self-assured factualism of sectarian writings.

It seems fair to say that, in myth, the idea, as presented in *Enoch,* of the Messiah having existed at God's side since Creation to await his great moment, might have been widespread. Akiba, the great rabbinic leader of the early second century A.D., is recorded in the Talmud as having said something like this himself;* yet we must be cautious in deciding how far to regard Akiba's remark as typical of early synagogue talk. He was, the Talmud tells us, very skilled in esoteric speculation; but there are signs that he never took Messiah-talk too seriously, as we know from the tone of his alleged announcement that Bar Kokhba, the great rebel of his time, was the Messiah. For Akiba, this was merely a conversational ploy, in line with a reply by one of his rabbi

*It brings to mind, of course, the opening words of John, "In the beginning was The Word" (that is, *logos,* an expression of Christ's existence).

colleagues: "Akiba, grass will be sprouting out of your cheeks, and the Messiah will still not have come."[8]

We have to recognize a paradox in this playful kind of talk about the Messiah. Faith could be pinned on his arrival one day, as long as one didn't take it all too literally. In later centuries, whenever messianism took hold of the Jewish people, it spelled disaster. The founding rabbis seem to have had a sound instinct on this. They sometimes toyed with Bible verses (especially from Daniel and Prophets) to work out the dates for the messianic age, but they were deliberately inconclusive about it. In any case, they said, the Messiah himself would only be the precursor of the Day of Judgment, which might be four hundred or maybe a thousand years later. Perhaps the Messiah had already been born, one rabbi said, and some of the messianic age had already gone. Another rabbi "cursed the bones" of anyone who made precise calculations. Most commonly, talk of the Messiah had a folktale character, as in the Midrash story of the Messiah being born at the very moment of the Temple's destruction. A farmer hears his ox lowing, which a stranger, passing by, tells him means that the Temple had just been destroyed. In grief, the farmer unharnesses his ox, who suddenly lows again. "Reharness your ox," says the stranger. "A redeemer of the Jews has just been born."[9]

If the rabbis talked about the Messiah only in this folkloristic way, it was because there was no firm doctrine on the subject. It was the *halakhah,* the Law, that one had to be precise about; the Messiah belonged to the realm of *haggadah,* storytelling and moralizing with no sense of precision needed. Even if, as seems likely, they felt free to indulge privately in philosophical or theological speculation of the kind spelled out in visionary books, these thoughts had to be kept away from ordinary folk. Against the sectarians who disappeared into the wilderness, leaving behind them, for our discovery, the kind of ecstatic and undisciplined writings that one would find today among the wild sects of California, the majority of Jews of Palestine were being encouraged to become safe and secure within "the fence" of the Torah, listening to it being read and expounded on the Sabbath, observing its rituals, and leading good lives in line with the homely sayings that the rabbis preserved from this period.

But if this is the comfortable view which most Jews absorbed of their past, we know today not to underplay the ideas we can follow in the visionary documents. In the talk that we find there of mass repentance and the expectation of a redeemer, we think inevitably of the background in which

Christianity emerged. If we look at the picture with this in mind, we shall find that the ideas of the visionaries did indeed straddle Jewish and Christian thought and also had parallels with Greek ideas that ultimately became more explicit in Christianity when the new faith developed its characteristic dogmas.

Behind the parallels there are many contrasts. One is that in the Jewish visionary documents, the Messiah is never conceived as coming quietly, a man of peace, to lead mankind gently toward a golden age. All accounts are centered, as in Daniel, on the background of sin and desolation that precedes —and in this case also follows—him. It is the same in *Enoch.* The storyline shows Enoch as a preacher of repentance, which calls to mind the teachings of John the Baptist; but there is a difference. The emphasis with the Baptist lies on the individual, in whose hands repentance can bring about redemption. By contrast, the general tone of the apocalyptic writings to which we now have access emphasizes the historical—almost cosmic—nature of the repentance called for. The centuries of anguish since the first destruction of the Temple, by Nebuchadnezzar, are the result of the earlier transgressions of the people of Israel that are still not wiped out, even with the Temple rebuilt. The intensity of this feeling seems to reflect the passion of small groups who feel that they alone have the secret of God's will for mankind. All routine life is material and evil: the elect alone can penetrate to God.

This concept of secret knowledge, *gnosis,* is one of the ideas which straddled Greek, Jewish, and ultimately Christian attitudes, not always to pleasant effect. In the first and second centuries A.D. some Christian writers built up their "secret knowledge" into a system (Gnosticism) with a dualistic conception of the deities of the world, in which Judaism's God and Bible stood for Evil, while Christianity stood for Good. The Jewish God's laws had to be turned upside down; and this strong antinomian attitude, despising the laws and standards of society in the name of one's secret knowledge of the truth, became for a time an element within the Church of passionate anti-Jewish feeling or, as it was later called, anti-Semitism.

It is perhaps ironic, in the light of this, that centuries earlier, select groups of Jews themselves, and Greeks around them, had developed elaborate and sometimes aggressive teachings on the basis of their own secret knowledge, coming straight from God. With the Greeks, mystery religions, including esoteric notions affecting the interrelations of gods, goddesses, and mankind, are associated with the mythical figure of Orpheus, who moved back and forth between earth and Hades. Apart from their sacrificial and Dionysiac aspects,

Orphic rituals put forward teachings on the liberation of the soul through mystic rites and moral purity from the "circle of birth and becoming," and included—almost in biblical style—laws for abstention on animal and other foods, rules against contact with pollution, and the practice of many "mysteries." These teachings were adopted in the sixth century B.C. by the philosopher and scientist Pythagoras, whose brotherhood gave a more religious form to the doctrine of the soul and its purification.

In these early times there was a free flow, between oriental and Greek ideas; and the Jews, based then in Babylonia, were part of this interchange. We shall never know exactly what they brought back with them to Palestine after the return, but by the third and second centuries B.C. they must certainly have had their own secret knowledge, due to find its way in subsequent centuries into the narrow exclusivity of sectarian writings. There is no need to predicate direct borrowing by the Jews of oriental mystery ideas from the Persians or from the Hellenists who were themselves influenced by these ideas. Yet the parallels are manifest.

One sees it, for example, in the persistence of dualist ideas among Jewish sectarians. Their writings are, of course, strongly monotheistic; yet they have clearly taken over some of the division of powers among the gods that is a feature of the Persian religion. In this, they allow far more than normative Judaism for an explicit dualism of Good and Evil. In the *Community Rule* of the Dead Sea sect, for example, it is laid down that after creating man, God appointed two spirits, Truth and Falsehood: "All the children of Righteousness are ruled by the Prince of Light and walk in the ways of Light, but all the children of Falsehood are ruled by the Angel of Darkness." This Angel of Darkness is not a symbolic figure, but real; everything evil in the world "lies under the rule of his persecution."[10]

The Dead Sea discoveries have greatly amplified what was already known about the ideas of sectarians in the last two centuries B.C.; but the historical thread is clear enough in the later rabbinic writings. Gershom Scholem is very firm in pointing to the disturbing character of the ideas of these visionary sects and their persistence later: "Of the existence of a heretical Gnosis of dualistic and antinomian character on the outskirts of Judaism there cannot be any doubt".[11] As later Jewish history was to show, the messianism that was based on secret knowledge drew much of its power and even justification from a reversal of normal moral standards, with obedience becoming rebellion and sin becoming virtue. We are aware of it most clearly in the seventeenth century messianism of Sabbatai Zevi.

Magic and Pietism

If the potentially explosive character of their secret knowledge made sectarian Jews, first in Hellenist and later in Christian times, more like their neighbors than they would have admitted, this was by no means the only area in which ideas were held in common with non-Jewish neighbors and widespread among all Jews. An obvious example was the natural acceptance of astrology and the presence among Jews of magic and healing through charismatic individuals. Here, once again, the later rabbinic writings attempted to soften the mention of these deviations, but without succeeding too well. Magic in all its forms—divination, sorcery, exorcism, communication with the dead—had been prohibited in the Bible as the hateful practice of non-Israelites, but it had certainly persisted. It can be assumed that much was picked up in these fields by the Jews of Babylonia and was active as a force in Palestine.

It is important to mention this because of the Gospel stories of magic and healing by Jesus. One should perhaps separate the two. Healing power is an attested gift found in all ages and does, of course, include an element of magic even when it operates simply by the laying on of hands. The idea is that sickness is the work of evil spirits who have to be expelled by this personal touch, and by magical formulae, for a cure to succeed. This was certainly the underlying assumption in the Near East, and it had become common among Jews in the pre-Christian centuries. In *Enoch,* for example, the angel Raphael (the name means *godly healing*) is entrusted with the task of throwing the wicked angels into darkness and fire so that the damage done through their sorcery can be removed; and there are many parallel stories. In general, the men credited with exorcist power in pseudepigraphical literature—Noah, Moses, Solomon, and others—are presented as going through prescribed rituals and uttering specific formulae to achieve the aim of exorcising the evil spirits. There are brief mentions of similar stories from rabbinic times, which one must assume reflect the strength of both the healing and exorcising traditions so often seen in Gospel stories of Jesus.[12]

Straight magic is another matter. For whereas healing (even through exorcising) is natural in its working—the recovery to normality—there is a kind of magic which means some demonstrable reversal of nature, as in the miracle of the loaves and fishes or Jesus walking on the water. The Jews of that period were familiar with many stories of magic, in this sense, in the Bible; and it is known from the Apocrypha and stories surviving among the rabbis that magic persisted in its folk form through amulets and magic formulae. In one case—told with ironic amusement—a certain rabbi demonstrates his skill by uttering a magic word through which a whole field is suddenly covered in cucumbers; a second magic word collects all the cucumbers into a heap.

But these stories are told as folklore. What the rabbis were really concerned with—and significantly for the religious ideas which had spread among Jews—was the kind of magic that was natural in its operation and yet contained within it a suggestion of a direct interrelationship, during prayer, between man and God. This was where the Jewish tradition, which includes the Gospels, puts its own stamp on the Near Eastern experience of magic.

One example of magic in this natural sense is the story in the Talmud of a man called Honi, who, during a period of drought, drew a circle on the ground and told God in his prayer that he would not move from the circle until rain came. The scene became one of defiance; but in the end God had to recognize Honi's power in prayer, and the rain finally came. Or there was Hanina ben Dosa, a rabbi whose intensity of prayer was so great that when a poisonous snake bit him he did not break off for a second and yet survived. When the prayer was over, it was the snake which was found dead. There is an obvious parallel to this story—and indeed to the subject of exorcism, too—in the Gospel passage in Mark (16: 17–18): "Believers will cast out devils in my name. . . . If they handle snakes or drink any deadly poison, they will come to no harm; and the sick on whom they lay their hands will recover."

It is clear that in ideas about magic and healing, the Gospel stories of Jesus reflected much that was common at the popular level among Jews of his time. At a more spiritual level, there is a close parallel, too, in the attitude to prayer. In rabbinic stories, the Hasidim are credited with a closeness to God in prayer. In the Gospels, the same thought is projected about Jesus. On all this, one notes the comment of one scholar that when the Gospel stories are properly analyzed, "Jesus of Nazareth takes on the eminently credible personality of a Galilean Hasid."[13]

Ideas on Immortality

If one had to pick an idea due to become of supreme importance in the Jewish faith which acquired its significance in the Hellenistic background, it would be the doctrine of the soul and its immortality. To this one must also add the concept of resurrection.

In its early form, this was a very vague area for Hebrew thought. The Bible had the concept of an underworld, *she'ol,* in which the dead lived a shadowy existence. In the centuries following the return under Ezra, the visionary books begin to think of a future existence in what one might call astral terms, as in Daniel (12:3), where it said of the righteous and the wise that they "will shine like the stars forever and ever."

The concept becomes more characteristically Greek in Enoch, who is shown in Heaven, the abode of the souls of the dead, and finds them divided, apparently, into different areas depending on their behavior on earth, some living happily in bright conditions which bring to mind life in the Elysian fields, others, in dark lands, condemned to retribution. This idea, Martin Hengel believes, is new for Judaism:

> Only now, as a result of the Hasidim, does there penetrate to the consciousness of further circles of the Jewish people the idea that after death the "souls" undergo different fates and can be punished or rewarded. This idea had probably been long familiar to the Greek world because of Orphic or Pythagorean doctrines; it occurs both in the philosophers, like Plato and the Stoics, and in the mysteries and in popular belief.[14]

It is hard to say what Jews thought at this stage of physical resurrection, an idea which took hold firmly in later times. According to Josephus, the Essenes spoke only of the immortality of the soul, in the manner of the Pythagoreans; and though there are some references in the Dead Sea Scrolls to the possibility of resurrection, this is thought to imply only a kind of corporeal form for the soul. But even with these physical ideas left vague, there is room for elaborate concepts of the scene of judgment in the afterworld: The deeds of men are written down by specific recording angels, which is paralleled in Babylonian myth by memorial tablets and in Greek myth by the memorandum of Zeus. In Greek myth, angels, or failed gods, are themselves punished when necessary, retribution being always by fire. As one scholar puts it dryly: "Hell is a Greek invention."[15]

Among the Jews, one striking result of the absorption of these ideas was that the immortality of the soul became a major issue between different religious groups in Palestine, with the Pharisees adopting the idea firmly, in contrast to the Sadducees, whose attitude was to stick to the Bible text and who saw no evidence for the idea there. As inheritors, under rabbinic guidance, of the Pharisee tradition, the Jews took over firmly the idea of retribution after death and envisaged physical resurrection quite explicitly, the ultimate hope being that the Jews of all history were destined to reappear in the Holy Land, perhaps rolling there underground from their graves everywhere. (To die or even to be buried in the Holy Land would make resurrection less awkward.) But if these crude ideas survived (and perhaps still do for some), the concept of immortality was normally presented in more spiritual terms, the central concept being the presence in each human being of an immortal soul, distinct from the body.

For centuries, the prayer book included a blessing on God "who restores the dead to life," but this had to be read in the context of a wholly spiritual affirmation of faith which appeared first in the Talmud (Ber. 60a) and is recited every morning on one's rising to life from sleep:

> O God: the soul which thou gavest me is pure; thou didst create it, thou didst form it, thou didst breathe it into me; thou preservest it within me; and thou will take it from me, but wilt restore it unto me hereafter. So long as the soul is within me, I will give thanks unto thee, O Lord my God, and the God of my fathers, Master of all deeds, Lord of all souls."[16]

These, then, are some of the ideas which developed among Jews in the centuries preceding the second destruction of the Temple at Jerusalem. The Hellenist background had affected them powerfully not only in the Diaspora but in Palestine itself; yet within this framework they had developed with new intensity a living philosophy of the Torah and of the purpose of Jewish existence.

4

Dramas in the Roman Setting

Understanding and Conflict

T IS COMMON ENOUGH to recognize that many of the ideas which flowed into Jewish life were drawn from the Hellenist background, itself reflecting Greek, Persian, and other oriental influences. It is less usual to come to terms with the Roman background; yet it was within the Roman orbit that the struggles took place which were to determine not just Jewish history but the whole of western history for the ensuing two thousand years.

It is astonishing, in retrospect, that the tiny Jewish people should have become the unconscious pivot for this historical process. Yet this is a legitimate way of considering what happened. The Romans brought law, order, and a highly civilized form of life to all the countries of the Mediterranean area, stretching soon across the Near East and the whole of Europe. When its military power waned, Roman culture, with its deep dependence on Greek culture, was rescued and developed for many centuries through a religious faith that had begun as that of a Jewish sect and taken root, with irreversible strength, throughout the whole of the Roman Empire. In this way, the intermingled product of the classical and biblical worlds became the common heritage of a very large part of mankind, spreading from the western world all over the earth.

Some will think that the spread of Christianity, through which this happened, was predetermined by Providence, with Jewish defeat by the Romans an essential concomitant. In human terms, things might have turned out very differently if, at an early stage in the story, some cards in the game had been played with a different style or emphasis. This is not to subject history to the fatefulness of trivial chance in the manner of Pascal's famous remark: "Had Cleopatra's nose been shorter, the whole history of the world would have been different." What might well have been relevant, however, was a more sustained acceptance of each other by Jews and Romans from the time when their paths began to cross.

One hypothesis of this kind has been played with rather wistfully by the historian Abraham Schalit, who talks in an essay of how different things might have been if the Jewish leaders of the time had consciously formulated a political position that took advantage of the religious toleration for which the Romans were famed. The Pharisees, he thinks, "should have opened the eyes of the people to the necessity of adopting a realistic attitude towards the Roman Empire. They could have done this without renouncing any essential features of the Jewish religion and way of life."[1] Instead, "they went on living in an ideal world of their own," leaving the political field open to aggressive nationalists. The Romans had no option but to put down the constant revolts, culminating ultimately in the great rebellion of A.D. 66–70. The loss to Jews of a national base in their homeland which followed was crucial to their later history but never inevitable. If it had not happened, the history of the world might well have been different in another central respect. Without Jewish dispersion, on the scale which followed the Destruction, "it is doubtful," Schalit writes, "if Pauline Christianity would have achieved the success it did."

Was there, in fact, an alternative scenario of this kind, in which the Jews would have retained Jerusalem, their Temple, and their homeland, contributing the message of their Bible to the world directly rather than through the extraordinary spread of the religion that grew out of Jesus? Could the Jewish faith have become universalist in a Roman setting, as Christianity did? Or does its whole character depend on its sense of distinctiveness, which history has lived with for these two thousand years?

It is true that during the long period of Roman direct involvement with the Jews of Palestine—a stretch of 350 years until the end of "the last revolt" by Bar Kokhba in A.D. 135—the Jews maintained a strong socioreligious separation, even if assimilated leaders did their best to behave at the same time as good Romans. But until the very last phase under Hadrian, this separateness did not produce insoluble problems. If a Roman prefect or his puppet Jewish ruler bore down heavily on the Jews, mostly in taxes or seizures of Temple wealth, Rome itself, when it heard of it, always found ways of easing the situation. It was not that the Romans had much respect for what the Jews were up to, as the Greeks had had, but they were prepared—sometimes sarcastically—to leave them alone if only they behaved with the proper respect to the government. For if Rome ran its imperium with power and style, it could work with a free rein and with what one might call good fellowship. Despite the cruelty and bloodshed of the Roman era, there was an eagerness to find allies everywhere, not as quislings but as active participants in the cosmopolitan system that they had established. By and large, the Jews in later centuries remembered the conflicts—overwhelmingly, of course, the Destruction of A.D. 70—but not the alliances which the great periods of Maccabean and post-Maccabean power depended upon.

Nor did the later generations of ordinary Jews recognize how Roman government—usually identified in rabbinic writings as Edom, the land of Esau, traditional enemy of the Jews—had provided, in fact, the essential conditions, in Palestine and internationally, for the development of what became Diaspora Judaism. The Romans were not themselves clearly visible on the Palestine scene until Pompey took over Jerusalem in 63 B.C.; but they were in the background for more than a century before this, when Torah Judaism was defining itself in what became rabbinic terms. In looking at the political history of the last two pre-Christian centuries, we see both cooperation and hostility between these prerabbis and those Jewish governmental figures—first among Maccabean rulers and then under Herod and his successors—who depended on Roman support. In nothing was the character of Roman rule more significant than in the complex setting—taking in Roman governors, Jewish kings, legal authorities, priests, messianic aspirants, military rebels, and ordinary Jewish teachers—that set the scene for the emergence and execution of Jesus.

Finally, it was the Roman setting of international law and trade which encouraged Jewish dispersion, long before the fateful destruction of Jerusalem in A.D. 70. The existence all over the eastern Mediterranean of these dispersed communities, some only partially Jewish and ready for a faith that could accommodate some elements of the pagan background, became all-important, of course, to the spread of Christianity. But Jewish faith, which enjoyed, to begin with, a kind of license from the Roman authorities everywhere, was able to build a strong sense of kinship in this long-established dispersion. Even when emerging Christianity became hostile, Jews had learned from this experience how to strengthen their roots in dispersion everywhere, and from that time to the present day they were prepared to show that the Jewish faith can sustain itself and the Jewish people by its distinctiveness and self-confidence.

The miracle of Jewish survival seems to lie in this: that in the pre-Christian centuries an outlook was developing among ordinary Jews that concentrated on Jewish values with remarkable indifference to alien pressures around them. This certainly became true later when Jews came to live in countries other than the Holy Land. But it would never have happened had this distinctive outlook not been developing during the earlier centuries, when being governed by alien rulers—which included assimilated Jews—was the familiar pattern of life. Let us trace the pattern of political rule in Palestine during these centuries in order to see how the indigenous Jewish outlook persisted in the Hellenist and Roman backgrounds and was ultimately able to define itself for long-term Diaspora survival.

Between Egypt and Syria

After the death of Alexander the Great in 323 B.C., the Jews of Palestine were subjected successively to the overlord rule of Egypt and Syria. If these Hellenist dynasties, the Ptolemies and Seleucids, fought each other fiercely for the control of Palestine, the outcome never seemed to make much difference, at first, to the Jews themselves, either in their economic situation or in the expression of their religion. The masses were poor in the manner of peasants, while a small minority of Jews, usually with links to the priestly establishment in Jerusalem, were very wealthy. In religious affairs, too, a change of master was hardly significant. Whoever was overlord, the Jews enjoyed in a limited way a sense of their independence, free to live, except at moments of crisis, by their traditional laws and customs, worshipping at their Temple, and obedient to their leaders, the tax system, and the courts.

It was out of this internal freedom that the Jews were able to develop, in time, the rocklike Torah culture that came into full effect when the state collapsed. Until that happened, a double process was at work. The pious looked inward, increasingly involved in religious movements of various kinds ranging from those who lived quiet lives concentrating on study and observance to apocalyptic groups who moved out to desert communities and recorded their wild ideas in writings, like the Dead Sea Scrolls, envisaging wars and total social upheaval. At the opposite extreme from all the pious Torah followers, whether conventional or revolutionary, were the official Jewish leaders, mostly the priestly families, who had to keep on close personal terms with the overlords, at first Egyptian and Syrian and, later, Roman.

One is first aware of the Romans in the background when the overlordship of Palestine began to give way, around 200 B.C., after about a century of control by the Ptolemies of Egypt, to the rule of the Seleucid dynasty of Syria. Diplomatic and military struggles had persisted even when Egypt was in the ascendant, and this came to a head in direct battles after the accession to the Syrian throne of Antiochus III (222–187 B.C.). His first victories over Egypt were in 219 and 218 B.C. An uncertain period followed, ending finally when the Syrians dislodged an occupying Egyptian force in Jerusalem in 198 B.C. But the position was never quite assured for overlords ruling from their home capitals, especially as different Jewish factions within Jerusalem itself alternated at this time between loyalty to Egypt and Syria.[2]

The main cause inspiring these loyalties lay undoubtedly in the pursuit of wealth and personal ambition by those at the top of the social pyramid. Those most directly concerned were members of the enormously wealthy Tobiah family, whose founder had married a sister of the high priest Onias II. The founder's son Joseph expanded his wealth as a tax-farmer in the period of Egyptian rule; but of his many sons only one, Hyrcanus, maintained the Egyptian link when Syria began to take over. The others supported the new overlord, identifying large sums in the Temple treasury which the Syrians could lay their hands on in return for political favors.

The current high priest Onias III attempted to thwart this and went off to Antioch to plead his cause. In his absence, his brother Joshua (Jason) had himself nominated as high priest, with a promise of still greater financial tribute. Jason was undoubtedly sincere in seeking to broaden Jewish life through greater Hellenization, and he was now seizing his chance with a new king, Antiochus IV (175–163 B.C.), who was due to become a familiar name centuries later to every Jewish schoolchild.

Antiochus was himself an enthusiast for Greek culture. It was while living at Athens that he had heard of the murder of the Syrian king, his brother Seleucus, and had rushed to Antioch to seize the throne. Once in power, he built pagan temples and supported Greek religious festivities with the greatest lavishness. He was thus in need of money and inclined to favor Jews like Jason who wanted full participation in Greek culture and sport and whose highest reward was to be given the honored Greek status as an Antiochian citizen.

It was in this background that the Romans began to have some indirect influence on the Jewish story. In 190 B.C., fifteen years before the accession of Antiochus IV, the Romans had defeated his father Antiochus III in the Battle of Magnesia, which lost for the Syrians the whole of Asia Minor north of the Taurus. Roman power was clearly spreading through the whole of the Mediterranean. Antiochus IV, new to the throne and ambitious for power and wealth, decided in 169 B.C. to attack Egypt while the chance existed. He was partially successful and in a further attack the following year won an outstanding victory. But the Romans had decided by now that Egypt was to be in their exclusive orbit, and Antiochus was given an ultimatum by them to renounce his conquest and retreat. Full of anger, he returned to Jerusalem and launched a persecution of the Jews that was to make him one of the villains of Jewish history.

On his first visit to Jerusalem, he had been suspicious of the pro-Egyptian party among the Jews and had met this by dismissing the high priest Jason and installing in his place an even more extreme Hellenizer, Menelaus, who promised still higher tribute and a more intense pursuit of Jewish Hellenization. Accusations, intrigues, and military revolts had proliferated during his subsequent absence on the Egyptian campaigns. In particular, Jason had brought together a small army to oust Menelaus, forcing him to take refuge in the Jerusalem citadel. With Antiochus now returning and clearly intent on punishing the rebels, Jason fled to Egypt. The Syrian force entered Jerusalem on a Sabbath, when there could be no resistance, butchered the citizens who stood in the way, and carried off women and children as slaves.

This was the setting in which Antiochus turned on the Jews with an edict forbidding, for the first time, all the practices of their faith. Rituals, circumcision, the Sabbath, and festivals were outlawed on pain of death. The Temple was turned into a sanctuary of Jupiter Olympus, images were erected, swine's blood was poured on the altar, sacred prostitution was rife. The Book of Daniel expressed it all in the phrase: "an abomination of desolation."

At this point, no one could have foreseen that the Jews, having been treated with more or less disdain for centuries by the empires of the Near East, were poised for an astonishing political renaissance under a new dynasty. In Jewish folk memory, the Maccabees secured the miraculous purification of the ancient Temple; but they have also become a symbol of military triumph even outshining King David in romantic drama. This is all the more astonishing since the rabbis of the Talmud, fired by a pacifist attitude, always played down military adventurism and hardly mentioned the triumphs of Judah Maccabee and his brothers.

Folk legend had a different stimulus. One is tempted to say that Judah Maccabee was the only military folk hero of the Jews between biblical Joshua and Prime Minister Ben-Gurion. The reality of Maccabean emergence was less assured; but it is worth examining how it happened because of the transformation it wrought in Jewish history.

Emergence of the Maccabees

The sacrilege of the Temple arose because the assimilating party among the Jews had sought a policy of active Hellenization; and even though these ordinances were far beyond what they had envisaged, there is no mention in the record of any attempt by them to soften the persecution. It was the Romans, later, who tried to introduce a spirit of compromise, but for the moment the mood among the ordinary people of the country was one of disgust and defiance.

The story is told in detail in the Books of the Maccabees and in Josephus. Wherever the Syrian soldiers appeared, demanding worship—even pretended worship—of the pagan gods on pain of death, the Jews refused. The wholly new concept of voluntary martyrdom made its first appearance, with simple people ready to die for their faith. Organized military defiance surfaced under the leadership, at first, of an aged country priest called Mattathias. When he died, his son Judah Maccabee* assembled a rapidly growing army of rebels who began to make their mark immediately in guerrilla attacks. The armed force dispatched by Antiochus to put down the revolt proved inadequate against the tactics and resolution of Judah and his brothers. To some extent, their task was easier because Antiochus himself had taken his main army eastward to cope with what seemed a much more serious rebellion by the Parthian province of the Syrian Empire.

But the Maccabee army was growing, and it was strong enough to meet an augmented Syrian force which approached Jerusalem from the south by way of Idumea (the Latin name for Edom). After a series of victories, Judah, though not able to dislodge the Syrian force from the citadel, had won control of the rest of the city and was able, above all, to enter the Temple (166 B.C.). The obscenities were removed. A new altar was built. The holy lamp was relit with a tiny vial of sacred oil, which, by a miracle, lasted eight days. An eight-day Festival of Dedication, Hanukkah, was therefore instituted as an annual holiday.

Resistance had triumphed; and Rome, with an interest in law and order, now sent word urging the local Syrian commander to arrange an armistice which would offer the Jews the restoration of full religious freedom in return for the end of fighting. By now, however, the fighters under Judah Maccabee had become heady with success and were set on forging their own political independence among the small nations who were in a constant movement of struggle and alliance within, or just outside, the shaky Syrian Empire. In continuing to fight, the Maccabees were to some extent merely responding to the developing military situation around them. The upheavals caused by the Syrian attacks had released pent-up feelings of enmity to the Jews among neighboring peoples—Ammonites, Idumeans, Arabs, and the inhabitants of the Greek cities that had proliferated on both sides of the Jordan who nursed a particular dislike of the Jews. When word reached Jerusalem of attacks on remote Jewish settlements far from the tight security of Judea, the Maccabees set out on rescue campaigns to all parts of the area, building up experience that was to turn them ultimately from a small guerrilla force into the creators of a new dynasty.

*The meaning of the word *Maccabee* is unknown. Suggestions linking the name as acronym to a verse of Psalms, Mi Camocha Ba'elim Yaweh, are dismissed by scholars.

It is hard not to see a parallel in all this with the situation exactly two thousand years later when enemies surrounding the new state of Israel decided, in 1967, to mount simultaneous attacks on it and met humiliating defeats. There is a parallel, too, in the fact that when the Maccabees demonstrated their military strength, they nevertheless turned for a guarantee to the great power in the offing, Rome, just as their descendants were to look to the beneficence and support of the United States. And though the new Jewish state that the Maccabees founded was due ultimately to collapse, it is well to recall that the independence it generated lasted in one form or another for more than two hundred years. In Professor Schalit's speculation quoted earlier (see page 81), it could have gone on forever.

Certainly, the pace of the first triumphs was startling. One Maccabean force under Judah and his brother Jonathan moved out across the Jordan to rescue a township of besieged Jews to the northeast and bring them to the safety of Jerusalem. Another force under his brother Simon rescued Jews in Galilee, driving the enemy army to Acre. In the south, Judah captured Hebron in the course of an attack on the Idumeans and was successful in another rescue expedition against Ashdod on the Philistine coast. During this time, leadership of the Syrian force in Palestine had been weakened through the death of Antiochus (163 B.C.) and quarrels over the succession; but now the local Syrian chief (acting as regent to his candidate for king) raised a really powerful military force—with elephants and cavalry—to crush the rebels. Judah was forced to break off his siege of the Jerusalem citadel and failed in a direct battle with the Syrians at Beth-Zechariah. Conditions for the Jews were now becoming pitiful, partly because the seventh year had come round in which the land had to lie untilled. One of the Maccabee brothers, Eleazar, had been killed in the fighting. Judah's force was besieged on the Temple mount.

It was a situation which needed the compromising influence of Roman power to satisfy all parties, a pattern which was to repeat itself many times in the future. At one level, it might be thought that the Jews involved were split in two irreconcilable halves, with the priestly and dynastic leadership eager to accept a role with the various overlords, while the religious masses (often in deadly rivalry themselves) detached themselves from the establishment. Certainly there was a splitting up of functions among the Jews which would cause confusion in responsibility, as was to happen over the death of Jesus. Yet in everyday affairs, people of different ideas found a place under the

Roman umbrella without obvious drama, as an unforced expression of the underlying political realities.

These realities included the recognition of the Syrians as the major power, while the Maccabees governed, for the time being, mainly on internal Jewish affairs. In this situation, with Rome watching from the background, the new Syrian king, through his representative in Jerusalem, offered a kind of peace to Judah and his supporters, subject to their acceptance of a new nominee, Alcimus, as high priest. But at this stage, peace was still premature.

The pietists, the Hasidim, among Judah's supporters regarded Alcimus as a traitor; he responded by enlisting Syrian aid to have many of them captured and executed. On a wider front, the Hasidim had begun to express doubts about Maccabean military and dynastic ambitions. The Torah was what mattered; and being pacifists at heart, they withdrew their support for Judah when it became clear that he was still ready to fight for political independence. His first campaign was, in fact, successful. When battle was finally joined in 161 B.C. with a small Syrian force under their general Nicanor—the main Syrian armies were pinned down in different parts of their empire—Judah won the day and entered Jerusalem in triumph. It was a decisive moment for the Maccabees, and Judah's first act as head of a would-be new state was to send a mission to Rome to win a friendship treaty that would guarantee protection against the Syrians.

Judah's triumph was short-lived. Within a year, the Syrians had put down their other rebellions and were free to send in a major army against the Jews. Judah was defeated and lost his life in the battle. His brother Jonathan took charge with hit-and-run fights against local enemies in the desert and elsewhere. It seemed a petty program after Judah's triumphs; but within a few years it had laid the foundations for the establishment of a new Jewish dynasty.

The key to independence from the overlord lay in Jonathan securing authority, for the first time, to assume the role of high priest. Rivalries for the Syrian throne in 152 B.C. between two claimants had led both of them to seek Jonathan's support. The final outcome of much negotiation was that one of the claimants handed over to Jonathan both independent political control over the Jews of Palestine and the role of high priest to go with it. The basis had now been laid for a true temple-state, strong enough in structure to survive and grow successfully if populist leaders would keep at bay religious dissension among the masses of Jewish society.

Jewish Populist Leaders

We inevitably have to deal here with what can only be called the Levantine politics that now came into full swing, with the rise to full power of the Hasmonean house.* This side of the story will be kept to a minimum, for these political struggles are not our main interest here. The Hasmonean and Herodian dynasties offer a tale of murderous infighting and passionate diplomatic and military struggles with small neighboring people, until all came to a head in the war with Rome, A.D. 66–70. The political story (which can be read in detail in Josephus) is interesting in its own right; but our concern here is to present what became the common heritage of the Jews in the two thousand years of the Diaspora, and very little of these political struggles appears in it.

What fills the common heritage is not history in general but what the distinguished historian Bernard Lewis calls, by a subtle distinction, "remembered history."[3] It is a striking fact that hardly any of the long postexilic stretch of Jewish history with which we are dealing trickled through into folk memory to become effective as part of the heritage. For the whole period, the names that lingered later in the minds of ordinary Jews can be numbered on one hand—Ezra (fifth century B.C.), Judah Maccabee (second century B.C.), Hillel (first century B.C.), and Rabbi Akiba (second century A.D.). But these peak figures presupposed a pattern of religious tradition that Jews took for granted, without specifying it in detail.

In this tradition, it was assumed that in these hundreds of apparently blank years there had been a continuous chain of Torah teaching, coming from Moses through Ezra and finally to the rabbis. Compared with this, the empires created by the Maccabean and Herodian dynasties left little sense of pride until they became "recovered history" (another of Professor Lewis's definitions) to bolster the ancestral pride of modern Israel. And this, one might say, was providential. If the Jewish tradition had looked to military triumphs to fill out the heritage, it would have faded away after the collapse of the temple-state, just as the ancient triumphs of Persia disappeared from Persian folk

*The name used by Josephus for the Maccabean dynasty. Its origin is unknown.

memory until the last shah of our time tried desperately, in a great celebration at Persepolis in 1971 to bring back to life its foundation by Darius twenty-five hundred years earlier.

The Jews did themselves no harm in "forgetting" the triumphs and disasters of their ruling dynasties in the pre-Christian centuries. In the first phase of these dynasties, the prerabbis certainly made common cause with the military leaders. Two hundred years later, they had written this off and launched themselves into a concentration on Torah study that would become, over time, the pivot of Jewish existence.

It is in this context that we can see, looking back, the origin of the group who came to be known as Pharisees and were assigned such a significant role in the Gospels. It is generally assumed that they must have been an offshoot of the Hasidim, who had first fought side by side with the Maccabeans but then broken away when these leaders began, after some victories, to work with alien authorities. The first signs of the split emerged when Judah Maccabee made a kind of armistice with the Syrians, but then opted to continue fighting. To the Hasidim, he was no longer resisting Temple desecration but fighting now for reasons of national and personal pride.

It is natural to assume that this was where the genesis of the Pharisees lay, though their precise origin and name, *perushim,* are still obscure. Since *perushim* has the sense of "separatists," some have thought that the name meant those who gave up all cooperation with the authorities. This seems unlikely, for the Pharisees never cut themselves off in this way. Indeed, a rabbinic dictum uses the same root, *parash,* to assert that one must not separate oneself, *tiphrosh,* from the community. *Pharisee* may just mean those who were separate, or stricter, in observance.

Far from cutting themselves off, the Pharisees tried to assert themselves politically wherever they could. They certainly never turned their back on the chance of working with Jewish leaders. Whenever a ruler surfaced with some apparent willingness to accept the populist religious leaders, the Pharisees were more than willing to cooperate. This was an essential prerequisite to establishing a pattern of Jewish observance among the population of Palestine that would ultimately have the power to survive the upheavals of the Destruction. The Pharisee leaders almost always had access to authority and could exercise an authority of their own as experts on the Law. Yet one still remains unsure about their exact role during the period of dynastic expansion in the pre-Christian centuries.

Alliances with Rome

If the political triumphs of the Maccabean-Hasmonean dynasty faded from Jewish populist memory, they were startling enough when first carried through. Judah's successor, Jonathan, who had extra authority as high priest, established a strong diplomatic position in dealing with Egypt, as well as Syria, and was able to expand his territories. His close involvement with one of the Syrian leaders led to his downfall. In a battle with a rival leader, he was defeated and killed (142 B.C.), but his brother Simon, who succeeded him as ruler and high priest, found the way open to still greater political independence and territorial conquests.

Simon was the first Maccabean to be fully recognized by the Syrians as king. But the high-level involvement in politics in those days brought with it its own hazards. Three of his brothers had been killed in battle; he himself was poisoned, together with two of his sons, by an ambitious son-in-law in the otherwise pleasant ambience of a family party. A surviving son, John Hyrcanus,* who succeeded him, was faced at first by a sudden massive attack by a new king of Syria and was able to escape only by agreeing to pay an increased tribute (131 B.C.). In time, this particular pressure was relieved, and John Hyrcanus was able to expand his domains hugely, pushing his boundaries to the limits once enjoyed by King Solomon. Significantly for the future, his conquests included the Idumeans to the south, who were forced to accept Judaism. Herod, due to become king of the Jews in 37 B.C., was from this newly converted Idumean background.

The approval of Rome was all-important throughout this story. Judah Maccabee had shown this by sending a mission to Rome after his first victories. By the time of Simon, the first king among the Maccabeans (142–135 B.C.), the relationship was more intense. After signaling his strength by capturing and destroying the citadel, which had long been the impregnable symbol of Syrian power within Jerusalem, he set out to bolster his position by sending a mission to Rome bearing a huge golden shield as a gift. The mission returned (139 B.C.) with a mutual assistance pact, agreeing, on the Roman side, that "if any attack be made on the Jews, the Romans shall assist them, as far as

*This Greek surname was borne by several Jews of this period. It may be connected with Hyrcania, a district south of the Caspian Sea, though why it was adopted by some Jews is unknown.

they are able." It was to be unlawful for "any that are subject to the Romans to make war with the nation of the Jews, or to assist those that do so" (*Ant.* 12:10).

It is not clear how valuable this guarantee was to the Jewish king in surviving the machinations of the rulers around him. Even with the fall of the citadel, the Syrians still exercised rights over Palestine, and deadly rivalries in Antioch meant that cash bribes and military support to this or that contender could quickly lose their effectiveness, turning alliances into wars. The Jews, therefore, were involved in a ceaseless to-and-fro of scheming and battles with rulers of the lands adjacent to Palestine. But while this was going on, the princes of the Jewish royal house would take particular care to spend a good deal of their time in Rome, partly for their education and entertainment but more importantly to store up allies in the struggles they were bound to be waging with each other.

One such struggle, which surfaced after the death of John Hrycanus in 104 B.C., illustrates the pattern of dynastic rule with Roman support that was ultimately to allow Herod, sixty-seven years later, to supplant the Hasmoneans and, though of alien origin, to establish his own line. John Hyrcanus had turned the Jewish state into what was almost an empire. On his death, the oldest of his five sons felt free, in the elegant manner of the time, to throw his mother and three brothers into prison in order to assure his position as king. When he died (apparently by an ordinary illness) a year later, his widow Salome Alexandra had the brothers released. As she was childless, she followed Jewish law in marrying the oldest surviving brother, Alexander Jannai, who was accepted as king and high priest. It was a long reign (103–76 B.C.) in which there was constant warfare on all fronts. In the background, the Roman involvement was clearly intensifying. When Alexander finally died, head of a very large domain, the struggle for succession brought the Romans in more closely still. But of equal significance to our story, we see in Alexander's long reign the first clear manifestation of popular opposition to a Hasmonean ruler, with the Pharisees establishing an important position of leadership.

Without doubt, a king engaged constantly in war and supported, both in foreign wars and at home, with legions of foreign mercenaries could hardly generate the simple Jewish patriotism of Judah Maccabee's days. For large stretches of Alexander's reign there was open civil war with large-scale slaughter of Jews by the king's soldiers. At one stage, Jewish enemies of Alexander even invited the Syrian king to invade. The outcome was murderous in the extreme. The details, as provided by Josephus, are grimly fascinating, especially in one bloody scene conducted in true Mafia style. Alexander, having suffered from a lack of Jewish support when he most needed it, invited his former enemies to a party at his harem where he crucified eight hundred of them, with their wives and children brought in to observe the scene.

Jewish Rulers and Rabbis

The story of another of Alexander's feasts is less bloody and more relevant to the future as illustrating the way in which the Pharisees had come to assert themselves in public life, not as politicians but as guardians of the religious tradition.

The drama arose because of the hostility between Pharisees and Sadducees. The Pharisees were known, at the time of Alexander, as a party devoted to observance of the Torah in full accord with its traditional oral interpretation, while the Sadducees—a priestly party named after Zadok, Solomon's high priest—were concerned only with the literal text of the Torah. This could lead to trouble.

The king, returning from a campaign, gave a feast to which both Pharisees and Sadducees were invited. On the advice of one of the Sadducees, the king appeared in high priest's robes and wearing a diadem with the Divine Name on his forehead. To the Pharisees, this was sacrilegious, since in their view he lacked the true qualifications for a high priest. But their fury was dwarfed by a fight later, in the Temple itself, which was at first merely lively, but then murderous.

It was on the Feast of Tabernacles, with worshippers carrying palms and citrons, as called for in the festival ritual. The king, performing the ceremony of water libation as high priest, did it in a manner which differed from Pharisee teaching, whereupon they shouted abuse at him and pelted him with their citrons. At this, the soldier mercenaries threw themselves on the crowd and killed six thousand of them. The breach between the Pharisees and the establishment now seemed irreparable.

But this is not what happened. If we are to trust the meager records we have, it appears that on his deathbed the king advised his wife Salome Alexandra to make peace with the Pharisees, leaning on the majority who were genuinely pious and had the ear of the masses, as opposed to the fanatics, a minority whose zeal could be inhuman and hypocritical—a distinction to bear in mind when one reads the strictures on the Pharisees in the Gospels. The dowager Queen, who kept the rule in her hands for the next nine years (76–67 B.C.) took his advice. Assigning the military command to one son (Aristobulus) and the high priestly functions to another (Hyrcanus), she also injected into the Sanhedrin, Council of State, a large proportion of Pharisees, whose advice became all-important on Torah-interpretation questions, though not necessarily on strictly political matters—a distinction important for the Jesus story. After the days of Salome Alexandra, one hears less of the Pharisee presence as a party, but in a sense their role in Salome's Sanhedrin put the seal on the transformation they had now wrought in Judaism for the future.

The main element in this transformation was the way they made it possible to worship God in the home and synagogue and not just in the Temple. Far from being hypocrites, as portrayed in the Gospels, this was their way of celebrating the spirit, and not just the letter, of the Torah.

In their view, God had to be worshipped in every act and every place. While the Temple, God's home, had a sanctity of its own, the Jew could reach God equally in every place of prayer, in the daily rituals of the home, and above all in the constant morality of conduct. As a result of these views, ceremonies originally part of the Temple cult were carried over to the home, while the synagogue as a place of prayer and Torah study, assumed exceptional significance.

In this transformation, a new ideal, the sincere scholar, was put forward in Jewish life. The priest had to be honored by virtue of his birth; the sage was adorned by the crown of the Torah. The hypocrites in both camps—the grasping priests, the pettifogging pietists—would be denounced, but even where leaders were wholly sincere and admirable, the weight of respect had now been changed. Judaism, as it survived, came to depend not on the Temple ritual but on study and practice of the Torah. This change had started with Ezra but clearly became concentrated in the century and a half before the political collapse of the state in A.D. 70.

It is intriguing to think of the dowager Queen Salome Alexandra having the good sense to enlist the support of the Pharisees, in the independent style of Queen Elizabeth I of England, rallying popular support to offset rivalries at her court. It is true enough that Salome had a peaceful reign; but when she died at the age of seventy-three, the predictable struggle between the two brothers for the succession took place. The direct fighting between them was resolved at first through a straight victory by the younger brother Aristobulus but was affected soon after by the introduction of a new element—the entry of the Idumeans onto the stage. The governor of Idumea, the neighboring country which had been conquered and converted to Judaism by Alexander Jannai, was a wily politician called Antipater. He now offered his support to the older but weaker brother Hyrcanus, collecting allies, too, among some disaffected Jews and Arab leaders. They met and defeated Aristobulus in battle. It was at this point that Rome made the fateful decision to take charge of things directly.

The Syrian Empire had fallen apart owing to successful rebellion by the Parthian leader Mithridates and his son-in-law, the Armenian leader Tigranes. It was the Syrian weakness which had given Aristobulus the freedom, originally, to oust his brother Hyrcanus. But these disturbances in the Near East had led Rome to send Pompey, a very high-level general, to the scene. He crushed Mithridates and Tigranes (66 B.C.) and incorporated the whole of Syria, including their territories, into the Roman Empire. He then sent an emissary to examine what should be done about the fighting between the two brothers for the control of Palestine. The emissary opted to support Aristobulus, and after much negotiation and fighting, Aristobulus promised to yield Jerusalem to the Romans. But suddenly, either in pride or with a loss of nerve, he barred the gates. In a foretaste of what was to happen a hundred years later, the city was besieged, and when it finally fell to Pompey (63 B.C.), the population was massacred. Aristobulus and his family were sent to Rome as captives; the other leaders of the sudden revolt against the Romans were executed.

The Temple treasures were left intact, and the rituals were now resumed, with Hyrcanus as high priest. But it was the end of the great Hasmonean Empire. The coast cities, the Greek cities beyond the Jordan, and many other areas of Palestine were taken away from Jewish control and annexed to the Roman province of Syria.

It is worth setting out the pattern of government which emerged if only to understand the complex political setting in which Jesus lived and died less than a hundred years later. For a time, after Pompey's takeover of Jerusalem, Palestine was put under the governor of Syria, with different districts under local leaders, responsible for order and taxes. Hyrcanus was left in charge of the Temple, with his political activities very much under the control of the Idumean Antipater.

Pompey had joined Julius Caesar at this time (60 B.C.) to form the first Triumvirate, and one direct effect on Palestine was that Crassus, as proconsul of Syria, plundered the Jerusalem Temple of its treasures in 54 B.C. When the Triumvirate broke down in 48 B.C., the enmity between Pompey and Caesar was echoed in the emergence of violent factions in and around Syria, supporting one or the other by arms.

Hyrcanus and his adviser Antipater took an important decision to throw their support to Caesar, especially in his fighting to control Egypt. Egyptian Jewry also supported Caesar; and when the dust had settled, with Caesar victorious, the rewards were that Hyrcanus was named *ethnarch* and given back some real political power in Palestine and much of the territory taken away by Pompey, including the port of Jaffa. Antipater was given Roman citizenship and immunity from taxation, a favored status that was to be of immense value later to the young Herod, his son. The Jews outside Palestine, notably the Jews of Alexandria and Cyrenaica, also had their rights confirmed by Caesar.

It helps to indicate the spirit of the time by setting out, as Josephus does, one of the orders of Caesar guaranteeing the freedom of the Jews, though this also establishes that there must have been much anti-Jewish sentiment against which this order was to contend:

> Caesar Augustus, high priest and tribune of the people, ordains thus: Since the nation of the Jews had been found grateful to the Roman people, not only at this time but in time past also, and chiefly Hyrcanus the high priest, it seemed good to me and my counsellors, according to the sentence and oath of the people of Rome, that the Jews have liberty to make use of their own customs, according to the law of their forefathers; and that their sacred money be not touched, but be sent to Jerusalem; and that they be not obliged to go before any judge on the Sabbath-day, nor on the day of the preparation for it, after the ninth hour. But if anyone be caught stealing their holy books, or their sacred money, whether it be out of the synagogue or school, he shall be deemed a sacrilegious person, and his goods shall be brought into the public treasury of the Romans. [*Ant.* 16.6.2].

Emergence of Herod

Despite this apparently tolerant, even warm-hearted, attitude by the Romans, it was not always reciprocated by ordinary Jews. For a mixture of religious and patriotic reasons, there was hatred and revolt in the air, especially in Galilee, against the Romans and their Jewish puppets. One guerrilla movement which broke out shortly before Caesar's assassination in 44 B.C., was led by a Galilean called Hezekiah and was put down swiftly by Antipater's son Herod, who had been made prefect of Galilee by his father. The Sanhedrin in Jerusalem, hearing that Herod had summarily executed Hezekiah and a number of his followers, without the careful trial that Jewish law demanded, summoned him to Jerusalem to stand trial himself. Herod, aged only twenty-five, treated the Sanhedrin with disdain. Hyrcanus had, in any case, received orders from the governor of Syria that Herod was to be acquitted. Shortly after, Herod was made prefect of the whole of southern Syria. He was clearly on the way to power.

After Caesar's assassination, Antipater and Herod transferred their loyalty to Mark Antony, who, following the decisive victory which he and Octavian (Augustus) had won at Philippi in 42 B.C., became master of the whole of the Middle East. Herod soon showed that he was capable of taking full advantage of this position.

At first, he had to meet the opposition of Jewish religious leaders, who sent deputations to Antony repeatedly, complaining of the behavior of Herod and his brother Phazael. Far from being removed, they were appointed tetrarchs, in effect superceding Hyrcanus politically.

The decisive turning point came, however, when Mattathias Antigonus, a Hasmonean pretender to the throne and high priesthood, secured some sort of Roman recognition in return for tribute and, with a good deal of military support, sustained himself in this ambivalent position for three years (40–36 B.C.). To cope with this, Herod went in to attack at Rome itself. First, he sent the women and children of his family to shelter in his fortress at Masada and then set off for Rome to secure the support of Antony and Octavian personally. They accepted him as a true friend of Rome, and the senate named him as king of the Jews. Returning to Jaffa in 39 B.C., he had to spend the next two years fighting Antigonus and his supporters in many parts of the area, while at the same time striving to win acceptance by the Jewish people. When his fortunes were at their lowest, Mark Antony came again to his aid, sending two Roman legions to help defeat the forces against him. To give his claim to the throne some sort of validity, Herod married Miriam, a princess of the Hasmonean house, so that her children at least would have some royal status.

The climax was now at hand. The Pharisees in Jerusalem had opposed Mattathias Antigonus as ruler and high priest and were only prepared to accept Herod as king if he had a separate and authentic high priest. Herod decided to act, storming into Jerusalem, with his Roman soldiers slaying and pillaging freely. His reign had now begun, and in a style of bravado, cruelty, and distinction that was to be maintained for thirty-three years (37–4 B.C.).

Until modern times, the murderous magnificence of Herod's long reign left little mark on the folk memory of the Jews except in one major regard. The huge western wall of the Temple that Herod built in Jerusalem was all that was left after the Temple's destruction by the Romans in A.D. 70, and it became—as it still is today—a symbol of great sanctity. In our own time, this has been matched in sentiment by the opening of the palace and fortress he built at Masada, where our sense of awe includes respect for the heroism of the rebels who chose death there, rather than surrender, in the Roman war. Ironically, Herod entered the Christian tradition as a villain much more forcefully than the Jewish, through the brief but telling reference to him in Matthew (2:16) as being furious to hear of the flight of Mary and Jesus to Egypt, which led him to order the slaying of all the children of Bethlehem —"the massacre of the innocents."

This story, apocryphal or not, is entirely in keeping with what we know of Herod's totally ruthless style as described in detail by Josephus. Having won the crown, he removed everyone who might possibly have posed some sort of threat, either in realistic terms or through his inflamed imagination. Though he had married a princess of the Hasmonean royal house, his sense of danger from the family never left him. His first act as king was to kill forty-five men of the Sanhedrin connected with the royal family; and subsequently, during different phases of his reign, he killed Hyrcanus (the king he had supplanted), the high priest Aristobulus (his wife's brother), all the other Hasmonean princes and potential enemies he could reach and, most bitterly of all, his wife, his own brother and sister, and his sons.

If all this never entered the folk memory of Jews—Herod never appears as a king or a villain in the Hebrew religious poetry of the Middle Ages—many thousands of literature Jews would have caught up with him by reading a popular version of Josephus, *The Book of Josippon,* which was written in Hebrew in southern Italy in the tenth century and subsequently widely translated. But even without this direct picture of the time when the Jewish commonwealth had been turned, under a ruthless potentate, into a powerful and obedient vassal of Rome, the sense of hatred for Rome engendered in that time stayed powerfully in the Jewish mind, linked to the undying memory of the Destruction. The hundred-year period which began with Herod's accession in 37 B.C. and ended with the Jewish-Roman War of A.D. 66–70 is always considered as the age in which the rabbis took root in Jewish life. But politically its main events, including the drama of Jesus, are shapeless unless it is seen as dominated by Rome.

One thinks of the Roman connection in terms of military force in Palestine or state visits to Rome. It comes home more intriguingly to find Herod, a Jewish king, actively involved in the Antony and Cleopatra saga as described in different ways by Shakespeare and George Bernard Shaw. Cleopatra was keen to get Palestine back under Egyptian control and, with strong support from Antony, was actually ceded the rich city of Jericho. She also persuaded Herod to start a fierce and costly war against some Arab chieftains who had not paid tribute to her. But in general, Herod, as Josephus suggests, was wary of her coquettish advances."[4]

The Roman connection surfaced also when Herod's protector, Antony, was defeated by Octavian at the decisive battle of Actium (31 B.C.). Herod decided very coolly to change sides, though with some circumspection. He executed all his potential rivals before leaving for Rhodes to submit himself with the greatest humility to the victor. Octavian (who became the emperor Augustus) saw the value of Herod as an ally and ceded large areas of land to him, including Jericho, the coastal towns, and some Greek cities east of Galilee.

From this base, and with the support of Augustus, Herod went on to extend his empire hugely and within it to become famous for building magnificent palaces, fortresses, temples, and theaters, and for his lavish cultivation of the arts. His authoritarian rule kept rebellion in check—ready to burst out after his death. But if he was regarded as a tyrant and in some sense (though not technically) a non-Jew, he did his best, within the limits that he himself set, to get along with the Pharisees. There were plenty of episodes of protest, such as when he had his great Jerusalem Temple surmounted by a Roman eagle or when he demanded a double oath of loyalty from the Jews—to himself and to Caesar. But as long as the rabbis of his time (who included the famous Hillel and Shamai) were content to study the Torah quietly, he left them in peace. He was always ready to stand up for Jewish rights, both within Palestine and abroad.

It is easy to see that Palestine was very fully a Jewish commonwealth, even under the alien rule of Herod. Though the high priest was a cypher, the ceremonies of the Temple were rigidly adhered to, and there was a strong element of self-government in the existence of the Sanhedrin. Originally, Sanhedrin members had been empowered to deal with many issues of government. But its composition and roles were changing under Herod, who took all political powers away from it, leaving it only with religious functions. As seen in the drama of Jesus, serious issues that might involve the death sentence were no longer within the range of the Sanhedrin, but this would not have disturbed Pharisee members. To judge from statements in the Talmud of their rabbi descendants, the Pharisees found the reality of capital punishment (as distinct from merely discussing it) quite distasteful. "A Sanhedrin that produces a death sentence once in seven years is called a murderous Sanhedrin," says one rabbi (as quoted in the Mishnah Makkot 1:10), to which Rabbi Tarfon and Rabbi Akiba reply, "If we had been in the Sanhedrin, no death sentence would ever have been passed."

This tolerant talk seems a long way from the bloodshed—public and private—of Herod's reign. Was the gap between Jew and Roman too wide to be bridged? Not necessarily, Josephus thought; for even as he tells the gory story of Herod, he gives credit to him for attempting to secure a modus vivendi between the two. Politically, Herod was a realist, as he had shown in switching loyalty to Octavian. More generally, he saw security for the Jewish people within the Roman Empire if they could accept the role of willing subjects. To fight imperial Rome was suicidal; a small people like the Jews could fit in well with the Roman idea, always provided they moderated their isolation and national exclusiveness. It was to this end that he poured huge sums of money into promoting Hellenist culture, not only by vast building projects but through importing Greek artists and writers into the area under his control and founding festivals and public games.

It has been suggested by Abraham Schalit that Herod had an even more original Roman-Jewish ambition at the back of his mind. In the Roman Empire, now reborn, emperor-worship was at the center of the cult. Herod, though a king, could not have hoped for worship; but might not the Jews be persuaded to consider him as the Messiah, precursor of the redemption of Israel as promised by the Hebrew prophets? We are told, in support of this view, that Herodian propaganda tried to suggest to the Jews of Judea that he was of Davidic stock, that his kingdom was as extensive as that of David and Solomon, and that his Temple was even more splendid than the original.[5]

It has to be said that the idea of the alien—and hated—Herod as a quasi-Messiah does not sound as if it would have gone very far;* but perhaps it had

*It is a reflection of Jewish distaste for Herod that his name surfaces only twice in the Mishnah, and then only as a technical term: "Herodian doves," meaning birds kept in captivity. See Emil Schürer, *The History of the Jewish People in the Age of Jesus Christ,* vol. 1 rev. by G. Vermes and P. Miller, (Edinburgh: T. and T. Clark, 1973), p. 310, n. 77.

a natural place among the wild messianic ideas that had been spreading in his reign, and that must be considered in relation to the drama of Jesus.

Messiahs and Rebels

As a young man, Herod had put down a patriotic anti-Roman revolt, led by a Galilean, Hezekiah. During his reign, he kept opposition firmly in check; but it existed beneath the surface and much of it had a messianic tinge, in which a leader—even of a tiny group—found it natural to borrow the terminology of messianic prophecies. With Herod's death in 4 B.C., revolts broke out instantly, one of them led by a son, Judah, of the earlier rebel Hezekiah. The revolts were put down with much bloodshed by the governor of Syria; but from then on one hears of rebel movements constantly, most of them with messianic overtones. It is into this background that one has to fit the political issues of the Gospel story, with Jesus seen as a political rebel (king of the Jews) or as a messiah (sent by God to fulfill the prophecies) or as someone combining both roles.

But, first, we must look at the political framework in which the drama of Jesus was to take place. Herod had not succeeded in establishing a firm line of succession, for though heredity was recognized as carrying some claims, it was subordinated to the need for Roman approval. Despite all the favors that Herod enjoyed, first from Antony and then from Augustus, the title of king could not be carried without the emperor's explicit sanction, with or without the senate's confirmation. As Emil Schürer's famous study of the period, now revised, puts it:

> The title was, as a rule, only conferred on princes reigning over large territories; lesser princes had to be satisfied with the title of tetrarch or something similar. The title held good only for the person on whom it was bestowed and became extinct on his death. . . . Ratification was refused if there were reasons for doing so, and the paternal authority was either bestowed on the son with its boundaries reduced and his title diminished, or it was given to another, or it was even brought under direct Roman administration, i.e. turned into a province.[6]

The succession to Herod illustrates this perfectly. In the seventy years between his death in 4 B.C. and the outbreak of the fateful Jewish-Roman War, members of the Herodian dynasty retained some kind of authority or respect under varying titles, but with a very attenuated relationship to their Jewish subjects. The course of events had the Roman stamp: authority exerted from the outside. This becomes clear enough over the death of Jesus, around A.D. 30, and equally in the disastrous series of events which made the Destruction inevitable forty years later.

After much agonizing over his successor, Herod had finally given the nod in his last will to a son, Archelaus. Before leaving for Rome to secure confirmation, Archelaus had to deal with riots that had broken out to secure revenge for the execution of two rabbis, Judas and Matthias, who had torn down the Roman eagle set over the Temple gates. Passover was approaching, when the pilgrim crowds could always be a danger to authority. Repressive action had to be severe. In the first phase, the Roman army commander, after looting the Temple, was besieged by anti-Roman rioters in Herod's palace. A group of rebels under Hezekiah's son Judah had also become active again in Galilee. In this urgent situation—to be repeated many times in the decades to follow—the Syrian governor Varus led a large force of Roman legionaries and Arab auxiliaries into Palestine, putting down the rebellion with great bloodshed. In Josephus' account, we hear that Varus sent his troops all over the country and had two thousand of the rebels crucified. Josephus calls this the bloodiest fight between the conquest by Pompey (63 B.C.) and that of Vespasion (A.D. 70).

Archelaus, having taken off for Rome, had been confirmed there not as king but only as ethnarch, with a narrower range of authority. A younger brother, Antipas, was made tetrarch of Galilee and Perea (Transjordan), while a half-brother, Philip, became tetrarch of the northeastern districts. Rome was tightening its hold; and though Archelaus retained his title for ten years, he proved weak in authority and was finally banished to Gaul. His territory—Judea, Samaria, and Idumea—was annexed and placed under Roman procurators, residing not in Jerusalem but in the city that Herod had made magnificent, Caesarea.

From now on, A.D. 6, the procurator (or prefect, as he was sometimes called) was in full charge, though he had to balance Roman justice and authority with local self-government. In the financial field, tax-collecting was leased to tax-collectors, *publicani*, for a fixed sum or to the highest bidder, so that much of the odium—echoed in the Gospels—fell on them rather than on the Romans. The dividing line was harder over the administration of justice. The procurator always had supreme judicial authority, as well as military control, but he tended to keep out of the ordinary administration of criminal and civil law, which would be left to locals. This was particularly true of Judea, since the Jewish religion, which the Romans treated with respect, was expressed so clearly in law. The Jews had their own courts or councils for which they had adopted the name Sanhedrin from the Greek *synhedrion,* meaning *assembly*. But though the Sanhedrin was clearly a crucial element in Jewish self-government, it seems to have meant different things at different times.

One would like to know as much as possible about this, since the Sanhedrin—or at any rate a council headed by the high priest—surfaces at different points in the Gospel story with great importance, and one wants to understand how it operated over the drama of Jesus.

In the writings of the time or soon afterward that mention the Sanhedrin, a number of overlapping concepts seem to emerge. In Josephus, some early references indicate a political (Sadducean) council under the control of the king-high priest and turned to for the approval of matters of state. Later, it is clear that Sanhedrin membership had been broadened to include Pharisees also, as in his account of a Sanhedrin episode in which the Pharisees opposed the Sadducees by securing permission for levitical singers to wear priestly vestments.

The references to the Sanhedrin in the Gospels straddle this period. When Jesus is brought to be cross-examined on Passover Eve in the palace of the high priest, it seems to indicate a priestly council, an ad hoc Temple committee, since it would have been against the rules for the Sanhedrin itself to have met, as this council did, at night and on the eve of a festival. On the other hand, when Paul is brought before the Sanhedrin (c. A.D. 60) to answer, as a Christian, a charge of Jewish heresy, we are told that he "was well aware that one section were Sadducean and the other Pharisees," which led him to seek support by calling out: "I am a Pharisee born and bred" (Acts 23:6). He had indeed identified himself earlier as a pupil of the Pharisee sage Gamaliel (Acts 22:3); and during the Sanhedrin trial of Peter and the apostles, it was Gamaliel, "a member of the Council," who pleaded for leniency in a famous speech of tolerance and common sense (Acts 5: 35–39).

The references to the Sanhedrin are, therefore, a little confusing and even more so after the destruction of the Temple, when the rabbis of the next century set out to describe the role of the Sanhedrin in a chapter of the Mishnah devoted entirely to the subject. Drawing on their memory or folk memory, they describe the Great Sanhedrin not as a Sadducean establishment body, meeting for state occasions, but as an assembly of sages meeting daily, from morning to midafternoon (except on Sabbath, holy days, and the evenings before) in a permanent location—the Chamber of Hewn Stone in the Temple. In this "remembered" view, Sanhedrin members were basically scholars, preoccupied with determining the *halakhah,* religious law. They would be consulted by the ruler when it came to the determination of how to carry out esoteric biblical ceremonies (for example, "the red heifer," Deut. 21), but basically they would be concerned with straight legal questions, both theoretical and practical. It is because of these overlapping functions, as "remembered" by later generations, that the references in the rabbinic literature are unclear. Sometimes they call it the Great Sanhedrin, at other times the Great Beth Din, court of law, headed not by a high priest but by two leading sages, one called *Av* (father) *Beth Din,* the other *Nasi* (president).

In both cases, the title "the Great" indicates the full assembly of seventy-one members; for less important questions, the quorum was twenty-three; and there is talk of a small Sanhedrin consisting of only three members (San. 88b). Some scholars consider that there may have been three small Sanhedrins of twenty-three members in Jerusalem, each with a different role, so that when they met together with a chairman and deputy-chairman they would have seventy-one members.

There are many other theories; but a prime issue of this discussion is to consider what light it throws on the so-called Sanhedrin that cross-examined Jesus on Passover Eve and decided that he had blasphemed and was "guilty of death." In the Gospel account, Jesus had been brought before the high priest who had with him "all the chief priests and the elders and the scribes" (Mark 14:53), including, that is, a number of Pharisees. In the light of what has been said about the many definitions of the Sanhedrin, it is already clear, as suggested earlier, that the group that saw Jesus that evening and decided next morning to hand him over to Pontius Pilate was not an official Sanhedrin including scribes and Pharisees but a Temple committee hurriedly called together to deal with a security question.

Someone had told the priest-officials that this man, a popular preacher who had already caused some riots at the Temple, had been heard to say that he would destroy *this* Temple, which was corrupt, and build another more spiritual one (Mark 14:58). Preacher or not, he was, in these terms, a pretender to power ("king of the Jews"). On this clear-cut issue, a Temple committee handed him over to the Roman representative. Stirring up political rebellion was a prima facie offense carrying the death penalty.

The committee itself had no powers of life or death but merely collected evidence relevant to state security. (The full Sanhedrin had death powers, theoretically; but was extremely reluctant to use them.)

The Gospel account (Mark 14) suggests that the Temple committee was equally concerned with a blasphemous statement by Jesus that he saw himself as "Messiah, Son of the Blessed One." He had taken the vision in Daniel (7:13) of "the Son of Man [who] came with the clouds of Heaven" and applied it to himself to yield "the Son of Man, seated at the right hand of God and coming with the clouds of Heaven" (Mark 14:62). We have no way of knowing if this is an authentic report or an imaginative reconstruction of the dialogue to establish the Christological issue; but it is clear that when Jesus is delivered next morning to Pilate, the crime is the political one: "Art thou the king of the Jews?" (Mark 15:2).

The political claim affecting state security was the issue because religious misdemeanors, to be judged by a Jewish court, had not arisen. Even if Jesus was thought to have blasphemed, this was not a crime in itself, as Gamaliel showed in cross-examining Peter later (Acts 5:35–39). The Pharisees may not have liked Jesus—the venom in the Gospels toward them seems to have a story behind it—but they never treated messianic claims as blasphemous. In general, they always hoped for a messiah, and there is no record of their having intervened on religious grounds in the many cases when messiah claims were made.

We have envisaged, so far, that Jesus would have been treated by Pilate as a political rebel even if his claim had only taken the form of applying Bible verses to himself, for there was no clear line between this and outright military revolt. The rebels who came to be known as Zealots were a case in point. We know them as fully active in the final war against Rome, but they were present in Jesus' time, linked to the messianic rebels whom Herod had disposed of earlier.

The Zealots expected a very different Messiah from the gentle Jesus of the Gospels. As they were themselves fighters, they counted on a leader who would appear, sword in hand, to destroy the Romans. He might not be the direct descendant of David (Messiah ben David) but his forerunner (Messiah ben Joseph), a great general who would lead the Jews to victory, though he himself would fall in battle. His death was, in fact, an essential prerequisite to the arrival of the full Messiah. This had become an acceptable way of interpreting the repeated execution of Zealot leaders: They were martyrs leading the way to the ultimate triumph.

In a different view, the Messiah was expected to emerge not as a battling leader but in the wake of a cosmic cataclysm. Following an age of total depravity, the world would be given a new direction. Sometimes this new world would just be idyllic in a Jewish way, as in the projection by the *Book of Jubilees* of an era in which everyone would study the Torah and be righteous in action. In other views (for example, in *The Assumption of Moses*) the sense of cataclysm would continue for a long—perhaps indefinite—time. According to an apocalyptic work known as IV *Ezra,* the first messianic age would fade away after four hundred years, with the universe turning into primeval silence for seven days, and only then would mankind be ready for the true messianic age.

Whatever the shades of view, messianism was in the air, linked at one end to the biblical prophecies and at the other to the sense of frustration and anger at the Roman occupation. Individual incidents could turn this feeling into active revolt, as had happened in Herod's reign with the rebel Hezekiah and after his death with Hezekiah's son Judah the Galilean. Judah seems to have escaped the wholesale executions carried out at that time by Varus, governor of Syria, for we find him leading a revolt ten years later (A.D. 6) in protest against a census put in hand by the Roman prefect Quirinius to ensure tax payments. This was the moment at which, after a weak period of rule by Herod's son Archelaus, the Romans moved in to take full charge of the country, with the census an administrative element in this.

At the time of the earlier rebellion by Judah, we hear also of other outbreaks, though with less detail given. Josephus tells us that in Perea (Transjordan), a former slave of Herod called Simon gathered a group of supporters and had himself proclaimed king but was caught and executed. Another claim to the crown was made by a former shepherd called Athronges, who held out for a long time but met the same fate.

The story of Judah's revolt at the time of the census has an interesting angle in that he was ardently supported by a Pharisee named Zadok, who gathered other Pharisees around him. We see here how difficult it is to frame generalizations on the character and conduct of different parties at the time of Jesus; for while the Pharisees are mostly seen as too preoccupied with Torah study and observance to take up arms, some of them undoubtedly formed the nucleus, like Zadok, of fighters who were also fiercely religious. These Zealots were never going to accept Roman rule. They must have fought as guerrillas constantly, getting what support they could. To attack the Romans openly in a full-scale war, as they did finally in A.D. 66, was obviously suicidal; but reason had nothing to do with it. They were willing to fight to the death, and ultimately did so.

Historical Issues on Jesus

On the assumption that there was a resistance movement led by the Zealots all through these decades and therefore covering the period of Jesus, some scholars have argued in recent years that Jesus himself was a Zealot, directly active in stirring up military rebellion. In support of this, they point out that he was from Galilee, where the rebels came from, that he could be hot-tempered (as at the Temple), and that he entered Jerusalem before his arrest and execution in a somber mood, foreseeing that his active role as a rebel would now certainly lead to his death. Other scholars argue that his teachings run counter to this. Essentially, he was a healer, which hardly goes with the idea of a resistance fighter. In his sayings, he showed himself to be a devout law-abiding Jew, condemning the hypocrites among the Pharisees (as the Pharisees themselves did), but asserting firmly that he had come not to diminish the Law but to fulfill it (or, in a better translation, "to add to it," in the sense of adding spiritual ideas).

Yet he was a teacher who gathered huge crowds; and if one adds to this the gnomic character of many of his sayings, he becomes immediately the kind of troublemaker that Roman authority had to get rid of. We know from Josephus that this was the motivation of the Jewish ruler Herod Antipas (son of Herod the Great) in having John the Baptist imprisoned and executed (c. A.D. 29). Josephus describes John not as a rebel but simply as a "good man" who urged the Jews to be righteous to one another and God, "and so to come to baptism" (*Ant.* 18.5); but when all the crowds came, "Herod [Antipas], who feared lest the great influence John had over the population might put it into his power and inclination to raise rebellion, thought it best, by putting him to death, to prevent any mischief he might cause."*

*The Gospels offer a different story, of course, for the reason behind the execution of John the Baptist. John criticized Herod Antipas for having married his brother's wife Herodias; and when his wife's daughter Salome delighted Herod with her dancing, his reward to her—her mother had suggested it—was the head of John the Baptist on a platter (Mark 6:17–29). G. Vermes says, "Josephus' view, independent of, and conflicting with, that of the New Testament, is likely to be genuine" (*Jesus the Jew* [London: Collins, 1973] p. 237, n. 47).

Because Josephus was quoted on the execution of John the Baptist, it is apposite to ask at this point what he has to say about Jesus and the motivations for his execution. The two dramas are close to each other in time—within a year perhaps—and one expects a full account of the Jesus story, especially since Josephus reports on many other rebellions and executions. What does appear on this subject in his *Antiquities*—or rather in the text that we now have—is, however, both brief and puzzling.

There are, in fact, only two references to Jesus, which has led to fierce scholarly arguments for many years on whether the text on Jesus is actually what Josephus wrote. *Antiquities* was an immensely popular book with Christians, and some have thought that the original text might well have been amended on this subject by a Christian copyist for propaganda purposes. With the same motive, passages on Jesus might have been cut out, if what was written by Josephus did not accord with the Christian message.

The issues are discussed in detail in an essay, "Josephus on Jesus and James," contributed by the late Paul Winter to the new version of Schürer's *History of the Jewish People.*[7] The essay is as fascinating as a detective story, and only some of the main points and conclusions will be summarized here.

Winter thinks that the shorter of the two passages (*Ant.* 20.9) does not present too many problems. It describes how in A.D. 62 a high priest called Ananus—an insolent man, "head of the sect of the Sadducees who are very rigid in judging offenders above all the rest of the Jews"—decided to put down the Christian sect and to this end brought before "the Sanhedrin of the Jews" James, "the brother of Jesus who was called Christ." The outcome was that James and the others with him accused of "breaking the law" were put to death "by stoning." One can accept this passage as it stands, for it does not imply that Josephus himself thought of Jesus as the Christ (Messiah). He was writing around A.D. 94 in Rome, more than sixty years after the death of Jesus, and was quoting the name by which Jesus was identified in Rome by his followers, known as Christians.

It is the second passage (*Ant.* 18.3–4:63–64) which offers the problems. It runs, in Winter's version:

(63) At about this time lived Jesus, a wise man, if indeed, one might call him a man. For he was one who accomplished surprising feats and was a teacher of such people as accept the truth with pleasure. He won over many Jews and many of the Greeks. (64) He was the Messiah. When Pilate, upon an indictment brought by the principal men among us, condemned him to

the cross, those who had loved him from the very first did not cease to be attached to him. On the third day he appeared to them restored to life, for the holy prophets had foretold this and myriads of other marvels concerning him. And the tribe of the Christians, so called after him, has to this day still not disappeared.

It is hard to believe from what we know of Josephus that he could have put down these clear Christian doctrines—"he was the Messiah," "if one might call him a man," "he was restored to life on the third day"—without pursuing the implications. The odds are, then, that they were insertions by a Christian copyist. Winter points out, however, that if one then abbreviates the passage by removing these Christian additions, it becomes "disconcertingly colourless," "amazingly brief" for Josephus. He had, after all, written up very fully the troubles that Pilate had encountered, after taking office, when he had sent his troops into Jerusalem bearing the images of the emperor on their flags. This had resulted in a riot, followed by another when Pilate had seized the treasures of the Temple in order to get the funds to build an aqueduct. We know from the New Testament that there were riotous crowds surrounding Jesus. Why is there no mention of this in Josephus?

Winter thinks that a passage on Jesus and his Crucifixion must have been included in Josephus and cut out by a Christian copyist because it simply dealt with Jesus as one of the succession of troublemakers who had to be put down by the Romans with bloodshed and distress. There is a clue to this in the words which open the section of *Antiquities* after the existing passage on Jesus: "About this time, also, another sad calamity put the Jews into disorder." This would have followed an account of the riots, the trial, and the Crucifixion, now omitted.

There is no need to assume, Winter thinks, that Josephus deliberately said very little about Jesus because the claims that he was the Messiah and that he rose again on the third day irritated him too much. He certainly didn't believe these claims but "was not unsympathetic to Jesus" on the whole. One can well believe that he saw the execution of Jesus as "a sad calamity . . . that put the Jews into disorder."

There is evidence also, in Josephus, about another point central to the role of Jesus. For reasons of his own, as will be seen when we come to the war of A.D. 66–70, Josephus always wrote about the Zealots and other political activists with the utmost contempt as "robbers" and "bandits." His relatively friendly attitude in writing about Jesus indicates, in Winter's view, that "Jews belonging to the circle to which Josephus belonged—a Pharisaic group, no doubt—had not at that time given Jesus a bad name as a heretic, or denounced him as a rebel." This is in line with the fact that men from Pharisaic circles entered into friendly relations with Jewish-Christians for a long time after the Crucifixion, in sharp contrast to the attitude of hard-line Sadducee leaders like the high priest who had James put to death.

It may seem surprising to find the Pharisees tolerant of Jesus, since the words about the Pharisees, ascribed to Jesus in the Gospels, might seem to indicate strong mutual dislike. The truth is that the Pharisees were presented in the Gospels by writers anxious to establish a basis for the view that it was the Jews, not the Romans, who had engineered Jesus' death. As a result the picture is out of key. There is something equally out of key in the idea that Jesus was a political activist, directly involved in Zealot or quasi-Zealot affairs. He was certainly tried and executed because Pilate had decided that he spelled trouble politically—"king of the Jews"; but there is no evidence that this represented popular, or Pharisee, opinion.

An attempt to reconstruct the drama against all these difficulties must keep in mind the alternating seesaw of cooperation and friction between Jews and Romans that was characteristic of everything involving official action. To be more accurate, one has to see this as a three-way struggle which includes the Jewish kings, for they always tried to establish some semblance of power and were able to do so when the Roman representative organized things this way. This picture is familiar to us in the drama of John the Baptist, with the Jewish ruler Herod Antipas having him executed. The opposite emerges in the story of Jesus, with Pontius Pilate, the Roman prefect, taking the fateful decisions.

The character and role of Pontius Pilate is particularly important for Jews, since the Gospel account paints him as a rather genial character, prepared to be magnanimous to Jesus, but prevented because of the united will of the Jews to have him put to death. In the account in chapter 23 of Luke, Pontius Pilate does send him first to see Herod Antipas, tetrarch of Galilee, who happened to be in Jerusalem at the time. But in the other Gospel accounts, Pontius Pilate is on his own. In chapter 27 of Matthew, he offers the crowd a choice between crucifying "Jesus the Messiah" and Barabbas the rebel; but the crowd have been drilled by the high priest, and "with one voice" they demand Jesus as the victim: "Crucify him!" In chapter 19 of John, the contrast between Pilate's innocence and Jewish guilt is even more explicit. Pilate tells Jesus that he (Pilate) has "no authority" to order the crucifying. He "tries hard to release him" (v.12), but the Jews keep shouting for his death.

It is somewhat ironic that we happen to know from other sources that this particular Roman prefect was the very opposite of the genial and fair-minded official that the Gospels project. Unexpectedly, one source is Philo, the philosopher of Alexandria (see page 57), in a communication addressed to Rome. Philo took part in a mission to Rome in A.D. 40 to protest the erection of statues of the emperor in Alexandrian synagogues and also the display of statues or images of the emperor in the Temple of Jerusalem. Pilate's first act as prefect was to send his troops into Jerusalem with images of the emperor on their flags. It was well known that the images were an offense to Jewish religious feeling, and previous prefects had taken care not to offend the Jews this way. Pilate had no such tenderness; according to Josephus (*Ant.* 18.3) he sent the troops into Jerusalem "to abolish the Jewish laws." It was done at night, and when the Jews discovered it, "they came in multitudes to Caesarea, interceding with Pilate many days that he would remove the standards."

He was equally fierce when he seized Temple treasures to provide funds for an aqueduct. Soldiers were sent out with clubs concealed under their tunics, and in the ensuing riots "a great many were slain and others of them ran away wounded."

Philo's book *De Legatio* includes a letter from the Jewish ruler Agrippa I summarizing Pilate's character. He was, Agrippa wrote, unbending and callously hard by nature, "a man of inflexible disposition, harsh and obdurate." This is in keeping with an account in one of the Gospels (Luke 13:1) that Jesus was told of some "Galileans whose blood Pilate had mingled with their sacrifices," suggesting that Pilate had killed a number of Galileans who had brought offerings to Jerusalem. But this is the only echo in the Gospels of Pilate's cruelty, with the other references painting an idyllic and clearly misleading picture.

5

The Roman-Jewish War

Buildup to the Conflict

T IS NOT DIFFICULT to see the fateful conflict of A.D. 66–70 looming up in all the stories of Roman-Jewish hostility; but side by side with this, one has to consider the close relationship also described by Josephus and the possibility that direct war might have been avoided.

One can follow this aspect of the story by considering the role that might have been played by the Jewish kings of the time, successors in the Herodian dynasty. Agrippa I, whose letter was included by Philo in his protest to Rome, was one of these Jewish kings. He and his son Agrippa II were in the background when the seeds of war were being sown and had a distinctive role entirely unknown to later generations of Jews—as a kind of third leg in the balance of struggle in Palestine between Jews and Romans.

Princes of the Herodian house were fully at home socially and politically in Rome, making the most of their hereditary position and used in this way by Roman leaders. By good fortune, this became important to the future Agrippa I, living in Rome as a young man when the Emperor Tiberius died in A.D. 37.

Tiberius' successor Caligula is described by one historian as "capricious and manifestly insane."[1] However, he wanted to do his best for his friend Agrippa, a grandson of Herod the Great, and appointed him king over the northeastern districts of Palestine, enlarged by including a section of Lebanon. Galilee was added to this in A.D. 39; and when Claudius became emperor two years later, Agrippa's title as king was extended to cover also Judea and Samaria. In this way his realm became, for a brief reign (A.D. 41–44), as extensive as that of Herod; and in many ways this descendant of both the Herodian and (through his grandmother) the Hasmonean house brought some pride to the Jewish scene, even if he was fully dependent on Rome.

Agrippa had shown the strength of his Jewish feeling soon after Caligula had accorded him the royal title. On his journey from Rome to Palestine, he stayed for a while in Alexandria, where the Jewish population, said to have numbered a million, gave him a warm reception. This provoked riots among the non-Jewish population, intensifying the fight between Jews and "Greeks" over the emperor-worship that Caligula demanded. It is clear that though the rich and sophisticated Jews of Alexandria were in many ways assimilated Hellenists, there were limits, which included idol-worship.

Flaccus, the Roman prefect, had thrown his weight against the Jews, ordering them to install images of the emperor in their synagogues. When they refused, the mob and troops were let loose; synagogues were desecrated and Jewish leaders dragged in chains through the streets and whipped. In this situation, Agrippa was able to do a good deal for the Jews, but not decisively. He had Flaccus removed, but the successor was not very helpful. Egyptian Greeks had formulated anti-Jewish views under the stimulus of a Jew-baiter called Apion. The outcome was that two missions set off to try and win support in Rome, one led by Apion and one of Jewish leaders led by Philo.

There was not much goodwill in Rome for the Jewish deputation, especially when news reached there of even wilder riots in Palestine over an order to the governor to set up the emperor's image in the Temple itself. At about this time, Caligula was assassinated (A.D. 41). Agrippa, who had gone back to Rome, found his territories increased under the new emperor, Claudius, and when he finally came to Palestine to take charge of his responsibilities, he was able to win the support of the Pharisees by his clear intent to rule with full respect for Jewish laws and customs. In Josephus' words: "It was his pleasure to reside continually in Jerusalem, and he meticulously observed the precepts of his fathers. He neglected no rite of purification, and not a day passed without its appointed sacrifices." (*Ant.* 19:6;1:294). He also set about fortifying Jerusalem against attack by building what became known as "the Third Wall," the remains of which were discovered and excavated in 1925–27.

It seems as if, with Agrippa I, the relationship between Jews and Romans had found a balance of mutual understanding that might, if continued, have prevented the catastrophic war of A.D. 66–70; but he fell ill and died suddenly in A.D. 44. His son, also called Agrippa, was only sixteen and seemed unfitted for the rule of this large realm. It was, therefore, all annexed as Roman territory and put again under the rule of procurators, subject to the governor of Syria. The young Agrippa did gain some respect within a few years and was given a certain limited authority as King Agrippa II. Though he took his position seriously, the real power now lay firmly with the procurators. Given their character, it was clear that trouble lay ahead, with riots, revolution, and the ultimate destruction of the state becoming more and more inevitable.

Schürer's magisterial work on the period confirms this, with a rather unexpected touch of sarcasm:

> It might be thought, from the record of the Roman procurators to whom, from now on, public affairs in Palestine were entrusted, that they all, as if by secret arrangement, systematically and deliberately set out to drive the people to revolt. Even the best of them—to say nothing of the others who totally disregarded every law—had no idea that a nation like the Jews required, above all, consideration for their religious customs. Instead of showing moderation and indulgence, they severely clamped down on any manifestation of the people's national character.[2]

This national character was being strongly developed during this period through the emergence of the class of teachers whom we now call the rabbis. For Christians looking back to this period, it was, of course, also the time when followers of Jesus, growing in number after his Crucifixion, were beginning to stand out more clearly in the sociopolitical scene. The relationship at that time between traditional Jews and Jewish-Christians was not a major element in the drift toward the Destruction. Yet it is of direct interest, since the war, when it came, put an end to what had been, until then, a flexible relationship between Jews and the future Christians.

The rabbinical leaders seem to have had a mixed attitude to those Christians who had not yet cut themselves off fully from their Jewish origins. We have incidents on this reported in the New Testament. Most vivid among them are mentions of the Jewish teacher Gamaliel, whom we known in rabbinic writings as Rabban Gamaliel, president of the Beth Din, or Sanhedrin, and the leading Jew of his time.

We are told (Acts 5:34–39) that when Peter and other Jewish-Christians (who used to meet, perhaps provocatively, in Solomon's Portico of the Temple to talk about their new faith) were arrested by command of the high priest and his Sadducean friends and brought before the Sanhedrin, "a Pharisee called Gamaliel," a member of the Sanhedrin, spoke up against punishment in sympathetic and realistic terms. If Jesus is an ordinary man, he says, his movement will collapse by itself. We have had many rebels "claiming to be somebody" and winning allegiance. There was Theudas who had a following and was ultimately killed. Then there was Judah the Galilean "at the time of the census," but he, too, perished and his following was scattered:

> And so now, keep clear of these men, I tell you; leave them alone. For if this idea of theirs or its execution is of human origin, it will collapse; but if it is from God, you will never be able to put them down, and you risk finding yourselves at war with God.

When Paul himself was arrested by Roman soldiers as a Christian and therefore a disturber of the peace, he defended himself first by asserting that he had been a Pharisee (that is, a devoted Jew), a pupil of the same Gamaliel. He claimed to be obedient to authority in going to Damascus under the orders of the harsh Sadducean high priest to bring the Christians there back in chains to Jerusalem. Later (Acts 21:39), he based his defense on his rights as a Roman citizen—"a citizen of no mean city" (Tarsus)—which secured his transfer to Rome for trial. In these events and arguments, one receives a lively picture of the new developments in the religious background, so significant for the future.

But for the time being they were transcended by the steady buildup of a fateful conflict on the political front, in which the whole future of the Jewish people was at stake. All attempts at understanding between the alien rulers and native Jewry were failing. The procurators were increasingly harsh both in stamping out rebellion and in asserting their authority in ways totally offensive to even moderate opinion.

We hear, for example, of the procurator Cuspius Fadus (A.D. 44–46) trying to take control of the Temple activities by seizing the priestly vestments. It was under the same Fadus that the rebellion of Theudas, mentioned by Gamaliel, was put down. Theudas had gathered a following by asserting that the Jordan would part for them, as proof of his divine mission. Troops were sent against him; he was killed and his head was carried to Jerusalem for display, as a lesson (*Ant.* 20.5).

Fadus's successor Tiberius Alexander (A.D. 46–48) was unusual in being Alexandrian-Jewish in origin—a nephew of Philo. He, too, dealt firmly with rebels, having two sons of Judah the Galilean crucified for their guerrilla activities.

But these troubles were small compared with what was to follow with the next procurator, Cumanus (A.D. 48–52). On duty with the crowds at the Temple during Passover, a Roman soldier, as Josephus puts it, "let down his breeches and exposed his privy members to the multitude, which put them into a furious rage" (*Ant.* 20.5). In the riots which followed, twenty thousand people were killed, according to Josephus.

Guerrilla fighting was mounting. Some Galilean Zealots were murdered in Samaria en route to Jerusalem, and their comrades took their revenge in a massacre of all the people of the village, including the women and children. In a follow-up by Roman soldiers, captured rebels were crucified and the ringleaders, Jews and Samaritans, sent to Rome for trial. It is at this point (probably about A.D. 52) that we begin to hear of a participatory role by young Agrippa II, now twenty-four years old. He happened to be in Rome and interceded on the behalf of the Jews. The Samaritan leaders were executed, and Cumanus, the procurator, was sent into exile.

But it was under Felix, the procurator who followed, that the die was fully cast. In Schürer's judgment, Felix's term of office (A.D. 52–60) "was the turning point of the drama which had started in [A.D.] 44 and reached its bloody climax in [A.D.] 70."[3]

Felix, a freedman of the imperial family, was a favorite of Claudius. If his elevation from lowly birth to the rank of procurator with military command indicated special qualities, he drew at the same time on cruder elements in his character, at least in the judgment of Tacitus, who wrote of him: "Practising every kind of cruelty and lust, he wielded royal power with the instincts of a slave."[4]

Felix seems to have used authority in a style that took him out of the ruck of more commonplace procurators like Pilate. For one thing, he married a Jewish princess, Drusilla, the daughter of Agrippa I and sister of young Agrippa II. The alliance was in violation of Jewish law since she was already married to a nearby foreign princeling; but if this disturbed some of the Jews, it was a small element in his friction with the nation at large. The spirit of rebellion was now rampant, with guerrilla gangs roaming the country, murdering and plundering. Sometimes, Felix seems to have found it useful to turn a blind eye, as when the guerrillas assassinated a high priest, Jonathan, who was too weak for Felix's purpose. We hear at this time of the tactics of the Sicarii, who moved among the crowds in Jerusalem carrying a concealed daggers, *sicarius,* which they used on sympathizers with Rome. The procurator was ruthless in arrests and executions, but the rebellion was clearly growing in strength, fueled by a mixture of religious and patriotic motivations that could appeal to all classes of society. By the end of Felix's term (A.D. 60), the country was in a state of anarchy, and it was clearly going to take little to rally a major part of the Jewish community into a suicidal war with Rome.

By this time, the young Agrippa, moving between Palestine and Rome, had been given increased imperial recognition, both in his royal title as King Agrippa II (with large territory) and in a stronger responsibility for supervising the running of the central institution of the Jewish state, the Temple. In some situations he could be a restraining influence, as when he dismissed the high priest Ananus, who had launched wild attacks on the Jewish-Christian sect by having suspects arrested and stoned. We see his role reflected clearly, also, in the incident (Acts 25:23) in which the procurator tells Agrippa about the arrest of Paul, who is then brought before the king and his sister Berenice, at their request, to talk about his Christian faith. It is clear that Agrippa lived in state in Palestine and was treated with deference; even so, there was little that he could do to remove the grievances of the Jews. The procurators were free to conduct rapacious raids on Temple funds, which was a constant source of fury to the Jews. Equally wounding were the insults to which the procurators subjected the Jews. It was an incident of this kind that led ultimately to the outbreak.

Felix had been followed as procurator by Festus (A.D. 60–62), and then by Alibus (A.D. 62–64). It was during the term of his successor Florus (A.D. 64–66) that rioting reached its peak. Florus plundered the country at large; but when, like his predecessors, he seized Temple funds on a large scale, the massing of crowds that hurled insults at the Romans led him to send in the troops. Inevitably, they pillaged freely, despite all protests. In addition, Florus demanded that two cohorts whom he had sent in from Caesarea should be accorded an official and friendly welcome by the Jews. The tension was too great. The rioting crowds were driven into the city, where they seized the Temple hill and cut the connection with the Antonia citadel.

Agrippa was, at this time, on a visit to Alexandria, where he had gone to pay his respects to the former procurator of Judea, Tiberius Alexander. Hearing of the revolt, he hurried back from Egypt and at Jamnia met some crowds who demanded complete suspension of the sacrifices that were offered daily for the emperor. This would have meant, in effect, a declaration of war. According to Josephus, Agrippa argued with them, "diplomatically turning resentment upon the Jews whom at heart he pitied, wishing to humiliate their pride, and by appearing to disbelieve that they had been ill-treated, to divert them from revenge." He appealed to them to consider the consequences of revolt: "Who and what are the Jews that they can refuse to submit to that nation to which all others have submitted?" (*Jewish War,* Bk. 2:345–401). But it was too late. The final rebellion was now launched.

The Course of the War

For a little time, the issue of a Jewish-Roman war was not clear-cut. Among the Jews themselves there was a peace party, primarily the chief priests, the Pharisaic notables, and those related to the Herodian house. They saw that argument with the rebels was useless and decided to try to oppose them by force. When they appealed to Agrippa for support, he sent in troops who helped the peace party to gain control of the upper city for a time, though they had soon to evacuate it because of attacks by furious mobs. The rebels set fire to the palaces of the high priest and Agrippa and a few days later captured the Antonia fortress, also.

At this stage, the struggle still bore the marks of a kind of civil war rather than a straight confrontation with the Romans. When the rebels laid siege to Herod's upper palace and captured it, they gave a safe conduct to Agrippa's troops sheltering there, while the Roman soldiers made their own way to the fortified towers within the palace orbit. These towers also fell to the rebels, which led to a massacre of Roman troops. The same pattern of struggle swiftly spread to other parts of Palestine where Jews and Gentiles lived side by side, each group conducting fierce and bloody attacks on the other.

Now, after careful preparation, the Romans turned this into a straight fight by launching a serious effort to put down the rebellion. Certius Gallus, governor of all Syria, moved up from Alexandria into Judea with the Twelfth

Legion, two thousand picked men from other legions, six cohorts, and four *alae*, wings, of cavalry, together with auxiliary forces supplied by friendly kings of the area, including Agrippa. Arriving near Jerusalem, Gallus repulsed an attack by the Jews and encamped on Mount Scopus, overlooking the city. But then, after an unsuccessful attack on the Temple mount, he began to withdraw his forces from the area. In retreat, his troops were caught in a gorge near Beth-Horon and had to take flight. The victorious rebels were able to enter Jerusalem, with a dramatic impact on those Jews who were still arguing for peace.

In effect, the idea of an accommodation with the Romans was now given up. Those who were inveterately pro-Roman or of pacifist temperament (like some of the rabbis) left the city, and those who remained turned to the organization of the rebellion in earnest. The leadership seems to have been taken over by the aristocratic class, though with the agreement of prominent Pharisees. A popular assembly held in the Temple approved the defense plans. The defense of the capital was entrusted to men of priestly lineage—Joseph ben Gorion and the former high priest Ananus. Other leaders with the same background were put in charge of the campaigns in Idumea and Galilee. In the latter area, the leader chosen was Joseph ben Matthias, whom we know as the historian Josephus.

Through the books which Josephus wrote in Rome when the war was over, we not only have a vivid account of the political, military, and religious background of the times but also a picture of the man himself in more detail than that of any other contemporary Jew.* Though of a priestly family, he had, as a young man, been very close to the Pharisees, which accounts for the detailed knowledge of the oral traditions revealed in his books. He had also been to Rome and had a great respect for its power and culture. Yet in his own account of the war, he claims to have been enthusiastic and even optimistic at first, proud, no doubt, to be given such an important command, and at the age of only twenty-seven. In Galilee, he established an advisory type of Sanhedrin, fortified the towns, and set about having his soldiers trained to Roman standards.

Perhaps the real clue to Josephus lies in the fact that the fanatical patriots of Galilee did not trust him to pursue the war with sufficient determination; and they seem to have been right in their judgment. The moving spirit in the

*Apart from the directly autobiographical *Life,* he is very revealing in *Jewish War* and *Against Apion.*

Jewish opposition to him was Johanan of Gish-Halav, who not only continued to act as an independent guerrilla fighter against all and sundry but even put in hand an attempt to have Josephus assassinated. As was to happen repeatedly later throughout the war, the bitter fighting within Jewish forces and parties was often more dangerous than that against the common enemy.

For the moment, both Galilee and the Jerusalem front did not have to face a direct Roman attack; but Rome was carefully marshalling a plan to offset the defeat of Gallus. Nero's decision as emperor was to send a prestigious general, Vespasian, to mount a war in proper Roman terms. Vespasian set up a base in Antioch and sent his son Titus to Alexandria to bring up the Fifteenth Legion for the fighting. With the other legions at his disposal, together with auxiliary cohorts and cavalry, Vespasian had some sixty thousand men to engage the Jews, and a strong base, the town of Sephoris in Galilee, which had asked for his protection.

In the account of his fight in Galilee, which Josephus gives in *The Jewish War,* the force with which he could meet Vespasian was quite inadequate and was dispirited by the prospect of an engagement. He could, therefore, offer no resistance, so that most of Galilee lay open immediately to the Romans, with only a few fortified places holding out for a time. Ultimately, what remained of Josephus' army took refuge in the fortress of Jotapata, where they were besieged under desperate conditions for two months. When Jotapata finally fell, Josephus and forty comrades escaped to a cave where they agreed on suicide by lot rather than surrender. Josephus claims to have drawn the last lucky number and to have survived this way. Whatever the truth of the story, it is clear that he escaped from the cave and surrendered. From this point on, he seems to have had favored treatment, even though he was held as a prisoner.

The story behind this is worth mentioning, since a parallel, yet significantly different version entered Jewish folklore later. In Josephus' account, he was favored because he was taken to Vespasian's tent where he prophesied that the general would soon become emperor of Rome. In the rabbinic story, which appears in a collection of anecdotes and legends called the Midrash, the leading rabbi of the time, Johanan ben Zaccai, escaped to Vespasian's camp and made the same prophecy to him of becoming emperor, whereupon he was given favored treatment. In the rabbi's case, he asked—as a reward for his prophecy—to be allowed to found a school for Torah teaching; it was from this small school at Jamnia (now Yavna) that the entire system of rabbinic teaching ultimately developed. The rabbinic accounts of this period do not betray any knowledge of Josephus or his books, which makes the parallel rather tantalizing.[5]

The fall of Jotapata unlocked the whole of Galilee to the Romans. Tiberias opened its gates to Titus. The fortresses of Gish-Halav and Tabor soon fell. Gamala, in the Golan, resisted for a time but finally fell, which signaled the reconquest by the Romans of the whole of northern Palestine. But the resistance leader Johanan of Gish-Halav had escaped with a body of men to Jerusalem, and this is where the decisive struggle was now to take place.

One knows of the long siege, conducted by the inhabitants with the utmost courage; but infighting within the walls was also desperate. The Zealots under Johanan of Gish-Halav were completely ruthless, putting to death anyone suspected of a leaning toward peace. Against them were moderate men, appealing for an end to terrorism; and these men had a good deal of popular support. The priestly offices were democratized, with the high priest elected by lot, so that any suspicion of pro-Roman elitism could be eliminated. The official leaders of the defense of Jerusalem were Ben-Gorion and Ananus; but by their side stood the leading Pharisee of the time, Simon ben Gamaliel, a descendant of Hillel.

The Romans made no move, leaving the city to be worn down in the first phase by hunger and terror, and this strategy was certainly having its effect. The Zealots had been pushed back by the ordinary citizens and taken refuge in the inner Temple court; but now they summoned allies—a band of fierce Idumeans who entered the city at night during a storm and set off on a campaign of murder and looting. Moderate leaders, including Ben-Gorion, Ananus, and another son of Gamaliel, were killed, sometimes after drumhead trials.

It is ironic, but in the nature of resistance fighting, that Johanan, who was doing his job as a leader by laying in food and strengthening the city with new fortifications, was himself subjected to attack by an even more extreme fighter, Simeon bar Giora, who had had some success in ravaging the countryside outside Jerusalem and now struggled for mastery within the city. There was a third contender for power in Eleazar ben Simon, who managed to get control of the inner Temple court.* Johanan held the remainder of the Temple mount, while Bar Giora held the upper city, as well as a large part of the lower city.

*Emil Schürer refers to Eleazar ben Simon as the son of Simon bar Giora, but this does not seem to be indicated elsewhere; see *The History of the Jewish People in the Age of Jesus Christ*, vol. 1, rev. by G. Vermes and P. Miller (Edinburgh: T. and T. Clark, 1973).

This was no peaceful division of the city for defense. The three leaders seem to have been at war with each other constantly, as well as with the ordinary inhabitants of the city. One story told by Josephus to illustrate the blindness of their mutual hatred is that they destroyed by fire enormous stores of grain in the city in order to prevent each other from obtaining it. Josephus so hated the terrorists that one is suspicious of his stories of them; but an almost identical story appears in the Midrash, and with even more detail. In this account, the aim of the Zealots was to force the rich citizens to give up the attitude of "life as normal" and face the real crisis. It even specifies the names of three rich citizens of Jerusalem whose storehouses were burned, each of whose stores of grain, wood and oil "would have been enough to feed the whole country for ten years."[6]

A Midrash story of this kind, even if its exaggerated detail always conveys a legendary quality, is in one sense more important to our purpose in this book than straight fact, since it expresses the unbroken folk memory which was to feed Jewish imagination for the next two thousand years. In this case, there is clearly some kind of factual basis; but in its elaboration of the incident, the Midrash becomes more fanciful, reporting that the leader of the Sicarii responsible for this wanton act of destruction was actually the nephew of Johanan ben Zaccai, the rabbi who got permission from Vespasian to found the Jamnia academy during the war, turning Jewish life from nationalist revolt to Torah study. It seems like deliberate irony, in telling the story, to produce the contrast between the rabbi and his wild nephew. The Midrash goes even further in suggesting that when the rabbi objected to what the nephew was doing, he was nearly killed himself. But this is all just one more example of giving Ben Zaccai a specially dramatic—or melodramatic—role in folk memory.

One wonders, sometimes, how a tiny people torn by such dissension could have fought the Romans and held off defeat for the four years of the Jewish-Roman War, A.D. 66–70. If the story was told later with a strong mixture of patriotic pride, the truth is that the Roman forces led by Vespasian were taking their own time and waiting for the outcome of the imperial succession before moving in to attack Jerusalem. Nero had died in June A.D. 68, at a time when Vespasian was building up his forces at Caesarea preparatory to launching his attack. Nero's successor, Galba, was assassinated six months later; and now Vespasian could begin to indulge imperial hopes. A rival, Vitellius (head of the army of the Rhine), seemed ahead but was murdered in December A.D. 69. The way was now open for Vespasian. He set off from Alexandria to Rome and was recognized there as emperor in the summer of A.D. 70, fulfilling the prophecies of Josephus and Ben Zaccai. During these uncertainties, he had handed over the conduct of the war against the Jews to his son Titus.

The four years in which there had been little to show of direct conflict had almost run their course by now. Titus did not reach even the vicinity of Jerusalem until Passover of the year A.D. 70. The defenders of the city launched a successful sortie against the Roman forces while they were digging in, and only when this was beaten off did the Romans' direct attack begin in earnest.

At first, their battering rams breached the most exterior third wall, built by Agrippa; five days later, the more interior second wall was breached in the same way. In this situation, the rival Jewish leaders within the city had suspended their mutual enmity and united for defense. The Romans set out to surround the whole city with a siege wall to reduce the city by starvation and at the same time built four great embankments to mount battering rams against the fortified towers. The defenders repeatedly undermined the embankments and the siege wall in order to keep their communications open, but within a few weeks, the fortresses fell and the Roman forces under Titus were in position for their final attack on the Temple.

In the destruction of the Temple which ultimately ensued, two fateful dates in the calendar stood out in the folk memory of later generations and were instituted as fast days. The first was the seventeenth of Tammuz, when the Temple rituals were finally suspended; the second was the ninth of Ab, when the Temple was set on fire and destroyed. What was remembered also was the intensity of the starvation that the inhabitants of the city endured, described in painful detail by Josephus, and paralleled, often exactly, in piteous stories in the Midrash.*

Many nations have endured sieges with heroic courage. What is striking about the siege of Jerusalem is that while the stories in Josephus were written down close to the time, the parallel stories of the rabbis—who had no access to Josephus—were retold orally for hundreds of years until they began to be written down in the fourth to sixth centuries A.D. At this stage, and for all the centuries to come, they were merged with other tales of suffering under the Romans and became part of a martyrology wept over in prayers and poetry but also generating a tangible note of pride—even satisfaction. Everything

*Though the Midrash is given as the source here, the stories are often paralleled in the Talmud. These are Midrashic stories, generally speaking.

about the fall of Jerusalem was converted into a positive feeling for the future. The more one groaned or wept, the more feeling one could put into the rallying cry: "Next year in Jerusalem!"

The Temple area was strongly fortified and had to be attacked, like other fortresses, by raising huge embankments against the walls. Throughout the siege, the daily rituals of the Temple had been continued. When they were suspended on the seventeenth of Tammuz (June), it was not just because of the famine to which the city was being subjected but also because of the shortage of men to perform the rituals.

For the three weeks that followed, the defenders of the Temple fought off soldiers who were trying to get into the area by climbing over the top of the rising embankments. We hear of great acts of daring and bravery by the Jewish fighters in repulsing these attacks, with heavy losses on both sides. When the embankments were completed, the battering rams were able to begin their work; but the Temple gates were strong and held them back. On the ninth of Ab, the gates were set on fire, and when they fell open, the whole Temple area began to burn. The soldiers poured in, killing and looting without restraint. Soon the Temple itself was fully aflame; and when the fires died down, all that was left, enshrining its holiness forever, was the western wall.

Aftermath: The Temple and Masada

To the Jewish people, the loss of the Temple was a hinge of fate, and in the events which followed, we begin to see a stirring of historical consciousness among rabbinical memorialists, even if they ignored what has become a heroic drama for our time—the story of Masada.

But on the Temple, and particularly on the survival of the western wall, their imagination was fully stirred. It is striking that this has come down, like the other episodes mentioned, in parallel accounts by Josephus and the Midrash, each with a special point to make.

Josephus, as always, is anxious to put the Romans in a good light, and in his account, Titus did his best to avoid the final act of destruction. His troops had taken the Antonia tower in June; at this point Titus held a council with his staff to discuss the fate of the last center of resistance—the Temple.

Varying views were expressed. Some thought that the Temple should be destroyed, "since the Jews would never cease from rebellion while the Temple remained as the focus for concourse from every quarter." Others held that it should be destroyed only if the Jews fortified it for purposes of warfare. Josephus records Titus as saying that he "would not in any circumstances burn down so magnificent a work" (*Jewish War* Bk. 6:236–41). But other historians question this assessment, stating that it was Titus himself who urged that it should be destroyed.[7]

With a different slant, rabbinical stories put Rabbi Johanan ben Zaccai again at the center of the story, but also—ironically for our own time—they link both the destruction of the building and the saving of the western wall to an *Arab* leader. The Midrash tells us that Ben Zaccai pleaded with the Roman general (it calls him Vespasian) not to destroy the Temple and that his plea was opposed by one of the Roman leader's auxiliary generals, Pangar, dux of Arabia, who, under a pretense of friendliness toward the Jews, argued for destruction. The Roman leader was persuaded by the Arab. Even Rabbi Johanan's request that the western gate leading to Lydda should be left open for a time for fugitives was not granted, and he was allowed only to secure the safety of some of his friends, the rabbis.

The twist in the Midrash account turns on how the western wall was left standing—through Pangar. It tells us that when "Vespasian" decided to destroy the whole of the Temple, he put the Arab leader in charge. But Pangar failed to carry out the task properly; and when the dust had cleared, he was summoned to the Roman leader to explain the failure. His excluse was that he had wanted to leave a monument standing to the Roman victory; but this did not save him, and he was executed for disobedience. It is interesting that the rabbis should have given Pangar this excuse, which is not as lame as it sounds. Josephus tells us that in the earlier campaign, Titus had left the Phazael tower (now known as David's Tower) standing "as a memorial of his attendant fortune, to whose cooperation he owed his conquest of defenses which defied assault (*Jewish War,* Bk. 6, #413).

It is hard to envisage that in a war between the might of Rome and the tiny Jewish people, the victory of Titus should be regarded as a triumph of the first order; yet that is how it was celebrated, first in the Near East and later in Rome.

Before this could happen, the campaign had to be wound down in an appropriately ruthless fashion. In Jerusalem itself, in the upper city, where the leaders Simeon bar Giora and Johanan of Gish-Halav still held out, ramparts were thrown up as before against the high fortified buildings to allow the battering rams to get to work, and over the next few weeks the rebels were pursued into every part of the area, after which all of Jerusalem, including the lower city long occupied by the Romans, was set on fire. In the spirit of the times—and perhaps of all warfare—the soldiers had a free hand in murdering and looting. Those of the defenders still alive were rounded up for execution or to be used as slaves or for the entertainment of the circus. The most handsome were reserved for the triumphal march in Rome. Of the two leaders, Johanan was sent to prison for life, while Simeon was kept as a victim for the triumph. After a festive sacrifice and banquet, Titus marched off with a large part of his army to his base and palace in Caesarea, leaving the Tenth Legion to garrison the destroyed city.

Three fortresses remained to be reduced—Herodium, Machaerus, and Masada. The first two fell without too much difficulty; but the Sicarii, under their leader Eleazar ben Ya'ir, had established themselves in Masada at the beginning of the war and seemed determined to hold out against the now concentrated attack by the Romans.

Leaving this task to Flavius Silva, a general newly appointed as governor of Palestine, Titus set off on a round of triumphal appearances in various cities of Palestine, Syria, and Mesopotamia, in which the entertainment was provided by Jewish prisoners killing each other in gladiatorial combat. From there he went to Alexandria, where he discharged his legions before sailing for Rome. In the triumph he was accorded there in A.D., 71, jointly with his father, Vespasian, and brother Domitian, the displayed prizes of war included the famed booty from the Temple—the Table of Shewbread and the Seven-branched Menorah, (lamp), reproduced graphically in his memorial arch. In accordance with custom, the enemy leader Simeon bar Giora was carried from the procession to prison and there executed.

The Arch of Titus has continued to evoke poignant memories of the war through the Temple relics it illustrates. If, by a miracle, the actual table and menorah had been rediscovered in our own time like so many other historic marvels, they would undoubtedly have served as a focus of Jewish pride; but they have disappeared into the void of the past. They had been deposited at first by Vespasian in the Temple of the Goddess of Peace, but this building was burned down. If the Jerusalem relics survived this fire, they may have been carried away by the Vandals when they sacked Rome in A.D. 435 and perhaps transferred to Constantinople when Belisarius destroyed the Vandal Empire in A.D. 534.[8]

It is all a sad story to a Jew. To have been able to gaze, in particular, at the original menorah—prototype of millions of menorahs in Jewish life—would have gratified the sense of history that is potent in the thought of the Temple and the war in which it was destroyed. However, something has emerged in our own time which goes a long way as compensation. The power of national pride has been reinforced by an episode of the war—the defiance of Masada—that had completely disappeared from folk memory and emerged only through the dramatic archaeological expeditions of Yigael Yadin, undertaken as recently as 1963 to 1965.

A visitor to Masada today takes in at a glance the problems that the Romans faced in capturing it. The garrison of Zealots had installed themselves there at the beginning of the war in A.D. 66 under the leadership of Eleazar ben Ya'ir, grandson of Judah of Galilee, who had led the Zealots sixty years earlier. The towering rock on which Herod had built his fortress and palace is so precipitous that it would clearly involve immense work to get the attackers and their siege weapons to its top. The Roman general therefore established a large camp, the remains of which can still be seen, at the base of the rock and set out to build a huge slope that would allow a great battering ram to be pushed to the summit. In due course, the Romans were able to breach the fortress wall this way, but they then found that the defenders had built an inner obstruction of wood and earth which was harder to breach. It fell, finally, to a massive use of fire by the attackers.

Josephus tells us that when defeat was clearly inevitable, Ben Ya'ir addressed the garrison, calling for death rather than surrender. They drew lots for the order of the slaying, and when the Romans burst in, they found the bodies lying there, victims—or heroes—of the last defiance.

Josephus had heard the story and wrote it up in grandiloquent language, creating a picture of noble courage, especially in the long speech he gave—imaginatively—to the Jewish leader. Until Masada was opened up in our day, no one knew how much credence to give to Josephus on the details of his account. There was nothing to support his story in the rabbinic memories of the Midrash, where Masada never appears. It was, therefore, a moment of immense significance to Jews when Masada came back into history, confirming the details of Josephus' story and offering visible relics that brought the period graphically to life. On the military side, one could now see the huge fortress, the Roman earthworks, the remains of the walls, the evidence of the fire. On the personal side, there were the bones and skulls of the defenders everywhere, the touching remains of individuals—a girl's plaits of hair, toilet articles, household belongings. There was a meeting hall (perhaps the earliest surviving synagogue from the period) and scrolls of writing, some biblical, some later.

In his thrilling book on Masada, Yadin says that if he were pressed to single out "the most electric moment" in the excavation, it would be their discovery, at one of the most strategic spots on Masada, of "eleven, small, strange ostraca [potsherds], different from any other which had come to light." Upon each was inscribed a single name, each different and intimate in style, as if a nickname. The daring thought leaped into Yadin's mind that these potsherds might be the actual lots which sealed the suicide pact as described by Josephus:

> They then chose then men by lot out of them, to slay all the rest; everyone of whom laid himself down by his wife and children on the ground, and threw his arms about them and they offered their necks to the stroke of those who by lot executed that melancholy office; and when these ten had, without fear, slain them all, they made the same rule for casting lots for themselves, that he whose lot it was to first kill the other nine, and after all, should kill himself [*Jewish War,* 7.6].

Most grimly, it was found that one of the ostraca bore the name Ben Ya'ir, which was surely that of Eleazar ben Ya'ir, the leader through whom Masada has become, in Yadin's words, "an undying symbol of courage." The centuries are bridged through the oath which every recruit of Israel's defense forces takes today: "Masada shall not fall again!"

Masada was the end not just of the war but of the long period in which one is able to follow history in the documented style of Josephus and some of the other contemporary writers we have referred to. For Josephus, it might be said, Jewish history was over. His task, as he now saw it, was as a chronicler. After his defection to the Romans in A.D. 67, he had been allowed to stay in Titus' camp, using his position there to plead with his fellow Jews from time to time to lay down their arms. In Rome, he was given citizenship and a pension by the emperor, partly, no doubt, to support him while he composed a formal book, *The Jewish War,* describing their triumph. If this book (written first in Aramaic and then translated into Greek) had an obviously biased aim, it is nonetheless a major work of history, as well as being exciting to read. It is, of course, a panegyric to Roman virtue and military skill; but at the same time it presents the Jewish people in a favorable light, pious and patriotic, though egged on to disaster by "brigands"—the Zealots and Sicarii whom he so disliked.

The book comes to a noble end with Masada; and though the Jews still existed in the Roman setting, the portrayal of this relationship was going to be more difficult now. The references to Jews in the works of roughly contemporary classical writers (for example, Pliny the Elder, Plutarch, Tacitus, Juvenal, and Suetonius) are casual and for the most part distorted, even before Christian historians, like Eusebius, turned on the Jews with total venom.

The Romans had had some respect for the oddities of Jewish religious observances when they were linked to a surviving statehood; without this basis, contact was negative. But if we have no Josephus to give us a coherent historical picture from now on, the rabbinical writings that look back to this period give us a lively picture of the background in which a new Jewish role was being formulated.

6

Outlook of the Rabbis

Development of the Tradition

STRIKING FEATURE of the rabbinical writings is that they are very rich in anecdotal history. Where the anecdotage of the rabbis can be checked, it has a strong factual basis. If rabbinic writing is unsystematic historically, it has, at least, given scholars ample material out of which to construct a functional picture of the times, very lively on the biographical side.[1]

At the same time, a vivid picture of the social texture of Jewish life has been put together by scholars from the detailed legal discussions that the rabbinic writings are concerned with. By the time the Temple was destroyed, Jewish teachers had been engaged for more than a century in working out an authoritative interpretation of the Torah that would have two complementary objectives. From one side, it spelled out the precise meaning of the words of the Torah when the text offered direct commands and ordinances; from the other side, it found Torah authority (often in complicated ways) for the pattern of life which had come down orally from generation to generation and had thus been hallowed as living tradition. In these ways it brought together the Written Law and the Oral Law.

This twofold study of the Torah was open-ended; but gradually a body of rulings had been emerging, covering every aspect of life for a Jew. The Pharisees were distinguished, as Josephus confirms, for the respect they gave to the Oral Law, which meant that Torah observance, as defined in this broad way, was to them a supreme expression of the love of God. From the time of Hillel (at the turn of the Christian era), we hear of these teachers as rabbis (the word *rabbi* means *my master*). The study classes of the rabbis had begun to have something of the authority of courts of law.

When the Temple—and the state Sanhedrin—disappeared through the Destruction of A.D. 70, these rabbinical assemblies grew more comprehensive in this form. Within fifty years, a collection of their rulings was being assembled and edited under subject headings. When it finally emerged as a comprehensive work, known as the Mishnah, in the second century A.D., it had become a huge reference book to the body of Oral Law that Jews had developed and lived by under rabbinic guidance. The Mishnah was broadened later by fuller discussion; and the whole corpus of legal rulings became known as the Talmud. It is the Talmud, then, that became a vast sourcebook for modern scholars seeking evidence on how Jews lived their lives as far back as Temple times and the immediately following period. The memory of those ancient times, put down much later in the Talmud, was not always accurate; but it helps to formulate the Jewish social history of this period as seen through the experience and intuition of rabbinic minds.

Life after the Destruction

The living picture in rabbinic writings has been illustrated graphically by a remarkable discovery only a few years ago, emerging out of the soil of Israel, or rather out of the stones and bat-droppings of a cave, the one in which Professor Yigael Yadin discovered the Bar Kokhba letters, to be discussed below on pages 140–43.

Together with the letters, Yadin found, hidden for safety under a deliberately arranged mass of heavy stones, a large archive of documents recounting in detail the intricate human and business relationships of a whole family, centered around the personal history of one woman, Babata daughter of Simon. She and her family had taken refuge in the cave during the Bar Kokhba rebellion, carrying her personal possessions—cooking pots, dishes, coins, keys, and woman's makeup kit. But transcending this in importance were the documents around which her whole life turned.

These documents, marvelously preserved through the dryness of the cave, are in Nabatean, Aramaic, and Greek. They demonstrate dramatically that the rule of Jewish and state law continued in full flow after the fabric of society seemed to have been destroyed; and for the validity of the rabbinic tradition, they conform in every detail to the style and legalities of the social system as evoked hundreds of years later in the Talmud.

It is a marvelous accident that Babata had had such an eventful personal life, fully reflected in her archive. She came from a property-owning family, and the documents cover her first marriage (her husband died, but there was a son), her second marriage to a man who already had a daughter, and so on. All these relationships brought up property problems. Apart from the wide range of contracts for sale and acquisition of houses, there are five deeds dealing with the custody of her son by her first husband, two covering property of her second husband's daughter, five claims by members of the family against Babata in connection with property of which she obtained possession, after the death of her second husband. There are the wedding contracts of her second marriage and of her step-daughter, set out in what became the traditional rabbinic style and therefore specifying money settlements in case of divorce. Above all, for the sociopolitical history of the period, the property documents refer to the leasing of land from "the ruler," identifying him as "Simon bar Kosiba," the real name of the rebel leader Bar Kokhba.

We know from Josephus that in the first phase after the Destruction, Vespasian had taken all the land of Judea as his private possession and leased it out for profit. When Bar Kokhba staged his rebellion in Judea some sixty years later, he boldly transferred these seigneurial rights to himself, though with problems that emerge in his letters. But through all this period, people like Babata were getting married and divorced, buying and selling property, and all under the protection of a system of law—criminal, as well as civil—that had now become entrenched in Jewish life with the ultimate authority of the Torah.

The Rabbis Hold Things Together

The role of the rabbis was all the more significant in that Palestine had ceased, in many ways, to be dominantly Jewish. Increasingly, new towns were founded with predominantly gentile populations. We know from various sources, including coins, of the building of pagan temples and the holding of games. We see even from Babata's archive that, linguistically, Palestine was very cosmopolitan. The Jewish community to which she belonged was evidently only one strand of a complex society.

In this society, the Jewish sense of kinship was being intensified for the future through the emergence of a new leadership. The Temple and Sanhedrin had been controlled by a Sadducean elite of birth and wealth that now had to give way to the Pharisees and rabbis. Jerusalem itself lay in such ruins that, in Josephus' words, "those who visited it could not believe it had ever been inhabited." It was now, primarily, a Roman camp, the base for part of the Tenth Legion, its baggage, and its camp-followers. Jerusalem never lost its emotional hold on the Jewish mind, but public life now had a different focus in the academy at Jamnia, where Johanan ben Zaccai drew around him a band of disciples who would give a new force to rabbinism. The most famous were Joshua ben Hananiah and Eliezer ben Hyrcanus, with their pupils Ishmael, Akiba, and Tarfon.

A central feature of the work of this academy was the application of its rulings to religious practice in daily life and civil and criminal law. In this sense they had become the new Sanhedrin, giving judgments that conveyed authority and that helped to carry through an adjustment to the new realities. Yet with equal intensity the rabbis pursued every aspect of a subject that no longer had reality: Temple worship and its sacrifices. Far from this being dealt with in abstract terms, it was treated with complete reality, which was a healthy form of adjustment. For behind this attitude lay an unshakable confidence in the future. Certainly, they had suffered a terrible disaster; but one day the old glory—including the Temple—would be restored, and they had to go on studying with this in mind. They had been punished because they had betrayed the confidence that God had put in them. If they would rid themselves of sin, the day of salvation would arrive, more certain now because of the horrors that had been suffered.

Two apocalyptic books that come from this post-Destruction period—

Baruch and *4 Ezra*—express this fully. It is also the perennial theme of the Midrash, which was written down much later but reflects sermons given in synagogues on these themes. Most powerfully of all, this combination of sorrow and hope emerges in the book of Midrash which is most closely linked to the Destruction: the Midrash on Lamentations.[2]

Messiahs and Rebels

Even after Masada, the spirit of the Zealots was never fully crushed. In the war which had just ended, their strongest motivation had been religious. God was their Master and could never be replaced as Master by the Romans, however powerful. In this argument, the religious motivation for disobedience became a military motivation for rebellion.

In the first post-Destruction decades, the spirit of Judea may have seemed subservient. We hear of few conflicts between Rome and the Jews for some forty-odd years. But then, under the emperors Trajan (A.D. 98–117) and Hadrian (A.D. 117–38), rebellions became widespread, surfacing at first among Jews living in great numbers outside Palestine and then turning into the massive revolt of Bar Kokhba (A.D. 132–35). Only when this last rebellion had been put down, and with ruthless ferocity, did the Jewish people adopt the passive attitude that was to be their hallmark for many centuries.

Folk memory can be erratic as well as heart warming. One of the oddities for Jews is in the contrast between the stirring image of the Bar Kokhba rebellion and the faded memory of the uprisings against Roman authority, fifteen years earlier, in countries all around the Mediterranean. Yet these were not only remarkable for their time, but a much truer projection of the future of Jewish kinship—worldwide—than was demonstrated with Bar Kokhba.

As Josephus was no longer available on this period (he died around A.D. 100), the story of these rebellions have been reconstructed from the outside, as it were, by scholars using some contemporary sources (the historian Appian and newly discovered papyri) and some later sources (the historians Dio Cassius and Eusebius). From the inside, one picks up references in the Midrash and Talmud that were once rather mysterious but can now be fitted into their place.

In all the stories of the widespread revolts against the Roman overlord in the years A.D. 115–17, it is the sense of Jewish kinship which is so striking. In the Midrash on the Destruction, we see the aftermath centered in a sorrowing Holy Land. What we now know is that the sense of shock was overpowering throughout the Jewish Diaspora. It is thought that there were more than 4.5 million Jews living in the Roman Empire outside Palestine;* and if they were at first stunned, it is clear that they were only biding their time to show their feelings.

It was when the Emperor Trajan was preoccupied with the conquest of Mesopotamia in A.D. 115 that the moment came for the Jews of Egypt and North Africa. In Eusebius' account, they began "to rise against their non-Jewish fellow-citizens as if possessed by a wild spirit of mutiny."[3] We have lost track of immediate causes; one has to assume that together with local Jewish—non-Jewish friction, the basic cause was the release of pent-up feeling against the Romans, the destroyers of the Temple. In Egypt, there were set battles between Jews and Hellenes in which the advantage swayed for a time between the two sides, and with many executions and deaths in battle. In Cyrene, further to the west, the rage of the Jews was even more intense. The Jews had a ringleader whom they hailed as "king"; and according to Dio Cassius, they were driven on in their fury to commit the most horrific atrocities, with 220,000 non-Jews massacred.

Allowing for obvious exaggeration, the nature of the outbreaks was clear enough, impelling Trajan to send battle-tested troops to handle the situation. The rebellion spread from North Africa to the Jews of Cyprus, where, according to the same sources, a quarter of a million non-Jews were slaughtered. In Mesopotamia, the Jews rose in the rear of the Roman armies with a fury that led Trajan to send in one of his best generals, Lucius Quietus. Lucius, who was a Moorish prince, is said to have put the revolt down with barbaric ferocity and as a reward was made governor of Palestine.

It is around him that rabbinic writings provide echoes of these rebellions. We read of a *polemos shel qitos,* war of Quietus, that may refer to his Mesopotamian campaigns or to revolts that broke out subsequently in Palestine itself. In a midrashic work of the second century A.D.,[4] the war of Quietus is recorded as one of the four great revolts of the Jews against the Romans, the other three being the war of Varus (legate of Syria at the time of the revolt over the census in A.D. 6), the war of Vespasian, and the "reign" of Bar

*There were 2.5 million Jews in Palestine itself. For more population figures, see page 219.

Kokhba.* The Midrash on Lamentations describes with great bitterness the massacre of the Jews by Trajan and Quietus: "the blood of the men, mingling with the blood of the women, poured on as far as Cyprus."†

One can visualize the rabbis telling these stories, sadly but also with a touch of black humor, if we are to judge from a story in the same Midrash where they offer a somewhat jokey reason to explain why Trajan so disliked the Jews. His wife, living in Palestine, had taken umbrage, they say, at two imagined insults by the Jews. They had gone into mourning when she had given birth to a child on the ninth of Ab (which, as the anniversary of the Destruction, is a Jewish fast day); and when one of her children had died, they had lit candles of joy (it was, unluckily, the Feast of Hanukkah, when candles are lit). She had therefore written to her husband: "Instead of subjecting the Barbarians [presumably the Parthians], come and subject these Jews who have revolted against you." Whereupon Trajan had set out for Palestine, arrived unexpected by the Jews, and massacred thousands.[5]

But the Jews felt they got even with him in the end, if only in myth. The Midrash has a story about two Jewish rebel leaders called Pappus and Lilianus who were caught and about to be executed on Trajan's command when a letter arrived from Rome announcing that Trajan himself was being recalled on the orders of the senate to be executed. In this way, Pappus and Lilianus were saved. The Jews of a later generation believed that Trajan's Day, a minor holiday, had been instituted in memory of the miraculous escape of the two leaders, though it more probably celebrated some small victory of the Jewish forces against Trajan. Trajan, as might be imagined, was never recalled to Rome for execution, but it is intriguing that Lucius Quietus was. It was Hadrian's first act as emperor, when he succeeded Trajan. The reason is said to have been that Quietus had become a symbol of Roman cruelty to the Jews of Mesopotamia and Palestine.[6]

A mollifying act of this kind may sound a little surprising for the emperor whose name is almost always mentioned with a curse in the Midrash of Lamentations: "Hadrian, may his bones be crushed!"; but the curse reflects his actions, fifteen years after his accession, in defeating the heroic rebel Bar

*The Mishnah (Sotah 9:4) mentions only three revolts: "the War of Vespasian, the War of Titus, and the last war (Bar Kokhba)." But one text reads *Qitos* (Quietus) for Titus. See C. Raphael, *The Walls of Jerusalem* (New York: Knopf, 1968), p. 39.

†Midrash on Lamentations, 1:45. The text reads: "the Cyprus river." It used to be speculated that this perhaps meant that the revolt was put down with the same ruthless severity as was the revolt of the Jews of Cyprus, and that there was, as it were, one "river of blood" from Jerusalem to Cyprus. (For details see C. Raphael, *Walls*, p. 39).

Kokhba and outlawing the teaching of the Torah. In the earlier years of his reign, immediately after the revolts had been brought to an end, Hadrian was spoken of most kindly.[7] The Jewish tradition believed that the leading rabbi of the time, Joshua ben Hananiah, was on friendly terms with him, and that Hadrian "issued a decree" that the Jewish Temple should be rebuilt (*Gen. Rabbah* 64). The Christian historians also report a strong tradition to this effect.* There is no evidence that, as some have suggested, the Jews made this promise a condition of their laying down arms. They could never have been in a position to dictate to the emperor. It is more likely that Hadrian made this promise vaguely as a gesture of concession. He had a passion for rebuilding cities, and without realizing what this particular promise—to rebuild the Temple—meant to the Jews, he probably began to rebuild Jerusalem as a beautiful pagan city.[8]

The first signs of rebuilding must have aroused great excitement among the Jews. They seem to have begun to collect money from Jews everywhere toward the buildings and furnishings of the Holy Shrine,† and even to have raised certain religious, *halakhic,* questions emerging out of the reconditioning of the Temple site.‡ But they were soon to be disappointed. Hadrian withdrew his promise, says the Jewish account. One tradition blames the Samaritans for playing their usual anti-Jewish role (*Gen. Rabbah* 64). As soon as the Jews realized that Hadrian's aims were only military and pagan, they themselves began to oppose the rebuilding. Indeed, it took all the oratorical skill of Rabbi Joshua to persuade the Jews not to take up arms again to avenge their disappointment and imagined betrayal.[9]

We hear of no open conflict during the next ten years, but beneath the surface at least some of the Jews must have been getting ready for a last struggle against Rome. There is evidence in a papyrus that Roman soldiers were in service in Judea in A.D. 128, indicating some warfare there. Jewish

*A passage in *The Epistle of Barnabas* (16:4) refers to the Jews expecting the Temple to be rebuilt at this time by the pagans and denounces the Jews for this—expecting a *physical* Temple—among other faults.

†*Genesis Rabbah* 64: "Pappos and Luliani, the heroes of the last revolt, set up exchange tables in Galilee and Syria, from Acco to Antioch, and provided with gold, silver, and other articles those who were coming into the country from exile." Heinrich Graetz (*History of the Jews* (London: Myers and Co., 1901), vol. 4, p. 129, n. 4 interprets this as meaning that they could exchange here for Palestinian money the coins they were bringing as contributions to rebuilding the Temple. S. Krauss (*Jewish Encyclopedia,* vol. 9, 512) holds that these were the preparations for a rebellion; but the context makes it sound unlikely.

‡Graetz, *History,* vol. 4, p. 129, n. 14, argues that halakhic questions raised in the Mishnah and Tosefta show that the Temple was being rebuilt.

blacksmiths are said to have manufactured weapons for the Romans so poorly that they would be returned to the Jews, who would find them useful. Caves in the mountains were converted into hiding places and fortifications connected by underground passages. Some scholars think that the rabbis traveled to other countries to enlist support for a rebellion.[10]

Hadrian's attitude was all-important. Traveling in Syria and Egypt, he came into contact with Jews and seems to have treated them in a tolerant and inquisitive, if slightly contemptuous, manner.[11] It is known from coins struck in his honor that he visited Judaea, and it was probably then that he gave orders that the rebuilding of Jerusalem should be resumed in pagan style.

About this time, too, Hadrian reissued an edict of the emperor Domitian prohibiting bodily mutilation; and though this was not specifically directed against the Jews, it became in effect a grave attack on Jewish religious practice, since the ban included circumcision. The attitude of rabbis to this ban would have been to ignore it, as they ignored Hadrian's later ban on teaching the Torah; but Jews of more militant character would be increasingly ready to rally around anyone who would lead them with confidence against the hated Roman power.

The Bar Kokhba Revolt

When at this stage there appeared a courageous fighter who began to conduct open warfare and score victories against the surprised Roman governor Tinneius Rufus, it was natural that this Jewish leader—Bar Kosiba—should attract to himself something of the aura of the long-awaited Messiah. In this spirit, he was given a messianic *nom de guerre* Bar Kokhba, the star man, fulfilling the Bible verse: "There shall come forth a star [*kokhab*] out of Jacob" (Num. 24:17). But no one can tell how far this messianic aspect of his ambition—implied by the later historians—was prevalent at the time.

Nothing is known of Bar Kokhba's early life. He appears on the scene when he has already captured many fortresses and open villages and imposed a strong, if uneven, leadership on his people. There are a few anecdotes about him in the Midrash, including one that might suggest that he was called the

Messiah by the leading rabbi, Akiba; but on the whole, the rabbis had little to say in his favor.

Until recently, therefore, he was a very shadowy figure. The classical and later Christian historians give us an outline, indicating that at first (A.D. 132) he had considerable success. Tinneius Rufus was unable to prevent the rebels from capturing about fifty strongholds and nearly a thousand villages, and when Publius Marcellus, legate of Syria, was sent to help Rufus, he too was defeated. Only when Julius Severus, the greatest general of his time, was recalled from Britain to lead the campaign, were the Romans able to force the Jews out of their strongholds. Some have argued, though on little direct evidence, that at one stage Bar Kokhba occupied—or perhaps one should say liberated—Jerusalem;[12] but we only know of him in fact as holding out in a small area of Judea, with headquarters at Bethar in the hills southwest of Jerusalem. Large numbers of Jews took refuge there, with the defense well organized. After his initial campaign, Julius Severus surrounded Bethar closely but was unable to capture it. It withstood the Roman siege for three and a half years until A.D. 135. Finally it was captured, and the revolt was brought to an end.

Until very recent times, this was all that was known about Bar Kokhba, and even this was uncertain. But by one of the marvels of modern archaeology, manuscripts of his period began to be discovered, only a few years ago, authenticating him completely and filling out his story with illuminating detail. The discoveries also lit up vividly the social pattern of the time, but above all, we now know what was the character of this last revolt, and we have been able to meet Bar Kokhba in person. From these and many other points of view, there could be no better illustration of what is called the romance of archaeology.

The discoveries began in the early 1950s in the area close to the border between Israel and Jordan on the west bank of the Dead Sea. The discovery of the Dead Sea Scrolls in the late 1940s by Bedouins had stirred them to continue their searches, and rumors began to circulate that they had been sensationally successful in finding in a wadi, valley, in Jordan territory, pottery, textiles, and even well-preserved manuscripts going back to the Bar Kokhba period. These had come from the Wadi Murabba'at, a few miles north of En-Gedi; but it was being said that some of the earliest Bedouin discoveries (including the manuscripts) had been ferreted out from caves on the Israel side of the border.

The Israelis decided that they would do their own searching of their caves. Bar Kokhba was, after all, a Jewish hero. Anything that might document his existence would carry a special bonus of pride. The decision was taken at a high government level to make units of the Israel army available to the archaeologists for a few weeks so that the search could be conducted with military effectiveness. (This was not so surprising since the leading archaeologist, Yigael Yadin, had been chief of staff of the Israel army during the war of independence in 1948.)

Two major searches of the caves were therefore mounted in March and April 1960 and March 1961.* Part of the area covered was found to have been ransacked, as had been feared; but at one base, Nahal Hever, in charge of Yadin, striking discoveries were made. After tireless efforts of burrowing through the accumulated filth of centuries, baskets and bundles were found hidden away under the stones, left by those who had fled to the caves in the last phases of the Roman advance and were bringing their personal archives with them.

Until that moment of discovery, which came just as the time alloted to the search was running out, the Israelies had been in despair. Scholars dealing with the material from the Jordan side had already published much of their work, bringing Bar Kokhba himself and the whole period to life. Now that the Israelis had made their own discoveries, pride was satisfied, and the realm of new knowledge could be increased cooperatively. The Israelis saw this as they unrolled the manuscripts that lay before them, perfectly preserved and completely readable. The work from the two sides of the border could now come together as an integrated whole.

The material from the Jordan side was published in a magnificent book called *Les Grottes de Muraba'at,* with the Hebrew and Aramaic documents deciphered and interpreted by a Catholic scholar, Father J. T. Milik.[13] Almost as ancient as the Dead Sea Scrolls, these Bible fragments are riveting, including, most strikingly, portions from what had been a complete scroll of the Twelve Minor Prophets, found next to a skull, which might indicate that the man's personal scroll was buried with him.

These writings are all on parchment. Others on papyrus include marriage

*After preliminary publication of the results in the *Israel Exploration Journal,* 1961 and 1962, a full description of the whole mission and its broad results was published in 1971 by Yigael Yadin in his *Bar Kokhba* (London: Weidenfeld and Nicolson, 1971). He stated that this was to be followed by a volume dealing with literary analysis of the documents in more detail.

and divorce documents, with details of property arrangements, all in the form transmitted later by rabbinic ordinance. There are contracts for the sale and leasing of land; an IOU; and private letters covering many subjects, including one—perhaps two—from Bar Kokhba himself.

These Jordan documents illustrate vividly how strongly Bar Kokhba had taken hold of the area, and perhaps even of other areas, as an administrator. One bundle of contracts deals with the leasing of land from him, and the form of the contract itself illumines the period. Each contract (and there are nine of them) consists of a declaration by the signer that "of his own free will" he had leased his right to farm the land from Bar Kokhba's administrator, the rent being an annual remission of a certain quantity of "wheat of good quality," which would be tithed and sent to "the Treasury" at Herodium. All the documents begin: "On the 20th Shebhat, in the Second Year of the Liberation of Israel by Simon ben Kosiba, *Nasi* [President] of Israel. . . ." After the signature, the phrase: "By the authority of Simon ben Kosiba" is added, which confirms his real name. The whole procedure illustrates that Bar Kokhba had taken over to himself the imperial right of ownership of all land.

Who could have dreamed that the Jews of our own day would see their legacy enriched in this way through the bringing to life of a man who until then had been merely a legend—as legendary to them as King Arthur to the British? And the documents mentioned so far are only a small aspect of the revelation. On Bar Kokhba's character—the clue to his rise to power—we have the forceful, even explosive, style of his letters, as in one addressed to the leader in charge of one of his military posts: "From Simon ben Kosiba to Joshua ben Galgula and the men of Ha-Bruk: Greeting! I call Heaven to witness against me that if any of the Galileans who are with you are ill-treated, I shall put you in fetters as I did to Ben Aphlul." But there is also a kinder side, as in another letter to Ben Galgula ordering him to send over certain quantities of wheat, but specifying that the messengers carrying the wheat should be accommodated with all possible comfort over the Sabbath. Then he adds, "Be of good spirit and keep everyone's spirits up."

And to have all this happen when a new State of Israel had just been founded! Across the centuries, there is a powerful link in the language Bar Kokhba used in these highly personal commands to his troops: not Aramaic, which was widely used as a lingua franca, but Hebrew, in a highly fluid style, like the language of the Mishnah (roughly the same period), and modern Hebrew.

One looks for perspective in reading these documents from an ancient war. What comes to life is the character of that brief and poignant period—A.D. 132–35—in which the Jews of a small area of Palestine tried to pretend to themselves that they could exist under their own ruler, going about their daily lives and holding the Romans at bay. Father Milik has used these documents to build up a vivid picture of the administration that the rebel leader maintained. The rabbis, he says, looked back with nostalgia to many aspects of this era: "The Midrash on Lamentations is the requiem for this period of prosperity."

Some of the same points emerge from the documents found by Yadin on the Israel side of the frontier, but luckily they fill out the picture and introduce many new elements rather than merely duplicate it.

This is strikingly true of letters from Bar Kokhba, of which a bundle of fifteen was found. One is on four slates of wood which open into one, providing a letter beginning in formal style: "Simon bar Kosiba, Nasi over Israel, to Jonathan and to Masbela: Shalom!" The letter, which in this case is in Aramaic, orders them to confiscate a quantity of wheat belonging to a certain man and to transmit it "in safety" to Bar Kokhba. Its tone is as firm as the "fetters" letter: "If you do not act accordingly, you will be punished severely." There are similar threats in a letter to "the men of Tekoa" who are engaged in "repairing their houses" instead of fighting. This comes out even more bitterly in a letter to the men of En-Gedi: "You sit in comfort, eating and drinking from the resources of Israel, and are not concerned at all about your brothers."[14]

For the normal life that was carried on behind the fighting, the Babata archive, gives an immensely detailed picture of family and business life among the people of the time. For a simpler and perhaps more charming sidelight on normality, there is, among Bar Kokhba's fierce letters on military supplies, one supply letter in a different tone. It reveals the effort made, in the middle of the fighting, to keep up the traditional observances—in this case, the ritual of Sukkoth, the Feast of Tabernacles. The letter says that two donkeys are being sent to his agents Jonathan and Masbela for loading with palms and citrons, myrtles and willows, all four being required for this festival's ceremonies, as laid down in the Bible. They are to be tithed and sent to the camp.

I have been unashamedly sentimental in lingering over these Bar Kokhba letters; more historically, the Bar Kokhba drama achieves its real significance in terms of what happened to the Jewish faith when the revolt was over.

The Growth of Rabbinism

To look for long-term developments is not to play down, in any way, the straightforward thrill of the Bar Kokhba manuscripts, which is recaptured by Yadin in a story he tells in the preface to a book he wrote on his discoveries.

In the spring of 1960, he says, the then president of Israel, Izhak Ben-Zvi, had invited him and his fellow archaeologists to his home. Also present were Prime Minister Ben-Gurion, the Cabinet, and other leaders of Israel. Until that moment, nothing had been said in public of what had been found. Yadin projected on a screen a slide with a photograph of one of the letters and read aloud the first line of writing: "Simon bar Kosiba, Nasi [President] of Israel." Then, turning to the president he said, "Your Excellency: I am honoured to be able to tell you that we have discovered fifteen dispatches from the last Nasi of Israel, one thousand eight hundred years ago."

The audience, he says, broke into "spontaneous cries of astonishment and joy." It was undoubtedly a great moment; but behind the pride, there was also a fateful echo in the words "one thousand eight hundred years ago."[15] The audience in the president's home knew that in this long stretch of time, the Jewish people had never again shown a military spirit as a nation until the birth of modern Israel. Bar Kokhba's defeat, then, was a turning point, yet not in the sense commonly understood. Defeat was a turning point for survival. In military terms, there was never the slightest chance of Bar Kokhba winning lasting freedom from Roman rule and perpetuating Jewish existence this way. Yet in the circumstances of the defeat, a new spirit was being fashioned ensuring that a heritage of distinctive character would now be passed on for all time.

What Jewish folk memory brought back from this time, side by side with some vague legends about a military hero, was an absolutely clear picture of the heroism of rabbinical leaders who fought the Romans not with arms but with faith. Hadrian had offended the Jews with a ban on circumcision and with his plans to turn Jerusalem into a pagan city. It appears, from various sources, that these aims were not pursued very seriously; but now, in the wake of a strong rebellion, Roman toleration gave way to a policy of ruthless religious repression. Circumcision, the Sabbath, and the teaching of the Torah were all outlawed. The Jewish tradition called this the Age of the Decree, *gezeirah,* or the Age of Persecution, *sh'mad.* The penalty for teaching the

Torah was death. The rabbis defied the orders and suffered martyrdom, described in the kind of detail always accorded, in all religions, to sainthood. When Rabbi Hananiah was executed,

> They wrapped him in the scroll of the Torah, set bundles of brushwood around him and set them on fire. Then they brought tufts of wool which they had soaked in water and placed them over his heart so that he should not expire quickly. . . . His disciples called out to him: "Rabbi, what do you see?" He answered: "The parchment is burning, but the letters are soaring out on high."[16]

The martyrdom of the great Rabbi Akiba took its place in folk memory because, "while they combed his flesh with iron combs," he continued to recite the *Sh'ma** with intense concentration over the final word *Ehad,* One. These rabbis were but two of the ten martyrs, a group known to folk memory, whose example inspired countless others and sustained Jewish faith through centuries of existence.†

But the rabbinical martyrs set only the high points of memory. To later ages, the whole of the Jewish people seemed involved in the Destruction, a war with the Romans that stretched continuously from Vespasian to Bar Kokhba—seventy years—and was treated this way in the rabbinic work which concentrated on it: the Midrash on Lamentations. For even if the Bar Kokhba war was limited in range compared with the war of Vespasian, the effects were appalling for the whole population of Palestine. The horror stories in the Midrash of enslavement, transportation, starvation, and brutality are paralleled by similar accounts in the classical sources.[17] We read in Dio Cassius that 580,000 Jews fell in battle and that those who succumbed to illness and starvation were uncounted. "The whole of Judea was practically a desert."[18]

Side by side with this picture of misery, there is the deep insult, conveyed in the same classical sources, of Hadrian's rebuilding of Jerusalem as a pagan city. The temple which he built on the site of the burned-out Jewish temple was devoted to Jupiter Capitolinus and contained statues of the gods and of Hadrian himself. Jews, we are told, were no longer allowed to enter the city area on pain of death, which offers a poignant contrast to the position before

*"Hear O Israel, the Lord our God, the Lord is One" (Deut. 6:4)—the central verse in Jewish prayer.

†Stories of different martyrs in various parts of the Talmud were edited into a consecutive account and described as if happening on one day. See C. Raphael, *Walls,* pp. 49–50, n. 4; pp. 192–94.

the rebuilding, when Jews might have been free to wander, however sadly, among the ruins. To get the flavor—however apocryphal—of these wanderings, one has to turn to the Midrash. We read of one occasion when Akiba and a group of the rabbis were going to Jerusalem, and at Mount Scopus, overlooking the Temple area, they rent their clothes in mourning. When they reached the Temple mount, they saw a fox run out of the Holy of Holies, and all wept except Akiba, who laughed. Holy Writ, he told them, had already predicted this in the verse: "For the mountain of Zion is desolate, the foxes walk upon it" (Lam. 5:18). But there is another prophecy, he said: "The streets of the city shall be full of boys and girls playing," (Zech. 8:5), and that was why he laughed. If one verse has come true, the other one will also. "Akiba," they said, "you have comforted us. May you be comforted by the steps of him that brings good tidings."[19]

There is a special reason for thinking of Akiba as we end this chapter, for we need him to consider a final aspect of the Bar Kokhba war which has gone curiously awry in folk memory. There is a popular conception that Bar Kokhba was hailed by Rabbi Akiba, the leading teacher of his day, as the Messiah. This idea has worked its way into virtually every history book on the Jews. It sounds cheerful and harmless at first glance, which is why it has always been repeated. But the Messiah notion is too serious to be treated casually, especially in the light of the growth of Christianity in Akiba's time. Moreover, the story is out of keeping with the spirit that was going to preserve Judaism from that time on under the guidance of the rabbis during the developing outright hostility between Judaism and Christianity. It is interesting and necessary to examine briefly the origin and nature of this legend that Bar Kokhba was acclaimed as the Messiah.

The story all turns on wordplay over names and Bible verses. We know from the letters now in our hands that Bar Kokhba's real name was Simon Bar Kosiba, with a hard *s.* His letters always use this name, never the messianic-sounding Bar Kokhba. In the few references to him in the Midrash, the name is always spelled *Bar Koziba,* which can mean, by a pun, *son of lies,* or *the liar;* and it is clear that the rabbis did not care for him too much, despite the stories told of his superhuman strength and bravery. At some point, these stories led to a different pun being made on his name, flattering this time: not Bar Koziba but *Bar Kokhba,* picking up the messianic aura long seen in the Bible verse: "A star [*kokhab*] shall come out of Jacob" (Num. 24:17). After the rebellion was over, this nickname seems to have been used as if it was a real name by those who did not understand its origin, for it has come down to us through the classical and Christian (not the Jewish) historians.* The use of a half-messianic name always arouses one's interest, for we can never know enough of what the concept of a Messiah meant in applying it to a rebel against the Romans.

The Jews of the time had long dreamed of being rescued from their troubles by a *messiah,* which is Hebrew for *anointed.* The word always went back in significance to the days of glory, when David had been anointed king.

The Messiah had at first been thought of in cosmic terms—symbol of a world turned over and transformed—in line with the visions of the last days in Daniel. By the first century B.C., with the Romans ruling Palestine, the concept of salvation had become more practical and military; "the annointed one" would either himself take the field against the Romans or would follow a more practical type of Messiah, Messiah ben Joseph, who would lead the fight, after which Messiah ben David would take over for his glorious reign. The prototype for the Messiah precursor was the prophet Elijah; but he, too, was always more than just a soldier. He had a divinely inspired mission, as John the Baptist felt in showing the way to Jesus. It was against this background that leaders of anti-Roman revolt, especially Galileans, sometimes claimed some messianic role and were accorded this status by followers.

After the Destruction in A.D. 70, few of the many rebellions were led by messianic claimants, as far as we know. The few stories told of Bar Kokhba in rabbinic writings emphasize his bravado and cruelty, and nothing of the closeness to God that the Messiah had to evince. With this in mind, we can ask ourselves what it could possibly have meant if on one occasion, as all the historians tell us, Akiba "hailed" Bar Kokhba as the Messiah.

We have talked frequently in this book of Jewish folk memory, and this has to be applied even to the apparently factual stories in the rabbinic writings. Stories were passed on orally and finally written down two or three hundred years after the events.

The whole story of Bar Kokhba as Messiah is based on a reported remark by Akiba, written down many years after his time. The point of the anecdote is to report a funny remark by a friend of Akiba. The anecdote is that Akiba, when he saw Bar Kokhba, said of him "This is the King Messiah." His friend Rabbi Jonathan ben Torta retorted: "Akiba! The grass will be spouting out of your cheeks, and the Messiah will still not have come!"

*Dio Cassius (second to third centuries A.D.) does not identify the leader of the rebellion. Justin (second century A.D.), Eusebius (third to fourth century A.D.) and Jerome (fourth to fifth century A.D.) used variants of Bar Kokhba.

It is through ben Torta's badinage that we can understand how seriously Akiba hailed Bar Kokhba as Messiah, if indeed he ever did. There is a longer passage in the Midrash in which some of the great feats of Bar Kokhba are described. One of them is that "he would catch the stones of the *ballistae* on one of his knees and hurl them back, killing any number of men." This, the story says, is why Akiba called him the Messiah. The story, like the imaginary feat which inspired it, is pure legend. The rapporteurs of rabbi-talk, hundreds of years later, have built up a scene.

What we need to understand, from the inside of Jewish history, is why successive Jewish historians felt called on to accept this tale as gospel and work it into the picture they projected of a messiah-type warrior, with the great rabbi at his side, fighting to the death against the Romans. Does it matter if anachronism invades history this way? In factual terms, obviously; but if it has satisfied Jewish historians to present history this way and satisfied their readers, this, in turn, becomes a "true" part of history.

Every age seems to need a construct of the past suited to its style; and there can hardly be a clearer example than the picture that Jewish historians, including distinguished ones, have built up, in modern, Israeli-flavored terminology, of Akiba's role in promoting Bar Kokhba's rebellion. To take examples almost at random: in Cecil Roth's *Short History of the Jews* we are told that Akiba's "whole-hearted adhesion gave the movement exceptional significance"; the great scholars Max L. Margolis and Alexander Marx said in their history that Akiba was "the soul of the uprising"; even Salo Baron, in his magisterial *Social and Religious History of the Jews,* feels able to say of the revolt "Akiba was the intellectual and Bar Kokhba the military and political leader."[20]

The fuller version, common to almost all the books, turns Akiba into a kind of typical Zionist leader. We are told that he traveled tirelessly to Jewish communities all over the known world to raise funds for the rebellion; and when the moment came to fight, he signaled this by proclaiming Bar Kokhba as the Messiah, in propaganda style.

It is as if historians are sometimes unwilling, or unable, to turn themselves back to the spirit of the time they are writing about; but it must surely be immensely important to do this in trying to evoke the spirit of the crucial post-Destruction period in which the Jews set down their roots for the future.

Akiba, as a teacher, was central to this; and here is a simple test which anyone can apply to the flat statement—as in Chaim Potok's monumental book *Wanderings*—that Akiba "regarded Bar Kokhba as the Messiah."[21] It was now a hundred years since the death of Jesus, so that a Messiah was already on the scene in the minds of some Jews or ex-Jews.

What would it mean to a Jew of Akiba's type to regard a man as the Messiah? It would not mean that the man was pious in Jewish ritual or a good scholar, still less that he was so strong physically that he could return the *ballistae* of Roman catapults with a flick of the knee. What it would mean is that a man had appeared on earth supernaturally and that his very appearance had transformed the world, with the rules of life and death suspended forever.

Akiba is quoted in the rabbinic writings more prolifically than any other rabbi, yet without the slightest indication—except for the three famous words in the anecdote—that the Messiah has appeared on earth, and that he (Akiba) has seen him. Nor is there a single word about Bar Kokhba in the rabbinic writings or elsewhere to indicate any kind of spiritual charisma that a pious rabbi could associate with. On the contrary the rabbis tell stories of his brutality and even blasphemy.[22] We can therefore suspend, in historical terms, any idea that Akiba hailed Bar Kokhba as the Messiah.

But the story has been worth pursuing here to illustrate that in the folk feeling about Jewish history, anachronisms are fully acceptable if they succeed in giving the ordinary Jew an affinity with the past, with time standing still. This concept enlarges the life of a Jew with its vivacity and imagination.

One sees this, without bringing in the Messiah, in the character, as now revealed, of Bar Kokhba himself. In endless ways, he exhibits the exact mixture of talents, virtues, and defects that have been demonstrated in our own time by the fighting leaders of Israel. His driving force is patriotic, not religious. He clearly has no patience with submissive prayer and addresses God with jokey familiarity in a devil-may-care speech before battle: "O God: neither help us nor hinder us!"; yet he supports the public observation of Jewish ritual, as is shown in his instructions about resting on the Sabbath, and in the letter arranging for the provision of palms and citrons for Succoth, the Feast of Tabernacles. He exacts blind obedience to discipline, as in the test he imposes on recruits to cut off a finger as a test of courage if they want to serve with him. For disobedience to orders, he threatens imprisonment "in fetters"; but he is also gentle with his men: "Be of good spirit, and keep everyone's spirit up." Above all, perhaps, he is clearly a military commander who leads from the front, like the army officers of modern Israel whose battlecry is "Follow me!" Here is where one gets the real force of the anecdote of catching and returning the *ballistae* with his knee, a folkstory that tells everything.[23]

Akiba's timelessness is of a different kind. His preeminence among the founding fathers of the Jewish tradition established him throughout the centuries as a man whose life affected everything that evolved for Jews later in their rootedness to the law and magic of the Talmud. Jews turn to him not as a hero or even as martyr but as a presence whenever they open their minds to the extraordinary mystery of how this tiny badgered people stayed alive, not on suffrance but by their own will.

There is a remarkable exposition of this feeling in the writings of a Jew of our time, Yaacov Herzog, son of a chief rabbi of Israel, and himself a rabbi until his untimely death at a young age. If, he says in one essay, Akiba—or any great Jew of any generation—rose from his grave and came to life again, "it would be as if he had never died, because we could talk to him as if all that had occurred in the meantime had never been, as if Jewish experience had been uninterrupted until this day." This is not because of "ethnic continuity" but "continuity of memory":

If Akiba were to come to life today, Jews would not only talk to him but question him—about his attitude to Bar Kokhba's war against the Romans, about his personal relationship with Bar Kokhba. They would talk to him—about the character of the Jewish people, his dialogue with the God of Israel, his dialogue with the Gentiles, the historical experience, the continuity of the Jewish people and its future—as if he had never disappeared from our midst.[24]

7

Judaism and Christianity

Strengthening the Base

IN MOST BOOKS on Jewish history, the emergence of Christianity is given a subsidiary place; but as our object in this book is to define the experience that Jews have shared during the nearly two thousand years of Diaspora, the story would be out of balance without a consideration of the Christian background.

It is not enough to talk of Jesus in his Jewish context in order to form a view of him as "a good Jew" or a rebel or an inspired teacher. Little of this, as it happens, filtered into Jewish consciousness over the centuries. What Jews in the Christian world were aware of—and constantly—was a hostile faith carrying with it power, passion, and danger. The picture of Jesus that seemed central to this faith was different from any idea that an ordinary Jew might have of a rabbi or teacher of Jesus' time; for if some of his sayings and even some of the Church prayers sounded familiarly Jewish, the credo that Christians had built around him—Virgin Birth, the Trinity, Resurrection on the third day, and the Eucharist "meal"—was as remote from Jewish consciousness as anything could be.

In the minds of most Jews, therefore, there was and still is a complex and abiding problem about Christianity. How did it emerge from the Jewish background? Was hostility there from the beginning? And if—as we all know—a strong hatred for Jews developed in Christian countries, does history explain it, or show how it can be met?

It is in this rather macabre sense, then, that Christianity is part of the Jewish heritage in Christian countries; but there is also a positive side to the picture. The Judaism that has come down as a heritage developed its basic character—a respect for the Written and the Oral Law—several centuries before the emergence of Christianity; yet it was against the background of Christianity that Jews closed their ranks to put rabbinic Judaism on a firm and lasting basis.

The Role of the Law

The great testing time for Judaism was, in fact, in the first century of the Christian era, when the rebellions against Rome tore the Holy Land apart. They had reached their full stride in A.D. 66, and continued off and on for seventy years. It might have seemed that these futile revolts would be certain to lead to the permanent annihilation of Jewish identity. But this did not happen; and one factor certainly was that in this century the Jews assessed their ancestral faith in a new way.

Until that time, Jewish thought had not been subjected to direct challenge. The Jews had learned to have a relaxed relationship with the pagan world outside; it never posed problems of belief to the genuinely religious, and within Jewish life itself there was no censorship of sectarian ideas. The situation changed after the disastrous end of the Bar Kokhba revolt in A.D. 135. From then on, the Jews not only continued to look inward, finding the strength they needed in a passion for the Law but in addition had to be particularly stringent in defending the purity of their doctrines against the newly burgeoning religion of those Jews who looked to Jesus as their Messiah and saw him replacing the Law.

Within two centuries, the Christian faith would become directly hostile under the influence of the Church Fathers; but by this time, the fourth century A.D., the Jews had made their own faith rock-firm in the Talmud and the way of life that went with it. The challenge of Christianity had been met and, in the deepest sense, mastered. In the centuries to follow, the Jews would suffer sorrows, often desperate in scale and bitterness, but at no point would their sense of identity waver.

It is ironic to recognize that it was Christianity, as a catalyst, which helped to secure this. Within rabbinic Judaism there was a wide range of attitudes, explicit or implicit, to the ancient faith. If being a good Jew involved observance of rituals, there was plenty of argument among the scholars on the minutiae and, equally, on how to interpret the sayings and teachings of respected rabbis. But if Jews were free in this to develop personal attitudes, they had no problem in defining themselves in relation to Christianity. Supernatural doctrines of the type ultimately confirmed in formal creeds of Christianity never found expression in Judaism. Metaphysical inquiry was left, among Jews, to dreamers, mystics, or mythologists. The ordinary Jew just recognized that life on earth demanded some kind of authority, and Judaism provided it.

Authority for the Jews lay in the law and ethics of action, and the rabbi was its interpreter. He had won this role thorugh study; and this was another pillar of the faith. The reverence in Jewish life was concentrated on thought. To listen to the words of a scholar brought one nearer to the secrets of the universe —and in any case was highly pleasurable. One might not measure up to the teachings expounded by the rabbi, but this was where security lay.

It can be said that this world of rabbinic Judaism took literary shape between the second and fifth centuries A.D. The Mishnah (code of law) was edited in the second century A.D.; the Talmud (which discusses the Mishnah rulings discursively and unendingly) seems to have been completed in writing in the fourth to fifth centuries A.D. But clearly, these enormous works, and the ancillary books that go with them, would never have carried the authority they did had they emerged suddenly. We know that the Bible was being expounded in immense detail in the second and first centuries B.C.—six centuries before the emergence of the Talmud in writing. What is astonishing, for history, is the way the literary, logical, and imaginative subtleties that emerged in the rabbinic writings developed from what might have seemed a primitive religious faith grounded on an elaborate ritual of animal sacrifices.

One has to talk firmly of the role of Temple sacrifices to establish that the respect for these sacrifices—supposed to have been laid down by Moses in immense detail more than a thousand years earlier—carried the Torah's authority in the same binding way as moral principles. Both were derived from the written text, and both were interpreted through oral traditions handed down through centuries. In the teachings of the Prophets, Jews had been reminded tirelessly that God had no "pleasure" in sacrifices if the person bringing them led an immoral life. But the full Jewish worship in Temple times had taken in both these sides of Judaism and both reflected the Law: the majesty of an ancient unchangeable ritual and the living, flexible quality of a life built around morality and Torah study.

This double view was certainly prevalent when Christianity was establishing itself in the last decades of the Temple. In the view of one scholar, it was a distinction as ancient as the days of the return from exile in Babylon:

> There were at least two forms of Judaism flourishing side by side in Jerusalem at the time of Ezra. One was headed by the High Priest, and the other by Ezra and his disciples and successors. The one had a static and the other a dynamic approach to religion. The former became the Sadducees, and the latter the Pharisees.[1]

If this is too formalist a distinction, it does at least highlight the essential feature of what was to become rabbinic Judaism: the dedication of scholars to the formulation of firm laws, *halakhot*, for Jewish life, linked to Torah but going beyond it. How is one to explain the origins of this intriguing attitude?

In general, the devotion of the rabbis to the Torah made them anxious to establish a textual authority for every *halakhah* they discussed; and the favored way was to draw this out through midrashic (homiletical) commentary on Bible verses. It becomes clear, however, in rabbinic writings that there are two kinds of *halakhah*, one clearly textual in origin, the other handed on by word of mouth, and therefore aptly described as Oral Law, *Torah sheh b'al peh*. The scholars who grew into the Pharisees were the guardians of these studies; and one has to accept that it was the very age of these mysterious traditions, side by side with the straightforward rules set out in the Torah text, which gave Pharisees respect for the Law, one of the lasting imperatives in Jewish life.[2]

The Synagogue as Study Center

As the Law was to become a central area of conflict between Judaism and early Christianity, the origin of its authority is more than an academic question. Something similar arises over the origins of another Jewish institution, the synagogue, if only because of the extraordinary hold that it had on Jews in the time of Jesus and the part it played in the emergence of Christianity. But in this case, oddly enough, the origins are even more shadowy than with the Law; and to some extent this helps to explain how synagogues and churches, though apparently so similar in function, came to play such different roles in the two religions.

Without any evidence, it has usually been taken for granted that the unique institution of the synagogue emerged among Jews during the Babylonian exile to replace the Temple worship in Jerusalem that they missed and particularly to offer them a chance to recite the prayers and psalms they remembered from Temple times. But this speculation is probably an anachronism. When we first hear of synagogues, in the last centuries of the Second Temple, they are not prayerhouses, but meeting places for hearing the Torah read, usually with commentary and sermonic interpretation. They existed for this purpose not just in remote places—as a substitute for Temple worship—but equally in Jerusalem and even within the Temple area. One scholar, thinking of this Torah-reading function, sees the origin of the synagogue in Ezra's meeting the people of Jerusalem for this purpose, after the return from exile.[3]

By the first century B.C., synagogues for this purpose were to be found everywhere in the Near East. There is no mention in Jewish rabbinic writings of any formal prayer service taking place there. The prayers that were laid down as standard for Jews—notably the *Sh'ma* and the Eighteen Benedictions—were obligations for the individual and could be carried out anywhere at the set times. Even later, when the synagogue had become the place for regularized prayer services, anyone was free to conduct them; and until relatively modern times, the synagogue was preeminently a study center with a concomitant easygoing atmosphere of social goodwill.

In sharp contrast, the church, which had begun, in Jewish fashion, as a place for Bible readings and sermons, soon began to reflect elements in the new faith that introduced a wholly different atmosphere. The Jewish prayers that were still retained—like the Lord's Prayer and Priestly Blessing—were straightforward enough; but a hierarchy of officiants soon developed, reflecting, through the three-tiered ranks of deacons, priests, and bishops, a formality that Jewish gatherings did not share.

The rabbi in a synagogue would be regarded with respect, or even, in some cases, veneration; but in Jewish prayer, a man was on his own before God. No one had died to save him. No salvation could come to him through faith in a mystery—God appearing on earth as a man—that was beyond comprehension. No mother of God could be turned to for intimate help as a special kind of mediator. No holy trinity of godly spirits could replace the all-embracing unity of the Jewish God.

Both faiths were, of course, built around a central mystery; it is the contrast between them that is so striking. In church, theological ideas were expressed with great firmness, being confronted directly at certain moments in the recital of the creed, and even more in the ceremony of the Eucharist. In synagogue, a Jew left theology floating in the air. The mystery he was absorbed in was the community of his people with the Creator. It was a communion he had been born into, and he accepted it not as an act of faith but as a simple reality of his existence.

To express the difference graphically, it is as if the Jew moved in these critical centuries from the elaborate rituals of the ancient Temple to a workaday ease with his God, while the Christian moved from the ease of the early synagogues to a highly complex establishment and ritual that drew for fulfillment on the mysteries of the ancient pagan world. The parting of the ways between Judaism and Christianity released a dynamism in each that transformed the earlier position.

Adjustment to a Changed World

Jews do not always see how deeply the Jewish faith was transformed at this time in the shadow of Christianity, since the more usual point made is that the Jewish faith has been unchanging since ancient times. Certainly, the sense of identity with the past is astonishingly strong for Jews, but this is partly because Christianity, when it began to emerge, gave Jews a heightened determination to be inflexible in their basic beliefs.

It is almost as if each faith took off, in reaction to the other, without realizing where it would lead. Christianity, which had begun as love for a Jewish teacher and healer who was cruelly executed, set out after a time to distance itself in almost every particular from its Jewish base, giving a wholly new meaning to the Jewish Bible, and drawing into itself ideas—pagan to Jewish minds—of the world outside. The Jews, with equal passion, set out to build a new kind of protective fence around themselves, first as a counter to the anarchy and persecution of the immediate post-Destruction years and then in defiance of strange, debilitating ideas that Christians were importing into the faith.

The Jews will never be understood if this protective fence, within which a Jew was to conduct his life in accordance with the famous 613 rabbinic rules of life, is looked on negatively, as a force making for denial.* Far more significantly, these rules imparted a form of sanctity to every personal and communal activity lying between birth and death. Observance had God's imperative behind it, as laid down in the Torah; and though it was accepted by Jews in an almost matter-of-fact way, there was a leap of faith involved, both religiously and socially.

Religiously, the uncluttered belief in one indefinable God made it possible for Jews throughout the centuries to accept that His direct link with the Hebrew people, as expressed in the Bible, had to be kept alive continuously in a ritual of precepts—an assortment of do's and don'ts as worked out by the rabbis. Socially, there was an air of miracle in the fact that the rigorous observance of the Law provided the protective and perpetuating device that the Jews needed in the wake of Roman, and then Christian, persecution. The Law was cohesive, stimulating, satisfying. The ancient miracle lay in the existence of the Bible; the Law, in its myriad forms, was the way Jews lived out this miracle. Jews treated it with reverence, but also with goodwill—even humor.

There is certainly a shift, which has to be identified, between the emphasis on simple moral principles as demanded by the prophets and the new interest in the Law. It is not that the old principles of justice and loving kindness were demoted, but that the Jews found a new framework for fulfilling the aims of the covenant with God.

*The rabbis calculated the biblical commandments were made up of 365 prohibitions and 248 positive precepts, 613 in all. They are set out graphically in "The 613 Commandments." *Encyclopedia Judaica,* vol. 5, cols. 760–63; see also Louis Jacobs, *A Jewish Theology.* (London: Darton, Longman, 1973), pp. 211–30.

The historian Salo Baron relates this shift in emphasis to the end of political independence. The Prophets had conveyed denunciation, especially of the establishment classes, and notably of the priests, for failing to live up to Bible principles. Religious leaders faced a different situation when the Jewish people no longer had their indigenous monarchy but were ruled by half-foreigners (Herodians) under Roman domination.[4] Those with ultimate political authority, he says, could not be accused of breaking the covenant with God, as they were foreigners. Nor was it appropriate to follow the Prophets in issuing ringing demands for justice, since this was a principle that all, including foreign rulers, claimed to believe in.

What mattered now, Baron says, were "details," cases of concrete application of the great ethical principles. By now, the scribes—unlike the Prophets—could point to an elaborate and binding set of laws readily applicable to every particular occurrence. This, then, became their theme.

But going deeper, Baron wonders if the social background was not more conducive now to "cooperative endeavors," rather than to the rise of great prophetic leaders in the old style. Little could be accomplished individually in a Jewish world consisting of millions scattered over many lands:

> Even early Christianity could become successful only after it had evolved a church, an organization carried on collectively. This was doubly true in the case of those who remained within the fold of a traditional creed and a living national organism.

Perhaps one should really regard the role of the Law as a principle which supplied the Jews with the sense of social independence, even if they were now shorn of any kind of political independence. Politically, they had fought desperately against foreign domination when it had invaded the religious independence expressed in the ritual purity of the Temple. Now, they rallied with equal courage to defend the independence symbolized in the Law.

It was in this setting that the Jews developed—for better or worse—the concept of martyrdom. When the practices of the Law were being attacked, Jews were prepared to die rather than submit. In the Maccabean stories, martyrdom for religious reasons had surfaced among ordinary people—Hannah and her seven sons. Josephus describes Jewish defiance in graphic terms; and even the literary hyperbole does not diminish the sense of realism:

> Racked and twisted, burnt and broken, made to pass through every instrument of torture, in order to induce them to blaspheme their lawgiver or to eat some forbidden thing, they refused to yield to either demand, nor ever once did they cringe to their persecutors or shed a tear [*Against Apion* 2.6.65].

The Maccabean martyrdoms became the model for Christian martyrdom. The Christians were less interested, it seems, in the dramatic Jewish martyrdoms that followed the Bar Kokhba war. Yet these were really more significant for the survival of Judaism, since the martyrs of this period were rabbis who refused to give up teaching the Torah. The Christians never dwelled on this because the Jewish attitude to the Law had already become a bugbear to Christians, and they in turn were now being persecuted for their own faith. But historically, the defiance of the rabbis during the Hadrianic persecutions before and after the Bar Kokhba war was a watershed in Jewish life.

Jesus Among His Fellow Jews

Christianity, as developed by Paul, saw obedience to the Law replaced by faith in Christ and therefore had no further use for it. This had not been the attitude of Jesus himself, despite some ambivalent passages in the Gospels. Even if the ultimate split between Judaism and Christianity made respect for the Law central, it had never been the issue on which the Jewish religious leaders felt called upon to criticize—far less to condemn—Jesus.

This is not to say that the Law was not a major issue which could lead to riots and bloodshed. We see in Josephus that in the period immediately before Jesus, there were quite a few occasions on which riots against Roman or Jewish authorities arose from a breach of some intricate point of the Law. One such occasion was the riot which erupted in the Temple during the ceremony of libation at the Feast of Tabernacles, when the king Alexander Jannai, doubling as high priest, poured the water on the ground instead of against the altar, as was the teaching of the Pharisees. The people were so incensed that they pelted him with citrons they carried for the Tabernacles ceremonies. More seriously, his predecessor Hyrcanus had been denounced by the Pharisees as unfit for the high priesthood because his mother had been a captive at one point—a technical blemish which became central to a civil war that raged for two generations.

Echoes of rabbinic rulings surface in this way in the Gospel stories, with the Pharisees usually represented as inhumane or hypocritical against the humanity and sincerity of Jesus. On one occasion, Jesus' disciples, being hungry, pluck some ears of corn from the field on the Sabbath, whereupon the Pharisees rebuke Jesus, who replies: "The Sabbath was made for man, not man for the Sabbath" (Mark 2: 23–28). They criticize him, too, for healing a man with a withered arm on the Sabbath, since one may only break the Sabbath when life is at stake.

Gospel stories like this show clearly the type of argument on the Law that might proceed between rabbis of the time; and it is ironic that they ring true particularly when the "liberal" statements of Jesus are, to one's surprise, found as statements of the Talmud! On the Sabbath, for example, there was a rabbinic saying: "The Sabbath is committed to your hands, not you to its hands" (Mekhilta on Exodus 31:13 [103b]).

It has been shown, indeed, that virtually every saying of Jesus in the Gospels can be paralleled in the Talmud. It is clear, therefore, that the reason for the estrangement between Jesus and the rabbis of his time has to be sought at a deeper level. Jesus, as many studies have now shown, has to be considered as a Pharisee or as one equally at home in the Law, but who brought an individual and different attitude to it.[5] He himself said that he came to fulfill the Law; but his judgements led him to interpret it in a way which the Pharisees may have found too lenient, possibly dangerous, and certainly not entirely Jewish. We can determine the character of the Pharisees of the time from the kind of reservations they had about him. It was not that he emphasized the ethical character of the Law too strongly, for this (as can easily be shown) was central to their teachings. The Talmud is just as scornful of hypocritical practitioners of the Law as is Jesus in the Gospels.

Nor could the Pharisees have objected directly to Jesus' practice as a healer, for we find stories of healers among the rabbis. If we are to judge from the reaction between Jesus and the Pharisees as echoed in the Gospels, they seem to have found him too individual in his views (speaking with authority), too publicity conscious, too daring in his concept of the approach of the messianic age, too dangerous politically. The crowds who came to be healed or to hear him preach or to watch him taking direct action in the Temple courtyard, might be incited to revolt against the Roman-Herodian rulers. He seemed to enjoy mass popularity in a way that sectarian Pharisees never would. He thought nothing of mixing with *amei ha-aretz*, simple people, like fishermen, farmers, tax-collectors, or with women the rabbis might have shunned.

The feeling must have grown among the Pharisees and others that Jesus was claiming too much. The apostles who had been touring Galilee on his behalf may have seemed to the Pharisees too lax over the Law. It must surely be correct that the Pharisees felt themselves distant from something in Jesus' attitude that disdained the full acceptance of the Law and included some apocalyptic ideas way beyond their sympathy. Yet none of this would present Jesus in direct conflict with the Pharisees. It was at a much more serious level that he was regarded as dangerous by the Jerusalem priestly establishment (the Sadducees) and the Roman authorities.

Scholars have argued endlessly about whether the Pharisees, as members of the Sanhedrin, had any part in the condemnation of Jesus by the high priest and in handing him over to Pilate. The consensus is that it is impossible to imagine this, in view of what we know of their theological views.[6] There is no doubt that they saw the need later to issue warnings on heresy when the belief began to spread among Jews, after his death, that he was the Saviour and had risen from the dead as prophesied. But, as we see in the attitude of Rabbi Gamaliel reported in Acts, the rabbis were ambivalent even then about persecuting his followers. They simply took defensive action to close their ranks against the defection when Paul and those with him began to spread teachings which were both dangerous in their direct criticism of the Law and blasphemous in their ascription to Jesus of a supernatural existence.

But this was to happen later, in a period which we can assess through documents that have survived. For the first decades after the death of Jesus, we have no firm ideas at all about the lives of those who followed him.

To some extent this is because we have no objective picture of the life of Jesus himself. The picture that surfaced in the Gospels and was expanded in Christian commentary to prove that Jesus fulfilled at every stage the prophesies of the Old Testament has great appeal as a story, but seems clearly tailor-made to fit these prophesies. In this sense, his biography, as has been said, "was written long before his birth." His sayings in the Synoptic Gospels certainly seem authentic and attuned to the Judaism of his day; but the theology and mysteries that are expressed in the Gospel of Saint John and that surface in the account given of Paul, take Jesus further away from what we think of as the traditional Jewish base.

There is, however, a problem on this. Our idea of what was normal at the time is based on what we now find in the rabbinic writings; but in some respects we cannot trust the rabbinic texts, for the rabbis often played down and excluded eschatological and mystical ideas of the type that we know were prevalent in Palestine of the time. This playing down may have been done deliberately in a reaction against the increasing spread of Christianity; but there is an element in it also of the rabbinical distaste for mystery. It is as if they were always on guard against danger. It was important to define and practice the Law and to behave ethically; but beyond that, theological ideas that might impugn the unity of God or that introduced the supernatural in daily life on earth spelled trouble.

Jesus as the Messiah

Dwarfing all other issues, the question that forces itself into the open with regard to the relations between Judaism and Christianity is on Jesus as the Messiah. We know from Josephus and from apocalyptic literature that a belief was prevalent throughout Palestine that a messianic age was imminent. The idea dominated religious discussion, both in Palestine and the Diaspora.

There was, of course, a huge variety of views on how the End of Days would come—by force of arms, by a cosmic cataclysm, by utopian visions of godliness and perfection. The mission of John the Baptist, as a forerunner of Isaiah, fits into this picture perfectly. Yet there is a clear gap on what Jesus himself felt. Why, one wonders, was there not a wider acceptance of him in this role, when Palestine was so anxious to welcome a messiah?

If, in fact, Jesus believed in himself as the Messiah, would it not have carried conviction to Jewish believers on a large scale, rather than to the small sect of followers whom he attracted not so much through messianic claims but by his healing powers and his brilliant preaching? Is there not, then, a case for trying to track down what was really said during his life about Jesus as Messiah, since this was due to become a riveting issue between Jews and Christians during the crucial centuries which followed, when positions were taken up on each side of the gulf?

Among innumerable books devoted to this subject, a recent study by an Oxford scholar, Geza Vermes, called *Jesus the Jew,* gathers together and evaluates with the greatest sympathy the evidence from the New Testament.

In the section of the book discussing what appears in the Synoptic Gospels, the opening words will perhaps startle some readers:

> That Jesus never asserted directly or spontaneously that he was the Messiah is admitted by every serious expert. . . . The traditional claim is therefore based, at best, on circumstantial evidence. This state of affairs is astonishing in itself, and to understand it four problems have to be settled, the last of them crucial:
>
> (i) What part, if any, did the figure of the Messiah play in the thought and teaching of Jesus?
> (ii) How did his alleged Messianic office strike his opponents?
> (iii) Was he held to be the Messiah by friends and companions?
> (iv) How did Jesus react towards those who proclaimed or challenged his Messiahship?[7]

On the first question, Dr. Vermes concludes, after surveying the evidence, that "messianism is not particularly prominent in the surviving teaching of Jesus." It is reasonable to suppose, he says, "that the early Church, for which Jesus was the Messiah, would have produced additional evidence to support her faith if such had existed."[8]

On the second question, it is striking that no one hostile to Jesus accused him of messianic pretensions before the moment of the Passion. Dr. Vermes believes the accusation on the Cross that he was being executed as Messiah (king of the Jews) was a trumped-up charge by those who saw him as a danger to law and order and therefore invented this political accusation. "Conflict concerning Jesus' Messiahship is attested in Jerusalem alone. It has no polemical antecedents in the Synoptic Gospels."[9]

On the third question, there seems no doubt that the apostles accepted Peter's affirmation at Caesarea Philippi: "You are the Messiah" (Mark 8:29). But Jesus' own view is more problematical. It is odd that after hearing Peter's view, he insists that the disciples should on no account mention this to anyone. In the scene with the high priest and Pilate, he refuses to state positively whether he is the Messiah or not. He is evasive, with his quoted words meaning either "As you say" or "It is you who say it." In the Synoptic Gospels, Vermes concludes, Jesus failed to declare himself as Messiah, "and there is every reason to wonder if he really thought of himself as such."[10]

There is a different attitude on this in the Gospel of Saint John, which is not surprising. In contrast to the Synoptic Gospels, which do their best to tell the story straight, John's account is written to project Jesus as the Messiah in the most positive terms from the beginning of his ministry. As early as chapter 1, Andrew informs his brother Simon Peter: "We have found the Messiah" (John 1:41); and Jesus is himself explicit in talking to the Samaritan woman (John 4:25). This is the view which swiftly became accepted among Christians, but for the Jews of Jesus' own days, the ambivalence of the Synoptic Gospels helps to explain why the great majority of Jews refused to accord him any supernatural role of this kind.

It seems evident from the Synoptic Gospels that among the many types of messiah who might come, the one that his followers had in mind for him was the rather monarchical role of a Davidic King Messiah, coming to power by force of arms. Some modern scholars have argued that he did, in fact, fulfill this role by taking an active part in Jewish military resistance as a Zealot;[11] but this notion, in Vermes's view, "fails to convince."[12] Yet if Jesus as Messiah was a concept left vague and undefined during his lifetime, how was it that it took hold of the early Church, not only with Jewish-Christians, to whom the idea of Messiah son of David was familiar, but with the gentile Church, to which, as Vermes says, "neither the Semitic Messiah, nor its literal Greek rendering *Christos,* meant anything at all"?

This is, of course, a central question for Jews and Christians alike; and Vermes suggests that the answer has to be looked for in the despairing social and political conditions of the time. As the historical story of Jesus was one of defeat—he had not taken over as King-Messiah and, instead, had died on the Cross—victory had to link itself to the triumph of his resurrection on Easter Sunday, a sign of his status in Heaven at the right hand of God, ready to return as universal king in the Second Coming. In this way, defeat was transformed into triumph; and the Messiah title was of "psychological and polemical value" in the debate with the Jews.[13]

Merged into this debate, there was a question whose treatment and solution was to have baleful effects on Jewish-Christian relations. Why was it that the Jews, so familiar with the messiah concept, had not accepted Jesus in this role? A Christian controversialist could not concede that this was because Jesus was not the Messiah. It must have been, therefore, because the Jews as a nation were too wicked to accept the obvious truth. The argument could be made watertight by showing that it was no new thing for the Jews to reject the words of a prophet. The Old Testament was full of instances in which the Jews turned their backs on the truth this way in obstinacy and wickedness. Over the Messiah, then, the debate would end in denunciations which planted the seeds for Jew-hatred in all the succeeding centuries.

Jews and Christian Dogma

The issue emerges very clearly in the account of early Christianity given in the Acts of the Apostles. There is a hint early on (Acts 2:36) that Jesus was not the Messiah in his life but only after he had been crucified, and this accords with the emphasis given in Acts to the real proof that Jesus was the Messiah, which was that Bible prophecy had pointed so clearly to his crucifixion. Isaiah had spoken of a suffering Messiah—despised and rejected (Isa. 53: 3–5)—which was clearly Jesus on the Cross. Similarly, when the psalmist expressed the faith (Psalm 16:10) that God "will not abandon my soul to death," this was a direct prophecy of Jesus' resurrection.

One gets a lively picture, reading Acts, of the way the argument was conducted from the Christian side during the early stages of Christianity. In this phase, the violence between Judaism and Christianity was not so sharp as it was to become later. If Stephen, speaking from slightly outside (Acts 7: 51–53) as a Jewish Greek, is eloquent in denunciation of the Jews ("was there ever a prophet whom your fathers did not persecute"), there are signs of freer argument, as in the tolerant or patient attitude toward the claims of Christians displayed by the rabbinic leader Gamaliel (Acts 23). How one wishes there were more such relics of what went on between Jews and Christians at this time. For the most part, one is working in the dark—and this is a period in which one of the most decisive movements in history was taking place. There would have been so much more to learn if only the Jews, like the Christians, had left contemporary records of what they were doing and thinking.

This is not a casual aside. It is intended to pinpoint a feature of rabbinic Judaism which was, then and later, both a sign of resilient strength and appalling narrowness. The strength is clear enough: By making the Torah—the Law—all-encompassing, the Jews found a shockproof formula for survival. But the obverse of this was a narrowness which involved a conscious shutting out of the cosmopolitan culture, both Greek and oriental, that still dominated the world of the Near East and could produce the kind of attractive history writing and polemic that the early Christians exploited brilliantly. If this narrowness had remained a permanent feature of Jewish life, the Jews, for all their religious intensity, would have become culturally sterile as a people. Luckily for their spirit, this kind of isolation was not to endure; for the narrowness of the world of the Talmud always carried with it a marvelously fertile seed which was to take root and blossom whenever Jews could reach out just beyond the rigorous fence of their lives. In the early centuries of Christianity, we have no record of anything like this taking place. But once rabbinic Judaism had established itself in its lasting position as the religion of a minority living in alien backgrounds, those Jews who had the good fortune to live in cultured societies were always poised, at the margin, to burst out with startling fecundity from the narrow bonds around them.

Yet one still laments the long gaps during these early centuries in the expression of Jewish thought and writing. The silence is all the more painful in contrast to their earlier fabulous achievement of Bible writing, in which Jews had recorded their history, poetry, dreams, and social aspirations in language that moves us today with its original power. One cannot believe that suddenly, perhaps at some time in the second century B.C. after the Maccabean struggles, the Jews stopped being philosophic, sophisticated, creative, and imaginative in their old style. They simply stopped expressing this, once Jewish life became monolithic in Palestine; and it is significant that wherever Jews stepped out, so to speak, beyond their narrow fence—as, say, with Ben Sira in Palestine, Philo in Alexandria, or Josephus in Rome—they were compelling and original. The clearest proof of the rich Jewish talent pushed beneath the surface was that when the early Jewish-Christian propagandists expressed their arguments and feelings in what can be called the cosmopolitan language of the time, it had a stirring readability in human terms, even if the doctrines expounded depended for their acceptability on a new concept of faith.

The contrast being drawn here is not between Jesus and his Jewish contemporaries but between Judaism and the Church. Everything recorded of Jesus himself—his ideas, his acts, his sayings—fits into a picture of Jesus the Jew. The doctrines—dogmas blown up later in the creeds—are a different story. Whereas the Jews of his time clung theologically to a clear, old-fashioned, ethical monotheism involving a God who had directed history with the Jews at the center of His plans, the Christian writers—notably Paul and John—proposed the most daring developments of these Jewish themes.

It is belittling the change to say that it basically expressed the belief that the Messiah, long expected in some form or other by the Jews, had now arrived. What they asked followers to believe—far beyond the vague Jewish idea about a leader who would be like a new King David—was that God had, as it were, suspended natural laws and given the world a wholly new conception of human existence. Mankind—the whole of mankind and not just the

Jews—could base their hope for the future on the attestation of a supernatural occurrence: Jesus had risen from the dead after three days and ascended to Heaven. It was an easy step from this fact to accept that he would come to earth again to change the whole nature of humanity. His Second Coming would redeem mankind; but even before this, man was saved by having faith in the doctrine. Faith redeemed man from sin.

Even in this bald summary of some of the very early doctrines of Christianity, one sees the enormous break with Judaism, in which man was responsible for his own salvation through repentance and good deeds and not redeemed through faith in a mediator. From another standpoint, it is the discipline of obedience to the Law—the commands of the Torah—which saves a Jew, for his life is sanctified in this obedience. To the Christian, the Law was only a stage along the road. Until Jesus was born, the giving of the Torah to the Jews through Moses on Sinai had been God's prime Revelation to mankind; but with Jesus born, the real fulfillment had been given to mankind and the intermediary stage of obedience to the Torah had come to the end of its purpose.

This, at least, is how the new faith began to define itself in doctrines preached by Paul and others to Gentiles or half-Jews in Asia Minor and other areas of the Near East. In this particular approach, the emphasis clearly lay in allowing would-be believers to escape having to observe the difficult rituals of the Jewish faith, such as circumcision and food distinctions. At the same time, doctrines were being attached to the basic story of Jesus that brought in familiar ideas of Greek myth and oriental mystery.

It was in keeping with these ideas—totally alien to Jews—that the new faith proved so acceptable. In the pagan world, there were gods who died and rose again, as Jesus had; and the father of the gods presided over a family, so that Mary as the Mother of God and Jesus as the Son of the Father were acceptable in an almost literal sense, as was the idea of a miraculous Virgin Birth of the God figure. To envisage a surrogate figure who would "die for our sins" was an equally remote notion to Jews.* At the philosophic level, all these mythological ideas could be given some kind of reality through the concept of the Logos—the Word—which was seen as the principle linking God and man through which the universe is guided. The Old Testament had given this role to the abstract concept "Wisdom." Philo had taught that God, remote from

*The idea of a scapegoat had existed among the primitive Hebrews (Lev. 16: 8–10) but had long ceased to have any relevance in Jewish life.

the world, acts in it through the mediation of the Logos. In the Gospel of Saint John, the Word is the foundation of the universe ("in the beginning was the Word"); and when God takes flesh and becomes man, the Logos is Jesus.

There were verses in the Old Testament which could be brought into play to justify any one of the doctrines, such as the verses on the sufferings of Jesus: "Surely he hath borne our griefs and carried our sorrows" (Isa. 43:4). On the mystery of Jesus' birth, other verses in Isaiah were interpreted as literal prophecy: "A virgin shall conceive" (7:14), or "unto us a child is born" (9:6). In later centuries, these echoes of pagan mythology and their refinements in philosophic or theological terms were erected into immutable dogmas of the Church that went far beyond any of the relatively vague ideas of early Christianity. In these dogmas—refined after endless controversy—Mary, mother of Jesus, was ultimately seen as a perpetual virgin, immaculate in her own conception and in that of her son Jesus, absolutely sinless, and in all these ways the unique intercessor on behalf of mankind. Through parallel controversies, the relationship of God and Jesus was finally established in a Trinity of three "persons"—the Father, the Son, and the Holy Spirit—which made Jesus essential to God (though without impugning His dominance) and left the Holy Spirit as the link between this elaborate Godhead and man.

Even in their early undefined form, these ideas were obviously unacceptable to Pharisaic teaching; and though there was normally no outlawing of the doctrines of minor sects, the moment came when Christian teachings had to be rebutted. We see from Acts that trouble began to arise among some Jews in the Diaspora in response to the active proselytizing that Paul was carrying out there. To some extent, this could have been a social protest; Roman authority had given Judaism the official status of a permitted religion, and Paul, in encouraging Jews or half-Jews to ignore the Law, was a troublemaker. We know that in Corinth Jews brought him before the Roman consul to be disciplined (Acts 18:6, 12ff), and there may have been other occasions too.

In Palestine itself, there was as yet little direct conflict. To the Jews, the small sect of followers of Jesus were of little import unless they deliberately denounced the Law, as Stephen had done. To the Christians, the Crucifixion did not, at this stage, create anger at the Jews, since this was regarded as the "fore-ordained purpose of God."[14] The great marvel that inspired them was the Resurrection; and this would have been regarded by the Jews as a harmless sectarian fantasy.

The real separation began after the destruction of the Temple in A.D. 70. The defense of Jerusalem was being undertaken by the political leaders; and with the city about to fall, religious leaders got out of the way, the rabbis to Jamnia, the Jewish-Christians to Pella, across the Jordan. The loss of the Temple was momentous to both, but in different ways. To the Jews, it seemed a disaster that God had brought on them for their sins, and the remedy was to intensify study and observance of the Torah, through which their strength as God's people could return. The Christian reaction was blunt and dismissive, in a tone that was to be baleful for the future. The fall of the Temple meant that "the sceptre had departed from Judah."*

*This phrase was used repeatedly to prove the emptiness of the promise that had been made in Genesis 49:10: "The sceptre shall not depart from Judah."

8

The Parting of the Ways

The Growth of Hostility

HE SCENE was being set for confrontation, but it took time to develop fully.

We know little about the first phase, except that around ten or twenty years after the Destruction, the rabbis felt called upon to insert in the basic prayer (the eighteen Benedictions) a few lines which sound like a curse on the Christians. In the form which has survived, this appears rather mildly as a curse on "slanderers," *malshinim.* The original version may have specified "Nazarenes," Christians, a word removed for safety later when the Christians were in power; but even in the safe form, it seems to express the antagonism very strongly:

And for slanderers let there be no hope, and let all wickedness perish as in a moment; let all thine enemies be speedily cut off, and the dominion of arrogance [the Roman Empire] do thou uproot and crush, cast down and humble speedily in our days. Blessed art though, O Lord, who breakest the enemies and humbles the arrogant.*

Yet there is another aspect to this paragraph. Its use in the synagogue service is thought by scholars to indicate that at this point the Nazarenes still thought of themselves as Jews and went to the synagogue. The sharp words were intended to smoke out those who refused to recite them, after which the argument could begin. It may be that it was in this background of increasing antagonism that the author of Matthew (written at this time) added the fateful words: "His blood be on us and on our children" (Matt. 27:25) to his account of the Passion.[1] The idea of the Jews uttering this bloodcurdling cry in unison at the Crucifixion is too ludicrous to take seriously; but the echo of the words as "reported" in Matthew was immeasurably sad in the weight it put on the Jews throughout subsequent history.

If the die appears to have been cast in this way by the end of the first century A.D., it took the next three centuries for the confrontation between Jews and Christians to assume its lasting form. When one looks at the stages of development in this long period, it might seem at first as if the confrontation of enemies describes the situation adequately enough; but within both religions there were developments which sometimes went against this black-and-white picture.

New Forms of Independence

Speaking generally, the most obvious trend among Jews in this new situation was a retreat into inwardness. One aspect of this was a check to their expansion in number. Earlier, there had been large-scale conversions to the Jewish faith throughout all the countries of the Near East. In the view of Salo Baron, this had been "one of the most remarkable movements of all time," but this phase of Jewish life was now over:

*Text in *Daily Prayer Book,* ed. S. Singer (London: Eyre and Spottiswoode, 1935), p. 48. In this annotated edition, Israel Abrahams argues that the paragraph was not a curse on Christians but was directed against antinomians and sectarians *(minim)* within the synagogue: "The statement which originated with Justyn Martyr that it is an imprecation against Christians in general has no foundation whatever. . . . The sectarians attacked were, beyond question, Jews" (p. xiv).

Precisely when Judaism seemed to be nearing the goal of its history—the reconciliation of its national and universalistic ideologies through a process of inner and outer growth as an ethno-religious unity beyond the boundaries of state and territory—it suffered a sudden reverse.[2]

This is a good example of what was suggested above in discussing the rift between the two religions: that it is necessary to look beneath the surface for full understanding. How could the force that had given Judaism its immense appeal have suddenly disappeared? The paradox that explains this helps us to understand, at the same time, why it was that the daughter-religion, Christianity, was able to adapt itself more successfully to expansion, so that within three centuries it came to full power as the heir to Roman supremacy.

The Judaism that had been developed by the rabbis during their expansion period had two main elements. As an ancient faith, linked to a literature full of delightful patriarchal stories and celebrated in heartwarming family and community festivals, it had obvious appeal everywhere, with the numbers of Jews and semi-Jews growing enormously. Palestine itself, expanded through Maccabean and Herodian conquests, is thought to have had a population of 2.5 million—including Samaritans, "Greeks," and Nabateans—at the time of the destruction of the Temple. The Diaspora included some countries where the Jewish population was vast, notably Syria, Egypt, and Babylonia, with 1 million or more each. All in all, there may have been close to 7 million Jews within the Roman Empire.

The numbers had grown not just because Judaism appealed in itself, but because the political and social background buttressed its expansion in many ways. Jewish captives were transported in great numbers after each invasion of Palestine and would retain their old loyalties. Migration and trade was facilitated through the splendid Roman road system and the building of ports for the greater movement of sea transport. Socially and intellectually, the spread of Hellenism had broken down frontiers and eased personal communication. Campaigns and trade had brought the East into the fashionable world of ideas. All this may have been more influential in making converts than the work of Jewish preachers, on which there is, in fact, little evidence except for the famed remark ascribed to Jesus in Matthew 23:15, in which the Pharisees (described as hypocrites) are said "to compass sea and land to make one proselyte."

In an age of syncretism, the philosophic attitude of Judaism may have appealed to many thousands of pagans who liked what they had heard about the rational morality of Judaism and the way it encouraged quiet, disciplined rules of living. For those philosophically inclined, links would be seen with the best that Greece had to offer; and in turning to Judaism, there would be no need to be too rigorous about dropping the pagan myths that were so familiar. The synagogues that had sprung up everywhere would include worshippers of varying degrees of attachment to the full scale of Jewish rituals.

This is where the limiting factor came to lie; for against the popular elements in Judaism, there was the burden of the Law which, if carried out fully, could be difficult and socially divisive. During the active conversion period, there might have been no firm insistence on full observance of all rituals; even circumcision might have been overlooked. But when the Jewish leaders felt themselves moved, in the wake of their national catastrophe, to close ranks and shut out all disruptive influences, this would drastically alter their basic attitude to conversion. There is a dictum in the Talmud that a proselyte would have to be barred from admission if he said he was willing to accept every commandment of the Law except one. There is no need to assume that this theoretical absolute would always have been used as a measuring rod. We know that there were many discussions among the rabbis at the turn of the first century A.D. about how the full rules might be adapted for a god-fearing Gentile who would become, as it were, a resident alien, *ger toshab.* But as time went on, the change in attitude clearly became decisive.

The Jews were, in effect, facing and coping with the disruptive effects of their former triumphs. Among these millions of Jews and half-Jews, there were so many extraneous influences, so many pagan sectarian movements drifting toward them, that a turn inward, away from all this cosmopolitanism, became inevitable for survival. It was a sign of the times that we find the rabbis of the second century A.D. setting out deliberately to reverse the former familiarity with Greek. The Greek language, spoken everywhere, could not be ruled out, but a firm disapproval developed toward the study of Greek literature and thought.

To some extent, this was a specific reaction to the spread of Christianity. The rabbis had become hostile to the Septuagint (the Greek translation of the Bible) because it was used contentiously, and in their view inaccurately, in polemic against the Jews. One of the Christian tactics was to interpret the Bible text allegorically, both to substantiate its "prophecies" about Jesus and to soften the need for literal obedience to the Bible-ordained rituals. The rabbis began, in sharp contrast, to emphasize *p'shat,* the plain meaning of the text. They never gave up their own use of allegory, but carefully differentiated this kind of homiletical Midrash from the legal exposition of the Law. We see the intensity of rabbinic feeling in the kind of remark (typical of many) which condemns those "who throw off the yoke of the Law, break the covenant [circumcision], insolently interpret the Torah, and pronounce the Divine Name as it is written" (Tal. *Shabb.* 63a).

It is perhaps a more unexpected aspect of the same tendency that the Jews at this time began to turn away not only from Greek but even from Aramaic. This was partly because Aramaic was being used extensively by Christian propagandists in and outside the empire. Jews had grown up with it for centuries, but now they began to re-emphasize the importance of Hebrew. Some important personal prayers (for example, the Kaddish, both a magnificat and a bereavement prayer) were still left in Aramaic; and it remained the language for rabbinic argument in the Talmud. But the turn toward Hebrew was firm, and its chauvinistic intent received typical exaggeration. A father who failed to talk Hebrew to his infant son and to teach him the Torah this way, "acts," it was said, "like one who buried him." A man must not use Aramaic even in his personal prayers, "because the ministering angels are not familiar with the Aramaic tongue." As time went on, this renewed emphasis on Hebrew made itself felt even on tombstone inscriptions, which had hitherto usually been in Greek or Latin.[3]

There is a certain sadness in thinking of rabbinic Judaism turning away from the world in this way; but one has to be on guard against facile generalization. It might be more correct historically to think of this inward emphasis as a healthy adaptation to reality, preparing a base on which Jews would not only survive but would draw a special kind of fulfillment from continued existence.

One sees this, to begin with, at the political level, where the despondency of the post-Destruction period seems to foreshadow the coming weakness of Judaism against the rising power of Christianity. But from a different viewpoint, the retreat of the Jews can be seen as *reculer pour mieux avancer.* In this period, the Jews of Palestine found themselves devising new forms of political self-government to replace the unreal independence of an alien Herodian dynasty, which had maintained only a pretense of power under Roman protection.

No one sat down and planned things this way, yet this was how the logic of the situation asserted itself, given the determination of the Jews to pursue their Torah life with a new devotion and given, also, the Roman disposition to respect self-government when it was true to its roots.

One positive factor was a stronger emphasis on maintaining a religiously satisfying existence in the Holy Land, instead of looking toward emigration. There was intense discouragement of the sale of land or houses, and an attempt was made to sustain the religious authority that the Palestine rabbis had long exerted over the Jews in the Diaspora. Once the Hadrianic decrees against Talmud study were withdrawn or modified, the rabbis came out from various hiding places and established a new Sanhedrin in Usha, a little town in Galilee, headed by a rabbi, Simon ben Gamaliel, whose family, descended from Hillel, commanded respect from Romans, as well as Jews.

Simon's son, Judah, whose life covered the second half of the second century A.D. and the beginning of the third, became known formally as Rabbi Judah ha-Nasi (the patriarch) and built up the new institution to considerable power. He was granted by his colleagues the right to nominate rabbis and teachers throughout Jewry; and his agents inspected communities everywhere and collected taxes voted for the upkeep of the patriarchate. The Jewish calendar was fixed by his authority for use even beyond the Holy Land, and with Roman approval, the rabbinic courts were given full civil, and even sometimes criminal, jurisdiction. It was as a natural corollary of Judah's status as patriarch that he collected and edited the corpus of Jewish law which became known as the Mishnah. His court and lifestyle reflected considerable wealth; and, without any written agreement with the Romans, he was nevertheless recognized as the source of law and order.

The Talmud in Palestine and Babylonia

Even without military power, Judah ha-Nasi had high status in the Holy Land, and with one crucial difference from the royal leaders of the late Herodian period. The authority of the patriarch and his rabbi colleagues was not alien but based on popular acceptance. As time went on, the tax burden imposed by successive patriarchs began to be resented, as under all political systems. But the money flowed in, with Roman approval, from Jews everywhere, some of it going to the Roman treasury, some of it to support schools and needy students. The real opposition came increasingly from Christians, who saw this quasi-Jewish sovereignty as a sign that the sceptre had not wholly departed from Judah and resented the fact.

By the fourth century A.D. the Church was in a position to make stronger demands where it chose to. Before this happened, however, the generative power of Talmud studies, which had contributed to authentic self-government under the patriarchate in Palestine, had produced a parallel and even more remarkable movement of the same type in Babylonia. This movement supplied the Jews there with representative government and, through the Babylonian Talmud, was due to exert authority over the Jews of the world. Babylonian Jewry was, of course, the oldest mass-settled group of Jews outside Palestine; and though the center of interest in the Jewish story inevitably shifted to the Holy Land after the return from the Babylonian exile under Ezra, the Babylonian community maintained its strength throughout the period of the Second Temple in both economic and religious terms.

By the time of the destruction of the Temple in A.D. 70, the Jewish population of Babylonia had grown to at least a million. Under the semifeudal Parthians, who were dominant in the region until A.D. 226, the Jews themselves had a kind of feudal independence, headed by an exilarch (*resh galutha* —chief of the exile) who claimed direct descent, through exiled Hebrew kings, from King David. In the battles of the Parthians with Rome, the Jews, who were settled densely on both sides of the border and were historically anti-Roman, were regarded as useful allies. This special position continued when the Persian Sassanid dynasty took over early in the third century A.D. The incessant campaigns between Rome and the Persians were part of the cause of the decline of Roman power in the third century. When the Emperor Constantine formally recognized Christianity in A.D. 313, there was an even stronger motivation for Jewish attachment to Persia, where they were free from the vilification that the Church was now beginning to turn in full force on the Jews.

Until this time, the Babylonian community had always given pride of place to institutions in the Holy Land, particularly when Judah ha-Nasi stood out as leader with such obvious authority. The Babylonian scholars were proud enough of their status, though there had been a certain movement of Jewish scholars from Babylonia to Palestine, a trend which, in earlier times, had included Hillel. But now, with Rome herself weakening and Palestine torn with uncertainty, a flow of scholars began from the Holy Land to Babylonia, signaled by the arrival there, in A.D. 219, of a distinguished rabbi Abba Arika, known affectionately, but with respect, as "Rab." Working with a Babylonian rabbi called Samuel, Rab founded a series of academies in which the fame of Babylonian scholarship became universally acknowledged.

In time, their discussions of the Mishnah code emerged in a Babylonian version of the Talmud which became standard in world Jewry for many centuries. The distinction in scholarship was paralleled by the rich living style of the exilarch and his court. When, in due course, this world fell under Muslim sway, the same built-in distinction survived for several centuries, with Babylonia the focal point for world Jewish authority, even if the aura of the Holy Land still exercised its indefinable appeal.

The Basis of Jewish Life

This, then, was the positive product of what might have seemed the negative attitude of the rabbis in turning inward after the destruction of the Temple and the loss of political independence. Partly in Palestine itself, but more powerfully in Babylonia, the authentic values of the Jewish tradition—starting in the Bible and continuing through the thought and writings of Hellenist times—had been put on a solid and lasting basis.

These values might seem to have been buried for centuries under the vast legal foliage of the Talmud; but this was never the feeling that the Talmud generated. It became and remained for centuries, a forcing-house of intelligent and ethical endeavor, unique in its concentration on the original text of the Bible but equally rich in its revelation of the social background of the times and the seriousness and wit of its authors and contributors.

In a strange way, this difficult and mysterious work, the epitome of inwardness, opened up Jewish life by helping Jews to look beyond the horizons of their immediate, and often parochial, existence. The Talmud was a force for communion among Jews everywhere. Scholars spoke and wrote to each other in its terms; ordinary folk knew that when their rabbi advised them on some law or principle of conduct, he himself was drawing (or claiming to draw) on this catholic expression of Jewish existence. Jews had a feeling about the Talmud as an embodiment of learning, even if most of them could never read a word of it. Everything they did or had heard about or were amused by was thought to go back to the Talmud; and in this way it was a reality which helped them to come to terms with their scattered position in the world.

The Jews had willed the end and found the means. Their purpose was to preserve a view of God and man which was unshakable in its certainty; the inner security which this reflected was more precious than mere survival. Even where material conditions were hard, the identification of a Jew with the Law gave life a sense of purpose.

It is worth quoting Salo Baron again for his judgment of what it meant to an ordinary observant Jew to encounter "his Jewish forms of living" at every point in his life:

> From the moment he awakened in the morning until he came to rest at night, his behavior was not only governed by the multiplicity of ritualistic requirements concerning ablutions, prayers, the type of food he was allowed to eat and the time he should set aside for study, but also during all his long and arduous working hours he constantly felt the impact of Jewish law and custom. It was in this vast interlocking system of observances and institutions, more and more fully elaborated by his rabbinic teachers, that he found his most integrated way of living as an individual and as a member of society. For the most part, he found this all-encompassing Jewish way of life so eminently satisfactory that he was prepared to sacrifice himself—here his indoctrination in martyrdom played a decisive role—for the preservation of its fundamentals.[4]

The Separate Road of Christianity

Historically, the Church had been propelled forward by the very opposite incentive from that of Judaism. Undoubtedly, some basic ideas drawn on by both religions surfaced in almost identical terms—the veneration of God, the belief in Revelation, the ethical life, the duties to one's fellowmen, and the fulfillment of these duties in love. Yet the background in which these ideas were pursued were to become diametrically opposite. The Jews looked inward for what was molded exclusively in their tradition. The Church reformulated Judaism in terms of the Greco-Roman culture around them.

It has been argued that the presentation by Paul and his successors of ideas that drew on the whole vast background of the Roman Empire was a great historical necessity. The mixed races and cultures of the empire had by now found some common ground that called for "an appropriate religious expression."[5] Orthodox Judaism could never have supplied this kind of homogenizing and leavening influence. It could not have accepted, as some Christian writings began to explain, that the Roman Empire had been fashioned by Providence to unite mankind and that this had been the prerequisite for the coming of Christ. Rome, to traditional Jews, personified evil. It was always referred to in Jewish apocalyptic writings as "Edom"—the land of Esau, the deep-dyed enemy of Jacob. To the early Christians, even when being persecuted, Rome was the world they belonged to, in the sense that the mythic and artistic culture that underpinned life was natural and acceptable to them.

One sees this coming fully into the open once Christianity became a permitted religion in A.D. 313 by order of Constantine. Before that, the Christians had undergone much testing of their faith through persecution and had been establishing a philosophy and creed that would make the ultimate merging of the faith with the Roman establishment possible and natural. A main element in this process was the progressively sharp separation of the Church from its origin among the narrow and despised Jews. In time, this became not merely an interpretative exercise but an attitude filled with extraordinary hate, bringing in its train many tragedies for the Jews.

But this came later. At the beginning, one is struck by what can only be called the miracle of Christianity's emergence in its tentative state, when it was a sect of scattered communities feeling their way toward the idolization of a Being—half-man, half-God—through whom they came to feel holiness and love. In the background, there was the thunder and beauty of the Bible, evoking an ancient world of patriarchs, kings, and prophets. Around them was the bustling life and culture of the Mediterranean. Transcending it all, there was the joy of coming together in synagogues or in homes for rituals and communal meals, where a visiting preacher would lead them to the ecstasy of faith. There would be betrayal and danger; but this, as all faiths know, gives life a cutting edge of willpower and excitement. One has only to read the Acts of the Apostles to recapture the flavor of these times, with nothing determined as yet but with the new faith on the march, in terms ever clearer, toward the dominance it was to win.

By the time Christianity had established itself with increasingly firm dogmas and under an organization found everywhere of deacons, presbyters, and bishops, the exact history bound up with Jesus' life and death on earth ceased to be relevant, since the saying and deeds now linked with him were all that mattered. It was a fact of the faith that Jesus on the Cross had been the literal fulfillment of Isaiah's prophecy of a suffering servant of the Lord; he had been "wounded for our transgressions, bruised for our iniquities." Most importantly for the faith, his suffering had been not only predictable but essential to man: "with his stripes we are healed" (Isa. 53:5).

No Christian cared to recall that the chastisement and execution of Jesus had come as a profound shock to his disciples. The man who was to have led them to triumph over the enemies of Israel had died like a common criminal. It was not until the word came that Jesus had risen from the dead that faith started on its new and assured path. To most ordinary Jews, of course, the Resurrection was a totally unacceptable concept; but it was one which worked magic among those familiar with the myth of a dying and rising god and who could therefore see Jesus in this context.

Something similar happened over the origin of the Eucharist. With their faith restored through the Resurrection, the apostles must have gone over every detail of their final meeting with Jesus at the Last Supper and tried to read the most intense mystical meaning into their having shared bread and wine with him. There is no way of knowing—except through faith—whether Jesus said of the bread, as reported by Mark: "Take, eat; this is my body" (14:22), and of the wine: "This is my blood of the new testament which is shed for many" (22:24), an affirmation which grows even firmer in John: "Except ye eat the flesh of the Son of Man and drink his blood, ye have no life in you" (John 6:53). It is a concept which was, of course, totally abhorrent to traditional Judaism. But this was not so in the gentile world; and it is easy to see how the ritual of the Eucharist, which emerged from this, could become the high moment of all Christian worship.

Yet there was little in this that caused much direct friction between the early followers of Jesus and ordinary Jews. For quite a time, there was no animus against the Jews, so familiar later, over the Crucifixion itself, since this was clearly an act of the authorities. Nor was the Law built up yet into an obstacle, as it became with Paul. The driving element in the faith of the apostles was that the Messiah had come, signifying that the End of Days was at hand.

Among these early Jewish-Christians, baptism was very familiar (as with some other Jewish sects); and this, with the sacrament of the Eucharist and a disposition to live in communistic communities (like those of the earlier communities of the Dead Sea Scrolls) was all that distanced them from the main Jewish community until the emergence of Paul.

Paul was both an intellectual and a visionary. The power of the vision of Jesus, which had transformed him on the road to Damascus, fueled his feelings for the rest of his life. But it was his intellectual qualities which proved so decisive for the growth of the faith, since he was able, through them, to synthesize the ideas and mysteries of the Hellenist world with the prophetic theology that had been expressed in the Bible.

What he achieved, at the same time, was to move the early faith in Jesus from its narrow base in Palestine to the broad space of the Roman world. He was, in the end, to meet his death in Rome; but before that, his endless travels through the Mediterranean enabled him to formulate doctrines which were increasingly acceptable to citizens of the empire.

It is certain that he always continued to think of himself as a Jew, even if he was ready to apply his brilliant intellect to devising ideas which, in effect, cut at the heart of traditional Judaism and opened the way to the full separation of the two faiths. The most fundamental was the idea that while the ritual Law in all its ramifications had been an essential stage in worshipping God and winning His forgiveness for our sins, this had now been overtaken, and indeed nullified, by the advent of the Messiah. To those who had faith, sin need be no more; and the proof of these "glad tidings" lay in the resurrection of Jesus. Quoting verses of the psalms of David, he drew the contrast repeatedly between the corruption that was endemic even in a man like David and the absence of corruption in the man whom God raised from the dead:

> Be it known unto you therefore, men and brethren, that through this man is preached unto you the forgiveness of sins; and by him all that believe are justified from all things, from which ye could not be justified by the law of Moses [Acts 14: 38–39].

In the same spirit, he showed that even if Jews continued to draw religious strength from observing the covenant of circumcision, the new covenant called for the "circumcision of the heart" rather than of the flesh. In this sense, the significance of the people of Israel was no longer based on an exclusive covenant. All mankind could be Israel of the spirit.

This emphasis on the spirit as opposed to the flesh was developed by Paul intellectually and became, in effect, a powerful philosophic tool which could accommodate mysteries like the Incarnation or the Trinity. Judaism had begun, and remained, a faith which was rooted in the realism of everyday life. Christianity under Paul set out to erect a creed which, in the hands of the Church Fathers, grew into a daring challenge to reality. Side by side with the retention of many of the simple tenets of the mother-religion, the highly elaborate creeds of the early Church could only be believed in *quia impossible*, with rationality suspended.

The Rift and Its Consequences

It is not surprising, then, that common ideas between Judaism and Christianity were mostly overlaid now with hostility and finally, on the part of the Church, by direct persecution.

Even where a modus vivendi was achieved socially, there were barbs in plenty between Jews and Christians on specific subjects. The Jews' need, some twenty or thirty years after the Destruction of A.D. 70, to insert a curse on slanderers (or perhaps even directly on Nazarenes) into their basic prayer may well have been a reaction to Christian comments, always contemptuous in the extreme, on the loss of the Temple. To them, the Destruction was a sign that the glory of the Jews was over; and this was spelled out, in the Fourth Gospel, by putting words of bitter hostility into Jesus' mouth, centering on the fact that "they who were his own received him not" (John 1:11). The Jews are portrayed not just as indifferent but as hateful, forever plotting to kill him. From then on, the insults and dangers multiply. By the end of the first century, the Jews were expelling Christians from the synagogue, which meant that they became "illegal," as detached from a recognized faith. The Christians in turn were increasingly convinced that they were now on their own because the mantle of holiness, spread out in the Bible, had passed to them. The Church had become the true Israel.

In itself, this may not seem a very strong base for the Jew-hatred which developed in the early Church and was undoubtedly a historical element in the growth of European anti-Semitism. A Christian who saw the Bible finding its full meaning in Jesus might have been led to respect the people who had produced the Bible, as indeed many Christians do.

But to the theologians of the early Church, respect for the Jews was inadmissable. The fact that the Jewish people had handed Jesus over to the Romans and thus engineered his death was only the latest of their acts of rebellion against God. Throughout the Bible, they had been denounced by

God and the Prophets for their constant sinfulness. The Christian had conquered sin through his faith in Jesus; the Jew was still sunk in his ancient and vile sinfulness. He was therefore to be treated by Christians in a manner appropriate to his evil nature.

It is a tribute to the power of ideology that these abstract and quite difficult concepts could push on one side, for many Christians, the image of gentleness and love exemplified in the Gospel stories and leave, instead, a compelling attitude of contempt and hate. Yet this is what happened. The process is analyzed in a major work, *The Conflict of the Church and the Synagogue,* published in 1934 by James Parkes, a Christian priest and distinguished theologian.

"We may at first wonder," he says, "why the attempt to prove the reality of the Divinity of Christ made it necessary to falsify the whole of Jewish history, as the Gentile Church undoubtedly did."[6] The answer lies, he thinks, in the need of the theologians to move far beyond the concept of Jesus as a gentle healer and teacher and to establish his full meaning as the Messiah. In this role, the whole of Scripture had to be geared to him, which meant that it had to be detached from the Jews. We see this thought put in precise terms by a Christian writer like Justin who could say of the Scriptures, in his dialogue with a Jew: "They are not yours but ours, for you, though you received them, did not catch the spirit that is in them."[7]

A Jew sees this, with some distaste, in the Christological interpretations offered as running heads in some English translations of the Bible. As Parkes puts it: "The Church turned the whole of the Old Testament into a vast quarry with no other function than to provide, by any exegesis however far-fetched, arguments for His claims."[8] The Jews, in asserting their links to Moses and Revelation, had, it was said, been sailing under false colors. The Bible showed that they had constantly been rejected by God, whereas Church history flowed in an unbroken line back to Creation. It was Christ (in one form or another) who "appeared to Abraham, gave divine instruction to Isaac, and held converse with Moses and the later prophets."[9]

It can be taken for granted that where Jews heard of these views or were directly involved in arguments with Christians over them, they would not take them lightly. But the evidence on Jewish thought and action toward the Christians at this time is scanty. Either it was not recorded or such references as might have surfaced in the Talmud were largely removed. Socially, Parkes thinks, there must have been many day-to-day contacts when they did other things than hurl abusive texts at each other's heads:

In daily practice their common attitude to the surrounding paganism must have often drawn them together, and their common interests must often have been more important to ordinary folk than the disputes of the theologians.[10]

It is all the more tragic, then, that in this period—the first three centuries A.D.—the view began to be projected by Church leaders, and was picked up later by historians, that the persecution that Christians suffered in their early stages was entirely due to the Jews. Parkes quotes Justin (second century A.D.) as saying that "the Jews kill and punish us whenever they have the power." Tertullian (c. A.D. 150–230) talks of the synagogues as "the sources of the persecutions." It is tragically significant that these and other statements by the Church Fathers culminate in an even more violent attack by the nineteenth-century German theologian Adolf von Harnack to the effect that the Jews "systematically and officially broadcast horrible charges against the Christians which played an important part in the persecutions." It was the Jews, Harnack wrote, who "instigated the Neronic outburst against the Christians"; and after this, "wherever bloody persecutions are afoot, the Jews are either in the background or in the foreground."[11]

This view of Church history was shared by virtually all of Harnack's contemporaries; and it is easy to see how fateful this idea was, both in its early genesis and later elaboration, to the position of Jews in the Christian world. The sad thing is that much of this picture of the Jews persecuting the early Christians is built into a series of stories that, in themselves, have the greatest kind of appeal—the heroism of the saints. All religions create myths about their origins. For devotional purposes, the brave stories of the early saints are perfect; but as they came to play an important part in creating anti-Semitism, one has to look at the evidence to see how factual it is.

For centuries now, the stories of the persecutions of the early saints have been laboriously collected by the Church; and to get at the truth of this crucially important matter, Parkes devoted a substantial part of his book to an analysis of this factual evidence. He reports that many of the stories in these collections "are recognized to be entirely fabulous, nothing more than novelettes produced in some monastic centre based upon a local legend possibly of pagan origin, or due simply to the ingenuity of the writer."[12] By using the Acts of the Apostles as a source for descriptive detail on Jewish enmity, the persecuted saint can be set in any country; only by a comparison does it emerge that the same detail from Acts is being drawn on. Most strikingly, however, all the stories, true or legendary, cease at the end of the first century A.D., so that in these terms alone, no picture of unrelenting hostility by the Jews can apply. In records of the persecution of Christians after the first century, and most particularly in the widespread persecution that culminated in a ten-year reign of anti-Christian terror under Diocletian, responsibility is imputed entirely to the Romans. Where Jews appear in the old records, they reflect occasional unsystematic violence of the individual or a mob.

It is not usually safe to argue a case by the absence of records, but it must surely be significant that the Jews are not identified over the major persecutions and completely absent in the second and third centuries A.D. One can conclude, Parkes says, that "the statement of Jewish hostility in general terms is based on theological exegesis and not on historical memory."[13] Certainly, the Jews were determined, after the Destruction, to oust Christians from the shelter of the synagogue; and it was in this period that doctrines were formed on the Christian side that were deeply offensive to the Jewish view of their unique place in Bible history. The situation changed in the second century A.D. when the direct confrontation ceased or disappeared. In Parkes's judgment, "The universal, tenacious, and malicious hatred referred to by Harnack, Corluy, Allard and others, has no existence in historical fact."[14] Not that this judgment can undo the bitterness and tragedy generated in the wake of the falsification; but at least it helps us to understand what was really taking place during the parting of the ways.

The Final Position

We move into a different kind of separation when both Jews and Christians set out to define their positions in decisive—one might say final—terms in the fourth century A.D.

For Jews, this was the century in which the long discussions on the Law stretching back for five centuries were finally brought together in the Talmud. The Jews did not develop a new theology in doing this; the essence of faith was identical with what had been propounded by the Pharisees in the first century B.C. The *halakhah,* law, was now made more precise but, again, without raising theological issues. The unending legal arguments that had taken place, and were to continue, were all within a fully accepted framework, which included a common theological viewpoint, even if it was never spelled out, or argued about, in theological terms. What was achieved by the completion of the Talmud was the presentation of an edifice of faith that represented, for all Jews, a triumphant synthesis of the Written and the Oral Law.

For Christians, the fourth century A.D. had a different kind of decisiveness. The Church had already built up a widespread establishment of bishops throughout all Mediterranean and Near Eastern countries, though persecution meant that they had often to operate from prisons or secret hiding places. In the middle of the third century A.D., persecution had weakened because the Roman Empire itself was fighting for its life against invading barbarians. But this did not prevent the authorities from launching themselves later, from time to time, into the most bloodthirsty persecutions, notably, the ten-year stretch under Diocletian beginning in A.D. 303. The memory of these persecutions—real and imaginary—has remained vivid throughout all Church history.

Yet to the outside observer, this period is just as remarkable—even more remarkable, in some ways—for bitter arguments within the Church, and these had repercussions on the Jews. Almost from the beginning, the Church had developed internal schisms of the most violent kind. Perhaps this was inevitable, given the difficulty of conceptualizing many of the Church's basic teachings, notably on the Trinity or Virgin Birth. The Church suffered, as it also benefited, from being the heirs of Greek thought, and the elaboration of teachings in philosophic terms by rival theologians resulted in accusations of heresy pursued to the death. One such conflict had arisen through the Gnostic teachings of the second century A.D. theologian Marcion, whose contempt for the Old Testament and its place in Christianity spilled over, inevitably, into a contempt for the Jews. Of longer influence was the schism which developed over the great heresy of Arianism. Arius, a theologian from Alexandria who straddled the third and fourth centuries A.D., had advanced the teaching that Jesus the Son had been begotten by God the Father before Creation and was therefore neither eternal nor equal with the Father, a teaching which struck at the heart of the accepted views on the Trinity. Athanasius succeeded in outlawing Arianism at the First Council of Nicaea in A.D. 325; but the heresy persisted, spreading out politically and militarily among rival nations throughout Europe.

The infighting on heresies had been active enough through the third century A.D., with many side effects on the relations between the rapidly growing Church establishment and the shaky but still powerful Roman Empire. One such argument had turned on how far it was permitted to the Church to cooperate with the State, for political reasons, on pagan sacrifice, since this was basically a secular, national, ceremonial. All this was put into a new framework, of course, when the Emperor Constantine decided in A.D. 313 that he personally would become a Christian.

Nothing could express more dramatically the contrast for the future between the roles that Judaism and Christianity were now to play in the world. Judaism was to stablize itself during this century in its resolve to survive quietly and live by its internal traditions. Christianity was to move on through Constantine's act to dominate world politics.

The Church Expands

The English Church scholar Henry Chadwick has provided a valuable sense of historical perspective on Constantine by pointing out, in his book *The Early Church,* that his conversion "should not be interpreted as an inward experience of grace. . . . It was a military matter."[15] Constantine had invaded Italy in A.D. 312 with inferior forces and "was sure that victory in battle lay in the gift of the God of the Christians." He was not aware of any mutual exclusiveness between Christianity and his own faith in the Unconquered Sun, which might be called solar monotheism. Nor, indeed, did Christianity feel that if pagans saw Christ as the Sun-God, this image had to be ruled out too forcefully at the beginning. One moved in stages. In due course, Constantine became serious about his new religion and was baptized on his deathbed in A.D. 337. But long before that, his conversion meant more than the end of persecution of the Church. He himself became seriously involved in the development of the Church, and the Church itself became more implicated in high political decisions.

The doctrinal arguments that had already riven the Church now assumed heavy political overtones, often with direct or side effects on the Jews through organizational questions in the vast territories now covered by the Church. There were about 220 bishops in attendance at the Council of Nicaea. If it has come down in history as the locus of the Nicaean Creed, which established, in opposition to Arianism, that "the Son is of one Substance with the Father," this first world council of the Church also tackled important establishment questions affecting relations between the Churches in many countries. This pattern of organization with councils and creeds was to be characteristic of the Church in its new established form, with baleful effects very often on the Jews, who must have wondered sadly, when decisions of these councils (such as the Fourth Lateran Council of 1215) bore down heavily on them, why the Church could not leave them alone. It is indeed ironic—if this mild word can be tolerated—that the Church found itself impelled to move into ever-increasing attacks on the Jews as soon as it was itself finally freed of persecution through Constantine's conversion.

Behind the new venom in Church writings there was a social factor, in that society in Rome, now adopting some kind of superficial Christianity, was traditionally hostile to the Jew, an attitude that had persisted ever since the Jewish wars against the Romans. This had showed itself in contemptuous remarks about Jews and their peculiar religious customs that became commonplace in classical writing. But it could not compete in intensity with the picture of Jews that began to be presented in fourth-century Church writings, in a style which can be paralleled only—a sad thought—with the obsessed anti-Jewish fury of *Der Stuermer.* One must see the reason in the determination of the Church, now that it was in power, to give its theological basis a final irrefutable logic. The Jew could not be taken out of the Christian story; yet to allow him to exist side by side, so to speak, with Jesus was to imperil the total revolution that had come into the world through Christianity. He must, therefore, be given a role as the evil against which Christianity had triumphed; and if he was to be recognized as evil, let this be presented with all the passionate feeling that was expressed in the Christian's love of Christ.

This was a phenomenon of early Christian writing that was never to appear again in the Church itself with the same vehemence; but it obviously left its mark forever. Few of us today read the writings of fourth-century Church Fathers, but their character can be gathered in the summary provided in Parkes's book.[16]

In these writings, Parkes says, the Jew is not a human being at all. He is "a monster," a theological abstraction of superhuman cunning and malice and more than superhuman blindness. This picture is rarely related to his current behavior but flows overwhelmingly from his nature as deduced from the most authentic of all sources—the Bible. In the pages of the Bible, the Jews are displayed in their wicked disobedience to God, despite all that He had done for them. It was entirely in character that after this history of unchanging and unrepentant malice and vice, they had turned their back on Christ.

A Peak of Hostility

Because this picture is based on the "truths" of theology, it is established that the Jews can never change. They have been given their evil role in history forever. One exposition of this is by the historian Eusebius (d. A.D. 339). He presents the Jews "classically," as one might say, with all the charges and crimes. In his view, one has to draw a distinction between the ancient Hebrews, who led a Christian life, and the Jews who came after them and are totally possessed of evil.

If this was bad enough, the violence is much stronger in the writing of Saint John Chrysostom (c. A.D. 347–407), reaching a peak of hatred and contempt in eight sermons which he delivered in A.D. 387 from his pulpit in Antioch. In Parkes's summary, "There is no sneer too mean, no gibe too bitter for him to fling at the Jewish people. No text is too remote to be able to be twisted in their confusion, no argument is too casuistical, no blasphemy too startling for him to employ."[17]

The quotations from these sermons that one finds in Parkes are appalling. The synagogues of the Jews are the homes of idolatry and devils. If Bible scrolls are to be found there, that makes the Jews even more detestable, for they have introduced these books "not to honour them but to insult them, and to dishonour them. As God hates the Jews, and has always hated them, it is the duty of Christians to hate them too."[18]

It would be too painful to go through the list of other fourth-century Christian writers, all pouring out venom in the same style. What one needs to draw from this phenomenon in relation to Jewish history is some kind of understanding. There is perhaps a clue to this in a rueful remark which Parkes himself makes about the motivation of Chrysostom.

Parkes is particularly perplexed on why a man like Chrysostom should have been impelled to let himself go in this way, since he was, by all accounts, a man of deep principle, much loved by the multitudes. His commentaries on the Gospels, one learns, are still read and studied in the Orthodox Church because of their deep spiritual beauty.

If, nevertheless, this saintly man (he was in fact made a saint by the Church) felt impelled into these venomous attacks on the Jews, it could have been, Parkes thinks, because in fact the Jews lived on good terms with the Christians in Antioch and Chrysostom felt called upon to put an end to this for theological reasons. The Jewish community of Antioch was rich and long-established, and though it was now hemmed in by numerous imperial edicts issued under Christian inspiration, this had not ruled out a warm and close fellowship with Christians at the business, and perhaps also the social, level. There are hints about this in warnings to Christians against taking these relationships too easily; and this suggests that there must have been a good side to ordinary Jewish-Christian relations, offsetting the horrors of the time that have been highlighted here.

Underlying Friendships

One has to bear this factor in mind throughout Jewish history. In looking closely at events and documents, one can surrender to the view that the Jewish-Christian relationship has always to be remembered for its tragic side. The dramas of horror are prominent enough to generate this judgment; yet one knows that these events do not tell us everything about the human relationships that have existed at the personal level, and of which one had striking evidence even during the greatest of all tragedies—the one we have all lived through.

Apart from what happened through natural friendships, we have to remember, also, that the teachings of Christianity often produced men and women who exemplified love and grace and who gave expression to these truly Christian attitudes not just in faith but equally in works. It has sometimes been argued that the Jewish ethic is superior to the Christian since Jewish teachings impose practical duties that are within human range, whereas the teaching of Jesus was unreal, calling on one to love one's enemy and turn the other cheek. Yet this kind of unreality has been capable of producing lives of incredible devotion and self-sacrifice. The men and women who, for love of Christ, went out to work in leper colonies may or may not have loved the Jews. One has no idea; but throughout Jewish history one does know of Christians who fought their own inherited anti-Jewish feeling in order to help Jews at the political or personal level, seeking, in this way, for identification across the centuries with the Jew who was their founder.

Against all the odds, much of this has rubbed off on Jews living in the

Christian world, just as many Christians have felt drawn both to the beauty of Jewish family and religious life and to Jewish writings which have interpreted it. There is no way of measuring what these expressions of Jewish-Christian sympathy over the centuries have added up to against the all too obvious tragedies of antipathy, exclusiveness, and persecution. One simply knows that they have been of enormous value.

And there is another factor in the equation that must be put in to get things right. For long periods, Jews and Christians pursued different paths culturally, but when the times were propitious, the Jews entered a world which had been fertilized by Christian feeling and made it part of their own. Ironically, they recovered in this way much that was stimulating from the pagan world they had so abominated.

From the beginning under Paul, Christianity had looked out into the pagan world; and it is a commonplace that as the Church found its feet it began to give expression to this rich cultural source not only in theology but also in every form of art. As long as Jews lived in their own narrow communities, they were inevitably excluded from any free participation in this kind of cultural life. But they were always avid for new experience, and when they managed, first cautiously and then with bravado, to break out into some freer kind of Jewish-Christian association, they became grateful inheritors of the cultural work of centuries. The fact that this tradition—especially in art and music—was basically Christian, has been irrelevant. What the Christians did (and equally the Muslims in their time) was to develop and deepen the long heritage of mankind. The Jews, if long excluded in some ways, brought an even more intense devotion to these fields of human endeavor when they were finally free. Today, to say the least, they are full participants.

There is no way of assessing this in relation to the dark horrors that have hovered over Jews and Christians since the parting of the ways, but it is there, as part of the historical picture, and one has to recognize it.

9

Diaspora Judaism: Beliefs and Rituals

The Constants in Jewish Life

N THIS and the following chapters, we shall take a bird's-eye view of how the inherited tradition of the Jews exemplified itself in their experience from the time they were increasingly dispersed over the world in the early Christian centuries until our own day. In this chapter, dealing with the religious faith and practices of Diaspora Jewry, we shall see what has been constant—virtually immutable—among Jews in every place and every century until close to our own time. In the two chapters which follow, dealing with broad history, we have what seems a complete contrast to constancy—a picture of social variety and dynamism.

Yet the chapters are complementary. Religious and secular issues were, for Jews, two sides of the same coin. On one side, religion was rooted in the practicalities of life; on the other, social and political experience, for all its constantly changing local coloring, reflected the constancy—the distinctiveness—that was a product of the inherited religious tradition. These two sides of Jewish life flowing together so naturally gave Jewish kinship its strength and lasting power. Jews might quarrel with each other endlessly on religious, social, and personal matters: They were expert at this and liked nothing better; yet it was always an argument from within. A sense of unity had been established under rabbinic guidance in the early centuries, evoking the infrangible unity and holiness of the Bible; and, except for one relatively brief moment of time, this sense of community has pervaded the entire Diaspora era. It is expressed in the Hebrew phrase *klal yisrael,* which the scholar Solomon Schechter translated as "catholic Israel."

The brief moment when it seemed to be in some peril began in the last century as a by-product of political emancipation and cultural "enlightenment." Many Jews who felt, in this situation, that they were being invited to become free and equal members of the world at large if they gave up their links with the Jewish tradition, pushed themselves into a complete change of identity. Others felt that the tradition could be modernized by dropping the kinship links, so that Jews became superpatriotic nationals of their new state with only one minor difference—they went to synagogue instead of church.

In Germany, the Jews affected by this attitude—a small but influential minority—defined themselves carefully as "German citizens of the Jewish faith." The attitude was echoed among some Jews of German origin in the United States and to a tiny extent in England. In practice, it meant that all the historical associations seen here as the springs of Jewish life were played down. The use of Hebrew in prayers was minimized. The age-old longing for Jerusalem was stifled. The poverty-stricken masses of Jews in Eastern Europe or Arab lands were looked down on as a lower breed, superstitious victims of the worn-out traditions of the rabbis. One might help them out of charity, but that was all.

It was a relatively brief moment in Jewish history, due to be reversed in an astonishing way in the last fifty years. The polarization that seemed threatened in Jewish life had a far wider base than merely in the self-deceptive attitude of early German-Jewish reformers. Quite apart from those who tried deliberately to give up all Jewish associations, and those who maintained some links in weakened form, there was a strong secularist movement at large in Jewish life as a whole, pervasive even in the great traditional centers of Eastern Europe. For many, the Jews were now turning a corner, leaving the old associations behind. Even the building of a national home in Palestine, as furthered by the Balfour Declaration of 1917, had, at first, a far from universal appeal. The future of Jews was to lie in full citizenship everywhere or within the idealism of an international socialist brotherhood, with distinctiveness played down.

Hitler, it might be said, was a prime element in reversing this, but by no means the only factor. Certainly, the horrors of Nazi persecution brought back to life the full consciousness of Jews as a people, suffering with each other, responsible for each other. No Jews felt less American or British for identifying themselves totally with their kinsmen in the greatest Jewish tragedy of all time. And the same sense of unity was soon forged equally over the building of the State of Israel. It was as if a force of enormous power was latent in Jewish life, ready for a demonstration of how strong the kinship had been throughout history, and how false it was to imagine that this could now trail into nothingness.

Even by itself, this reinvigoration of ancient feelings would have been remarkable; but it is only one aspect of a new attitude to the Jewish religion as a whole, which is why it is singled out for mention in this chapter on Diaspora Judaism. Everyone observing Jewish life today has seen how the negativism that was common a few decades ago has given way to new forms of involvement with the tradition, pursued in many ways, some intellectual, some mystical, but all releasing strong, even passionate, feelings and interests. This is not to say that secularism is a spent force: far from it. But unlike other secularists or agnostics whose position might be fully defined by these terms, Jews always add something. Even secularists are aware of a religious-historical tradition which demands understanding fertilized by empathy. In the return of many Jews to a sense of full community with *klal yisrael,* they are returning also to the world in which *klal yisrael* expressed itself in the long Diaspora centuries. For most Jews, this is not a descent into the past as an abnegation of the present; it is an unfolding of the past in a hundred unexpected ways, all of interest to a Jew.

In the expression of this interest, the constancy of Jewish life in the religious and intellectual spheres has been reasserted. The evidence of this lies open everywhere. At the synagogue level, Reform Jews have reintroduced Hebrew and given new emphasis to ancient rituals. The Bible has taken on new meaning through its physical identification with Israel, and through the archeological discoveries that bring it to life in its true ancient setting and not simply for its ethical teachings. In a true sense one can say, now, that every word of the Bible has endless meaning, as it always had—though in a different way—for our ancestors. The vast treasure house of the Talmud has also opened its doors not simply to provide authority for conduct and not simply for the light it sheds on comparative law, linguistics, and philosophy but for the delight it offers in the realm of argument, a transforming process that has always lain at the heart of Jewish life.

In what is for many a new association with the Jewish past, much of the aridness that seemed to characterize the rabbinic tradition has yielded in this way to a richer kind of awareness. An excellent example of this change is seen in the work of Gershom Scholem, who showed that the emphasis given to rabbinic life as dominantly legalistic left out the immensely strong mystical and poetic influences that were active throughout Jewish history, establishing a common thread stretching from Talmud times through the Kabbalah and on to Hasidism.[1]

The springs of Jewish life, it can be said, are in full flow today. For strongly orothodox Jews, this is valid in a totally traditional and fundamentalist way; for others, the involvement with tradition has new forms, linked to our own time and place. But with *all* Jews affected this way, the result for Jewish life has been to lay the groundwork again for the enjoyment of a quality that was always the most heartwarming feature of inheriting the common tradition: that a Jew traveling to the furthest reaches of the world was immediately at home with fellow Jews in the rituals of home and synagogue. Religion as a constant in Jewish experience also had another aspect, in the realm of poetic imagination. As the prayers and rituals were unchanged from rabbinic—and even, in many cases, from Temple—times, it was taken for granted that if, by the grace of God, a Jew happened to drop in from a far-off century, he would be perfectly at home with the kinsmen he found. We saw this illustrated in the fantasy quoted earlier (see page 150) of Rabbi Akiba coming to life to talk to us with perfect ease about the unchanging issues of Jewish experience.

The constancy in Jewish religious life has always included within it a dynamic which takes shape through discussion. The Bible scholar Robert Alter has stressed this point in relation to the Jewish distaste for dogma. The Jews, he says, have made some efforts to systematize their religious ideas, but "it has been far more typical for Jews to articulate such ideas and values through textual commentary, and often, indeed, through commentary on commentary."[2]

One bears this in mind in setting out, now, a brief summary of the beliefs and rituals that have been at the heart of Jewish life in the Diaspora, and have been revived today for many who seemed at one stage to be wandering away from them. A book on Jewish tradition demands a catalogue of this kind, even though a catalogue is only a basis for discussion. One is reminded of the instruction conveyed in the *haggadah* at the Passover Seder: "The more one talks about the Exodus, the more praiseworthy it is."

Beliefs

To pick up the point made by Robert Alter, Judaism has rarely put much emphasis on theological dogmas. Though Jews always felt impelled by traditional ideas and practices, there was a strong tendency to avoid projecting them as a creed.

A Jew was defined in one sense by birth and in another by observance of rituals handed down generation after generation. These rituals were based on the Torah (Pentateuch) as interpreted by the rabbis. They carried with them implicit acceptance of religious ideas arising in the Bible, even if these ideas were not usually defined; and the same approach was evident devotionally in the recital of the psalms and the traditional prayers. Put this way, it would seem that one could say that a Jew was a Jew was a Jew. One was born of Jewish parents (technically, a Jewish mother was essential), and one spent one's life in ritual practices and in a social ambience with socioreligious overtones that were far more identifiable and fulfilling than would emerge from a theoretical creed.

This does not mean that beliefs implicit in this generalized attitude could not ever be defined. Attempts were, in fact, made to do this with variable success. But before we look at would-be comprehensive and formal creeds, it may be more to the point to pick out two basic religious ideas which seem to have been paramount in the concept of God that Jews drew instinctively from the Bible.

The first is the extraordinary weight given to the unity of God. This emerged first in the Bible in the idea of a single God as opposed to the pantheon of gods worshipped by surrounding pagans. Theologians sometimes stress that in earliest Hebrew times, this was not monotheism, belief that there is only one God in the universe, but henotheism, that is, belief in one's own god but recognizing the existence of others; for one hears repeatedly in the Bible that the God who is so protective of Israel is also superior in power to other gods. It is safe to say that though these comparisons survived in psalms and prayers, they long ceased to be relevant to the concept of God that Jews felt flowing from the Bible. Pagan gods had long been satirized contemptuously in their dead state as idols. The God whom Jews worshipped was incorporeal and universal, even if He could be addressed as a personal Being. And all this was summed up in the idea of God as One, paramount, universal, and totally unique in essence.

It was as a symbol of this that the *Sh'ma*, the verse in Deuteronomy—6:4—"Hear O Israel, the Lord our God, the Lord is One") became charged with mysterious power, even for Jews whose temperament might be cool and prosaic and infinitely more, of course, for those of mystical instincts. It is true that after Christianity emerged, the affirmation in the *Sh'ma* of God's One-ness always carried a silent defiance of the idea of Jesus as a second Godhead and even more of the Trinity. But there was much more to the *Sh'ma* than its assertion of unity. Even ordinary Jews heard in the word *Ehad* (One) a mystical cry toward God's power as the Creator and Sustainer of the universe. One was told that in reciting this word one should linger on the long *a*, prolonging it as long as one could, to open one's mind to the staggering concept of a Being who is the source of life and of everything. One saw the rabbi reciting the *Sh'ma* with eyes closed, lost in rapture as the word *Ehad* brought him into the most intimate feeling of God. One knew that as life ended, every Jew sought to recite the *Sh'ma* with his or her last breath.

The other Biblical concept that penetrated Jewish life with mysterious power was God as Judge. Whereas God's One-ness expressed the Infinite and was in this sense remote and beyond all human ken, God as Judge was a Being to whom one was responsible for one's moral behavior; and this was a concept that riveted Jews when they wrestled, however indirectly, with religious ideas.

The Bible had inculcated the sense of sin in the most thunderous terms. Repeatedly, the ancient Hebrews had been told—and every Jew repeated the words in endless Bible readings—that if one obeyed God's commandments one would be rewarded and if one disobeyed, punished. In the Torah, these commandments seemed to concentrate on the minutiae of law and ceremony—Sabbath and festival ordinances, civil and criminal regulations, agricultural practices, ritual cleanliness and Temple sacrifices. But wrapped up in them were ethical principles—honesty, kindness, consideration for the poor, respect and responsibility for human life—which were seen as a rationale (sometimes explicitly, but always devotionally) for the obedience that God demanded in His Covenant on reward and punishment. This covenant was still in being; and every Jew faced the fact that God as Judge was bound to find him wanting.

In Temple times, the annual Yom Kippur, Day of Atonement, ordained in the Bible had been celebrated in awe-inspiring ceremonies by the high priest, in which God's forgiveness was sought for the sinfulness of the people of Israel. In the Diaspora world, atonement had to be won by every individual Jew personally through the admission of guilt and sincere repentance. Throughout the world of Jews, therefore, the Day of Atonement (and the New Year Holy Days preceding it) gave expression to the most intimate religious feeling in Jewish life.

All the ceremonial days of worship had their importance; but on Yom Kippur a Jew grappled with the meaning of God's power as a Being who had given man an ethical purpose. At this level, the meaning was universal, like God's One-ness; but within Yom Kippur, a Jew also felt the special attachment of God to Jewish existence, and, by this token, a special culpability for failing to rise to the standards demanded by this relationship.

In ordinary day-to-day conduct, one knew that one had failed. Facing God as Judge, His *gezeirah,* decree, had to be adverse unless one found a way of reaching Him through a new kind of spirit in one's life. Amid all the prayers that express this in the New Year and Atonement services, there is one climactic affirmation that rings out with the power of the *Sh'ma.* After a long recital of the issues of ethical conduct, the worshippers cry out: "Repentance, Prayer and *Tz'dakah* [justice-charity] will avert the dread decree."

These two concepts of God as One and God as Judge were felt instinctively by all Jews. When scholars went further than this in trying to give Jewish beliefs a fully comprehensive and philosophical shape, it was, by definition, less instinctive, even if it brought in additional aspects of belief that rang true to Diaspora Judaism.

We will look briefly at these quasi-creeds, always remembering that for all ordinary Jews, Diaspora Judaism was defined not so much in dogmas as in rituals and practices that were absorbed automatically in the household, the Torah school, and the synagogue services.

The first formal list of doctrines of Jewish belief was produced by the twelfth-century philosopher Maimonides in his commentary on the Mishnah, the code of law compiled by Judah ha-Nasi in the second century A.D. There is a brief passage in the Mishnah discussing what kind of heresy would deprive a Jew of a place in the World to Come. One definition was that this would apply to someone who had denied resurrection or who had said that the Torah did not come from Heaven or was just generally a skeptic, *epikoros.* Other rabbis, including Rabbi Akiba, put forward alternative views; but this passage was obviously too vague for a clear definition of belief.

Maimonides, who was born in Spain in 1135 and absorbed much of the sophisticated culture of the Arab world of that time, felt a special obligation to spell out in his voluminous writings the underlying structure of Jewish law and faith. Taking this Mishnah passage, he opened it up methodically, in the style of Muslim theology, and offered Thirteen Principles of Faith which he saw as fundamental to Jewish belief. They can be summarized as belief in:

1. God's existence, which is sufficient unto itself and is the cause of the existence of all other beings
2. God's unity, which is unlike all other kinds of unity
3. God's incorporeality: the anthropomorphisms in the Bible are metaphors
4. God's eternity
5. God alone as the Being to be worshipped directly and without any mediating persons
6. Bible prophecy as valid
7. Moses as the greatest of the Prophets
8. Revelation of the Torah to Moses on Mount Sinai
9. The immutability of the Torah
10. God's knowledge of the acts of human beings
11. Reward and punishment for obedience and transgression of the commandments
12. The coming of the Messiah
13. Resurrection of the dead

These Thirteen Principles of Faith were clearly designed to correspond to and amplify what Jews felt instinctively. In due course they were paraphrased into a credo in the prayer book and used as the basis for many hymns, most particularly the very popular *Yigdal* hymn which is sung in synagogues universally in the Sabbath Eve service. The Principles also stimulated much discussion among Jewish scholars, culminating in our own time in a major work by the theologian, Rabbi Louis Jacobs, which examines the Thirteen Principles individually to ascertain how authentic each has been to the religious ideas of Jews throughout the Diaspora and to what extent they might now have to be modified in the light of contemporary thought. (In his own case, for example, he enters reservations on Maimonides' Eighth Principle, that the whole of the Torah was handed to Moses by God.)[3]

Yet despite the activity of many writers in spelling out, amplifying, curbing, or regrouping the Principles as set out by Maimonides, there was never much disposition to hammer out a creed in terms which would make adherence crucial to fulfillment as a Jew. One of the outstanding theologians who participated in these discussions, the fifteenth-century Hasdai ibn Crescas, explicitly argued, indeed, that while some dogmas were basic to Judaism, others might diverge into heresy without danger to the faith. In the same century, the writer Joseph Albo saw only three root principles in Judaism—God's existence, Revelation, reward and punishment—with everything else following from this.

Some scholars went further in denying that there was any validity in formulating a credo. Moses Mendelssohn, the great scholar of Enlightenment, argued that the Bible called for moral conduct expressed in action rather than belief. The self-evident truths underlying the Jewish religion call for ever-deepening understanding, rather than recital as a credo.

The English scholar Israel Abrahams (1858–1924) brought the varying views on Jewish beliefs together into a rather typically English compromise. "Judaism," he wrote, "is a discipline of life rather than a creed . . . but behind our actions must always stand our beliefs. . . . Judaism has no formal dogmas put forward by an authority with power to enforce its decisions, but it must have dogmas in the sense of clear, settled opinions." Despite all the arguments, "the Thirteen Principles of Maimonides still remain for many Jews true and adequate."[4]

It will be obvious that the doctrines referred to here in the briefest summary indicate only a common ground of belief affecting all Jews in the most general way. As a picture of Diaspora Judaism as a whole from the first to the twentieth century, it would need at least two basic qualifications.

The first is that by concentrating on what one might call simple or straightforward ideas emerging in the practices and prayers of daily life, it leaves out of account completely the elaboration of these ideas in devotional, poetic, or mystical (kabbalistic and hasidic) forms that completely captured the hearts and minds of masses of Jews at different stages in this period.

The second qualification arises from strong tendencies in the period following nineteenth-century Emancipation to harmonize Jewish beliefs with ideas entering from the world outside. This was strongly developed in a movement of Reform which first manifested itself in Germany at the beginning of the nineteenth century and expanded its range there (and also in the United States) from the middle of the century. At first, Reform was mainly preoccupied with the length and style of the services (shorter, less Hebrew, more decorum, et cetera). But it soon began to alter the content of prayers and the practices of Jewish life to take account of more modern ideas on Revelation, the role of *halakhah*, resurrection, and other points in Maimonides' Principles.

The Thirteen Principles of Maimonides have, therefore, to be qualified as a guide to the pattern of Jewish belief after his time; yet they hardly affect the broad picture. The later pietistic and hasidic movements were still grounded in the basic ideas we have summarized. The Reform movement is only a late gloss on what Jews have believed in this long period. There is a separate point, however, that we have to look at if we want to understand the source and character of religious belief that Jews carried with them in the Diaspora.

The Feelings Behind Belief

When one discusses, as we have here, what do Jews believe, it is not enough to present the answer as if it were a recording of fact in the way one might reply to questions like how does electricity work or who won the World Series in 1981. Maimonides, it is true, would have claimed to be factual in his Thirteen Principles, yet he would have had to admit that their truth was a reflection of a religion that already existed rather than a set of doctrines that had some outside objectivity. This would never have lessened the reality of these doctrines to Jews. On the contrary: Those who thought that the Principles rang true endowed them with absolute reality. God *is* One; Moses *did* receive the Torah from God on Sinai; men *are* punished for evildoing; the Messiah *will* come. Jews had been brought up to believe this, generation after generation. Their apperception of each belief was like a picture of something in the round—totally convincing. The joy was that it all fitted together almost by definition, forming a world not just of Jewish belief but of something much stronger, much more enduring, much more affecting: a world of myth.

Myth, in this sense, is not something legendary and unreal. It indicates a received tradition, limitless and indefinable in its range, that embraces and thereby transforms the routine activities of living, lifting the individual into a community of history and faith that far transcends, in its effects, any standardized affirmation of religious belief. In this sense, a Jew reciting the *Sh'ma* is not simply asserting his belief that God is One. He is reaching back to his infancy when this was the first sentence he learned in Hebrew. He hears it read from the Torah scroll in synagogue. He is told of the martyrs who recited it in ancient days or in the death camps of our time.

In this and countless other familiar recitals—in the joy of a psalm or the solemnity of the memorial Kaddish—a Jew does not test by objective reality the validity of the magniloquent religious statements being made about God, His power, and His relationship to the Jewish people. The truth of these statements is attested by their place in Jewish feeling; and this is something which has always enveloped a Diaspora Jew in an absorbing context of kinship and responsibility. In some situations, one expresses this historic kinship in automatic support, in any situation, for fellow Jews in need. But at a different level, one needs words that penetrate to the source of this kinship. A saint or a poet might frame his own words for this; an ordinary Jew reaches out to words that have been heard in Jewish life for thousands of years. One murmurs: "The Lord is my shepherd, I shall not want"; or one surrenders, in bereavement, to the magnificat of the Kaddish: "Glorified and sanctified be His great Name in the world He has created by His will."

Jews are not alone in inhabiting and being governed by a world of myth in this way, where statements of religious mystery are received happily with a compelling emotion that disdains theological clarification. Here is a Christian parallel that comes readily to mind to someone writing in England.

One of the most beautiful buildings in England is the fifteenth-century chapel of King's College, Cambridge. Annually, on Christmas Eve, a service of carols and Bible readings on the Nativity is televised from there and is received by the whole population of this mythically Christian country with an intensity of feeling as compelling, one might say, as that which surfaces among Jews at the Kol Nidre service on the eve of the Day of Atonement. In both cases, the words read or sung have no rational compulsion. On the surface, a carol at Christmas is as far from active Christian dogma as acting in a Nativity play at school at the age of eight. The Kol Nidre prayer—probably the most sacred moment in the whole of the Jewish religious year—simply seeks relief from vows undertaken and unfulfilled. But this is not at all what it stands for. Like the carol service, its power flows from ancient associations,

associations, thoughts, and feelings irreducible to words, Keats's "unheard melodies"—soft pipes that play not to the sensual ear.

But if parallels of this kind can be drawn to show how powerfully the belief in any religion is affected by a world of myth, there are many reasons why the Jews' absorption in their myth had a pattern and intensity all its own through the long centuries of the Diaspora.

In the forefront of this was a social phenomenon: that Jews, uniquely, were literate in the darkest of centuries, employing this literacy—from earliest times and throughout the Middle Ages—to the reading of the Bible and the prayers in whatever situation they found themselves. As wanderers or settlers, all Jews read the same prayers and were taught the same rituals and traditions, with only minor variations. As a result, the myth they were born into was never sectarian or heresy hunting but absolutely solid, making the members of this apparently homeless people at home everywhere with kinsmen who shared their feelings and thus made the myth universal.

Linked to this was the fact that the Jewish religion as practiced was bursting with the most varied and joyful opportunities for fulfillment, day by day and week by week. If Jews were poor and scattered, family life was enriched with Jewish involvement and by the standards of pride and responsibility that had come down with Jewish tradition.

Most pertinent was the paradox that the discrimination—and often the persecution—that was the lot of Jews brought out among them not just defensive qualities of courage and patience but an outlook of self-confidence and enterprise that lived out the inherited tradition with resilience, enterprise, and—where at all possible—with wit. When the Jew drew on tradition to enjoy and act out the beliefs that had come down to him, the world he drew on was rich with imaginative stories that expressed a cheeky kind of familiarity with God, side by side with reverence.

If the traditional Diaspora Jew could accept every doctrine of Maimonides' Thirteen Principles as literally true, surrendering in this way to mysteries about God and the Jews that are beyond comprehension or proof, this mysterious Power was at the same time a Being one could talk to, who had a direct interest in one's success or failure in business, whose presence was vivid in one's life as a friend as well as a judge. The tales that had come down through rabbis or popular preachers took this familiarity to extremes inconceivable in a religion sticking to a credo. One learned through this world of myth of arguments that God had with his direct agents, the angels, in creating the

Universe. One heard of the dramatic scenes in which He had offered the Torah to a whole variety of nations before the Jews accepted it. At the individual level, one was told of argumentative conversations that God had had with Moses, echoing in style, of course, the very "Jewish" argument that Abraham had conducted with God (Gen. 18) to get Him to lower the price for cancelling the decision to destroy Sodom and Gomorrah. Folkstories extended these conversations to bring in rabbis and other favored teachers, very often in humorous ways. And yet this was the same God to whom every Jew turned in prayer and worship: "Glorified and sanctified be His great Name. . . ."

One has to present all these paradoxes to get within reach of answering what sounds like such a simple question: what do Jews believe? We have had to allow for the way religious belief is wrapped up for Jews in family and community associations. This, in turn, has always been affected by the social position of Jews, pulled in opposite directions by the loneliness of discrimination and the delights of kinship. The definition of belief has clearly to be more flexible than one might have thought.

Yet the world they were born into still left Jews with what they felt were straight affirmations. We can consider a telling example of this. Jews talked about God in imaginative fantasies as a friend one could argue with in the most intimate way; but this God could never have been thought of as a Being who could become flesh and blood, and walk on earth in any form whatsoever. Behind all the fantasies lay the concept of an incorporeal Being, whose essence was Infinity and whose purpose was open to Jews only if they could summon up the unity, under Him, of all life and matter, as expressed in the word *Ehad*, One.

A believing Jew always reached out to religious affirmation within his world of myth; and there is a sense in which this has also operated on those Jews who are by nature secularist.

The events of the last fifty years have given a new kind of life to the deep instinctive loyalties that were once embedded in Jewish religious faith and reflected in the mythic experience of being born a Jew. In itself, these loyalties can be thoroughly secular in tone, as they are heavily in Israel itself; yet side by side with this, there has been at least a partial reaching out toward the religious ideas that were once the central issue in Jewish feeling.

This is partly due to the revival of a wide understanding of Hebrew, which allows many Jews today to savor intimately the power of Bible poetry as it was expressed thousands of years ago and to wonder at the impulses which generated this astonishing literature.

But this is only a small element in a revival of religious faith that flows today —even if in limited form—from a reconsideration, forced upon us, of what the Jewish story has meant, and still means, to the world. The innumerable books that now explore the Jewish heritage open up not merely straight history but the ideas and feelings which fed experience in the Diaspora in imaginative and poetic ways that many now understand for the first time. This has certainly happened through the insights of Gershom Scholem into the world of Jewish mysticism. In a different way, one has seen a remarkable new interest, among all kinds of Jews, in the folktales of the hasidic world and in the religious enthusiasm that Hasidism generated—and still does.

Perhaps to their own surprise, many Jews who were previously indifferent seem led today toward an association at the level of faith and ritual with the millions before them who expressed their heritage in this form. Even those who have left most of the practices behind like to feel that they can recapture some sense of the fulfillment that the rituals of Jewish life afforded the faithful.

Rituals

Jews assumed, correctly, that the formal rituals all flowed from the Torah and that this gave them total authority. Even though the rituals were carried out without question, they had a rationale, within Torah terms, that was always fully understood. Readings from the Bible—say, on the observance of the Sabbath or on kindness to the poor—established this, and the devotional meaning of prayers and practices was always liable to be spelled out at length in synagogue discourses by a local rabbi or a traveling *maggid,* popular preacher.

The Judaism of the Diaspora was what we would now call Orthodox, allowing no deviations from the rulings that had been determined in the Talmud and interpreted subsequently by later rabbis. Ordinary Jews never questioned this as the norm, even if many were not always rigorous in observance.

This chapter lists the festivals, rituals, and practices of the year for Orthodox Jews. The Feasts and Fasts are described in more detail in the appendix where some explanation is given briefly of their origins and devotional purposes, though this really requires a book of its own.[5]

The same is true of trying to present a picture of the qualities and attitudes that Jews aspired to, apart from carrying out the formal rituals. One has the feeling that Jews had developed by osmosis, over the centuries, a clear picture of what turned an observant Jew into a really good Jew, an outstanding exemplar of what Jewish teaching intended. Without doubt, the great preachers labored these points, as some of us know at first hand from listening to a classical *maggid* even in our own times.

What one can say, as a generalization, is that Jewish involvement was never a meek or neutral sideline to the business of living, in the way sought by early Reform Jews, attracted by the model of once-a-week church-going Christians. To be a Jew involved political tension, a struggle with the outside world and with one's fellow Jews, lived out in a socioreligious framework that was always full of excitement and could generate danger and joy simultaneously. Even where Jews lived in mass poverty, in Eastern Europe or North Africa or the early slums of New York, the flatness—or hopelessness—of life never extinguished the sense of constant involvement through prayers, festivals, and rituals with the reality of being a Jew.

Prayers

Traditionally, Jews turn aside for formal prayers, either individually or with others, three times a day: in the early morning, afternoon, and evening. As always, there is a Bible verse to go with this: "Evening, morning and noon will I pray and cry aloud; and He shall hear my voice" (Psalm 55:17). The practice was established also as a substitution for Temple sacrifices at these times of the day. The first tractate of the Mishnah opens, indeed, with a reflection of this: "From what time in the evening may the *Sh'ma* be recited? From the time that the priests enter the Temple to eat of their Heaven-offering."*

Recital of the *Sh'ma* is an essential part of the morning (*shahrit*) and evening (*arvit*) services, though not of the late afternoon service (*minhah*). † The *Amidah* (Eighteen Benedictions), special prayers, and psalms are included in all three.

*Strictly speaking, the regular daily sacrifices were only in the morning and late afternoon. The evening sacrifice was a priestly ritual related to purification from uncleanliness (Lev. 22:4–7)

†The Deuteronomy passage (6:4–9) which includes the *Sh'ma* sentence ("Hear, O Israel") calls on a Jew to think of God's commandments "when thou liest down and when thou risest up," that is, evening and morning, leaving afternoon out!

In addition to these formal prayers, a Jew turns to God at many other times in the day. There are private prayers or blessings on waking up or before sleep, set prayers before and after meals, blessings on individual foods and drink, and blessings tailored with great ingenuity to the variety of special occasions that come one's way. On hearing thunder, one blesses God "whose strength and might fill the world"; on meeting a great sage—"who hast imparted of Thy wisdom to them that fear Thee"; on seeing a king—"who hast given of Thy glory to flesh and blood."

For all the eventualities in life from birth to death, special prayers (and psalms) are set out. One of the most intimate, uniting every Jew to the Torah, occurs during the reading of the weekly portions of the Torah in the synagogue service. Before and after each section of the reading, a Jew, "called up" to stand by the reader, blesses God "who has given us His Torah" and "planted eternal life in our midst."

With prayers burgeoning on this scale, their recital can often seem to take on a routine air. Many sections of synagogue services seem to be gabbled through by some worshippers; but this in no way lessens the religious relationship established in these prayers through a joint act of worship in different modes. Some parts of the service are recited loudly and communally, others silently and with an intense concentration called *kavanah.*

The range of feeling is symbolized by two prayers *Kiddush* and *Kaddish,* both words being from a Hebrew root *kadash* meaning *holy.* The *Kiddush,* blessing over wine, is always cheerful; the *Kaddish,* a bereavement magnificat, is always solemn; and this is perhaps a typical echo of the many-sided expression of Jewish religious feeling.

The Sabbath

To rest on the seventh day of the week is the Fourth of the Ten Commandments (Exod. 20:1–17) and has been central to Jewish life throughout the Diaspora.

Observance includes an absolute prohibition of all work, a command which covers the entire household. God had rested, *shabbath,* on the seventh day of

Creation, "blessed the day and hallowed it"; and Jews rejoiced to echo this celebration.

The Sabbath begins just before dusk on Friday evening and ends at dusk on the Sabbath day. Its framework of prayers follows this sequence, and it is during the major service on the Sabbath morning that the scriptural portion is read directly from the Torah scroll.

The Friday evening service includes a famous hymn, *lechah dodi,* which welcomes the Sabbath joyfully as a bride, and this is the mood which is sustained in the home on the Friday evening. Wherever one traveled during the Diaspora centuries, one would know that even in the poorest of homes, the workaday world would have been banished: The table would be spread with a fresh cloth, Sabbath candles would glisten, their light reflected in the cup of red *Kiddush* wine, the *challah* loaf ready for its blessing, followed by the Sabbath meal, perhaps the only good meal of the week, and with guests always welcome.

Returning from synagogue prayers, the father would bless his children with the familiar: "May the Lord bless you and keep you . . ." and then recite quietly to himself the long passage in Proverbs (31:1–31) extolling the virtues of the mother: "A valiant woman who shall find: her price is above rubies. . . . The heart of her husband trusts in her . . . strength and majesty are her clothing, she laughs at the time to come . . . Her children rise up and call her blessed, her husband also . . .."

What is the work that is forbidden? Endless argument in the Talmud refined the rules with the utmost precision. What emerged for ordinary Jews, when ordinary life was possible, was a magic day on which a family could be together, eating good food, singing *zemirot,* songs, enjoying a respite from daily troubles in a spirit of gratitude and holiness.

The Religious Calendar of the Year*

There are three major festivals of the Jewish Year *Pesach* (Passover), *Shavuoth* (Pentecost), and *Succoth* (Tabernacles). All three festivals were linked to the

*See appendix: Feast and Fasts of the Jewish Year for details.

harvest timetable in the Holy Land but also had historic significance. Passover celebrated the Exodus from Egypt, Pentecost the giving of the Torah on Sinai, Tabernacles the years of wandering in the wilderness.

There are memorable features for all these festivals. During the whole of Passover (prescribed in the Bible to last seven days) *matzoh,* unleavened bread, is eaten instead of bread. On the eve of Passover, there is a family feast, called *Seder,* of enormous appeal. The story of the Exodus is told in the *haggadah,* in reply to four prepared questions put by the youngest child present. There is much jollity. Four cups of wine are drunk by each person present; and the prayers and psalms are interspersed with songs.

Pentecost, a summer festival, is enjoyed with flowers and dairy foods. Tabernacles is celebrated by meals held in booths constructed in the garden to recall the temporary dwellings in the wilderness and during harvest time.

The Jewish New Year is held in autumn, which was the time when growth began again in the Holy Land after the droughts of the summer. The first ten days of the New Year are given over to a serious contemplation of one's conduct and the fate that may be in store during the year ahead. The period begins with special celebration of the New Year, *Rosh Hashanah,* and ends with a twenty-four-hour fast called *Yom Kippur.* These grave occasions are known as "The Days of Awe."

There are two important historical festivals in the calendar, both occasions of great joy. The first, called *Hanukkah,* the Festival of Dedication, usually coming in late December, recalls the victories of the Maccabees in 166 B.C. over the Syrians. It is an eight-day feast of lights, with a *menorah,* lamp, containing eight candles. Starting with one candle on the first night, the number lit is increased by one each night until eight is reached. The other festival is *Purim,* Festival of Lots, which comes a month before Passover and celebrates the deliverance of the Jews of Persia from the wicked Haman, as recounted in the biblical Book of Esther.

In addition to *Yom Kippur,* there are other fast days in the Jewish calendar. One is a twenty-four-hour fast in memory of the destruction of the Temple on the ninth of Ab, usually in July, while the others are relatively minor fasts —from sunrise to sunset—for a variety of devotional reasons. There are also days for joyous celebration other than the major ones mentioned above. Some celebrate memorable deliverances; others are associated with the agricultural calendar in the Holy Land or with the new moon.

Imperatives of Personal Life

Sabbath, the festivals, the Days of Awe, and these minor occasions clearly established a strong framework for Jewish living. But with equal or even greater strength, the daily life of Jews reflected ordinances and attitudes existing quite separately from those engendered by the calendar. Formal and informal prayers for all occasions filled a Jewish life; linked to this, there were rules and principles affecting every moment of one's awareness of being Jewish. We can see them, perhaps, under two heads.

The first relates to practices in daily life which had the force of explicit law for a Jew because they had been derived directly from the Bible as interpreted by the rabbis. The outstanding example of this was the elaborate system relating to food and drink, in which what was permitted was *kasher* or *kosher*, correct, while the forbidden was *t'reifah*, abomination. The Bible had laid down precise rules over what meat and fish might be eaten, in Leviticus 11 and Deuteronomy 14. Animals had to have a cloven hoof and to chew the cud (which excluded the pig); fish had to have both fins and scales (which excluded all shellfish). Some fowl were permitted, but no rodents or "crawling things." The method of animal slaughter and the preparation of meat had to take account of an absolute prohibition of consuming blood. In addition, a Bible verse ordering "thou shalt not seethe a kid in its mother's milk"* had been taken to mean that meat and dairy foods (and the dishes they used) had to be kept separate. "Milk" could only follow "meat" after an interval of hours.

In recent times, some apologists for what might seem absurd in these regulations have attempted to show that many of them grew out of useful folk knowledge and that their rigorous observance over the centuries kept the Jews healthy. Whether this has some truth in it is quite irrelevant to the way the dietary laws were followed by traditional Jews and the purpose they saw in them. The laws were observed with the most minute precision because they were God's will, as expressed in the Bible. The purpose was not to make Jews healthy but to make them holy, by which was meant that they enabled Jews, through obedience, to identify themselves with the overall purpose of the Jewish faith—a life of self-discipline as commanded by God.

*Exodus 23:19. The command is repeated in Exodus 34:26 and Deuteronomy 14:21.

Taboos on food were not felt as primitive. They established an area of daily life in which a Jew recognized some things as pure and some as impure. The rationale of the classification might not be understood and did not need to be spelled out (except in synagogue homilies); but the nature of obedience to them was always understood. They were an integral part of the tradition that Jews had been born into. The same complete obedience covered many other rules on personal life drawn from the Bible, such as those separating a wife from a husband during menstruation and the ritual bath, *mikvah,* which formalized the end of the separation. Rules were derived and applied in the same way affecting permitted categories of marriage and the procedures in divorce. If there was an implicit principle behind all this, it was the Bible's rejection of hedonism, spelled out in fierce rules condemning prostitution, adultery, and many other deviations from the straight and narrow path. In everything they did, Jews were guided not to act on impulse (especially the impulse for pleasure) but to be aware of the virtue of acting on principle; and it added authority to the Jewish conception of decent family life to find everything supporting it in the Bible.

This Bible authority was also symbolized in somewhat unusual visible ways. In morning prayers on weekdays, a Jew attached small boxes, *tefillin,* containing Bible texts to arm and forehead by leather straps in fulfillment of the injunction following the *Sh'ma* in Deuteronomy to bind God's commands "as a sign upon thine hand and as frontlets between thine eyes" (Deut. 6:8). Every Jewish home proudly displayed on the doorpost a small case, *mezuzah,* with Bible verses in it, fulfilling the injunctions in the next verse to write these commands "on the doorposts [*mezuzoth*] of thy house and upon thy gates" (Deut. 6:9).

All these and many other Jewish activities were directly based on Bible instructions. But side by side with them were principles of conduct flowing rather from ethical principles in the Bible that grew organically into an integrated Jewish attitude to life.

At the heart of this attitude was a concept of the *mitzvah,* commandment, that went far beyond obedience to a command. A mitzvah became an act of grace, a deed or an attitude that God would like. One looked for a chance "to perform a mitzvah"—an act of honesty, kindness, or generosity in the personal field. The opposite in this field—equally difficult to define—was the commission of an *aveirah,* transgression. This might be an act of slander, revenge, or deceit. One had to fight against this all the time, knowing that one often failed; and when the day of reckoning came on Yom Kippur the prayers set out included a thousand mea culpas in the personal field, an intense expression of what was seen as the truly moral life that Jews must aim at.

Less formally, Jews were identified by certain traits of character which had somehow established themselves in Jewish life. The word *hesed,* loving kindness, which appears constantly in psalms as applied to God was a feeling that Jews felt impelled to strive for themselves. This ideal was reflected in a talmudic saying that Jews have three characteristics: "They are merciful, modest, and engaged in acts of kindness." In the same vein, the twelfth-century philosopher Maimonides said: "One must suspect the Jewish credentials of anyone who is cruel."

The most widely attested characteristic of the Jews was that they had a very strong attachment to family life, showing great consideration to parents, and endless loving—perhaps too much—to their children. As part of this, they put children to Hebrew school from infancy and did everything possible, usually in difficult conditions, to widen the sphere of their education.

All these qualities had made their presence felt in Jewish life in the early centuries and are expounded repeatedly in the rabbinic writings. It was the founding rabbi Hillel who had asserted as the basic principle of Jewish life: "What is hateful to you, do not unto others" (Tal. *Shabb.* 31a), reformulated in the Gospels as the Golden Rule. An anthology of rabbinical sayings known as *Ethics of the Fathers* quoted the rabbis discussing the good life and gave precedence to one dictum: The way to the good life was "to have a good heart." This formula was favored because "it included all the others."[6]

These are all aspects of the heritage that Jews took with them and lived with in the long centuries of the Diaspora.

10

Patterns of Experience

A Search for Meaning

IS IT ENOUGH to say of the Jews that they are possessed by an indomitable will to live? In the course of this book, we have seen the sources of this in ancient times; and we set out in the previous chapter the pattern of life that filled every day of the year with expressions of these beliefs and traditions. But there is one question unanswered: What happened when this pattern of life became a pattern of death?

Until fifty years ago, it would have been wrong to let this question dominate an examination of Jewish history. One certainly knew of suffering and persecution in every one of the preceding twenty centuries, and one could never regard this as a minor—a kind of accidental—aspect of Jewish existence. The Jews had insisted on remaining distinctive, and it was this, in one form or another, that had attracted the distinctive (and usually unpleasant) attentions of the world at large. Spelling this out, one could make a horrifying list of attacks, discriminations, expulsions, and murders surfacing everywhere. And yet this would not have been the true story of Jewish history, for the Jews had clearly risen above these persecutions. They had gone on living; and in this sense the most murderous attacks were, in the long view, peripheral.

Indeed it could have been said, fifty years ago, that the hostile attitude to Jewish distinctiveness was, until that point, part of the armory of Jewish life. Jews, forced to live on the qui vive, had developed an alertness that fleshed out their distinctiveness with enterprise, imagination, and courage. The fact that they, like their ancestors, often suffered for being Jews imputed a sense of importance to their heritage. They never doubted that their history, as revealed in the Bible, had established morality and idealism as the basic tenets of mankind. It could never be—except for the timid—something pale and insignificant. If Jews suffered, it was because there was something powerful in their tradition that made them a focus of attention. They could see a positive expression of this in the cohesiveness, the comradeship, that was always intensified in the shadow of special suffering. And if Jews were so often looked down on, something opposite to this was also true: that in every generation their élite had a flavor which was as distinctive as everything else about the Jews. Against all the contempt and discrimination that seemed to be the fate of Jews, they were heard of, at the same time, in the choicest positions in a country's life, leaders in government, finance, business, and the arts. No one measured out the proportions of this; but it was an evident fact that Jews (or half-Jews or former Jews) were a palpable element in the political and social ferment of the Western and Middle Eastern worlds.

Until the rise of Hitlerism in 1933, Jewish experience was, therefore, a part of the living picture of a very large section of the world. From within, it often sounded like a recapitulation of the Lamentations of Jeremiah; but with the hindsight of history, one can see a constant give-and-take. The expulsions from Spain and Portugal at the end of the fifteenth century had established a rich and cultured Jewish life in the Ottoman Empire. The pogroms of Russia in the 1880s had led directly into the emergence of a vast new frame for Jewish existence in America. At every stage of these and a hundred other migrations there was pain; but life went on.

Suddenly, with the rise of Nazism, it was being decided that Jewish life was *not* to go on. Every Jew within range of Hitler's power was to be annihilated. Even today, it is hard for ordinary men and women to comprehend the scale and character of this operation. One would rather not know that people existed who secured the secret annihilation of six million men, women, and children as an act of government policy, shooting them down in remote woods and ghettoes or herding them for mass murder, with all the efficiency of German power, into the Nazi gas chambers.

One never doubts that this was an act of horror unparalleled in anything one knows in history; but in trying to understand it in the context of a book on Jewish experience, one finds two questions in one's mind: Was it, in some sense, a "logical" conclusion to the unending discrimination and direct persecution that Jews had suffered everywhere in the Diaspora; or was there something in the German setting which was unique and powerful enough to trigger this unprecedented crime against humanity?

A Jew has to ask these questions not from the outside, as an exercise in historical analysis, but from some place within his consciousness as a Jew that will let an answer emerge. Is there any way in which these events can be accepted as consistent with what we have heard for 3,000 years about the interest of the Creator in His chosen people? Is there, after the Nazi experience, any meaning in Jewish history, or must one simply turn to the wall in despair?

Many answers have been put forward by theologians, and these may satisify those who are at home in what often sounds like a particular kind of gobbledigook; but for others, an answer has to come from oneself. One cannot make any demands on God. If, in a posture of self-reliance, one wants, as a Jew, to live with what has happened, there are, I think, two possible attitudes, very different from each other yet in a certain sense not mutually exclusive.

Both attitudes express a reaction to history. In one mood, one lets the factual picture take over, living with it existentially; in the other, one leaves the facts on one side for ideas that one tailors into speculation—not too realistically, perhaps, but with a self-indulgent sense of comfort. Ultimately, both attitudes are undogmatic. If the theologians know what is in God's mind, that is fine. Others accept that Jewish history, like all human history, yields no meaning that can be set out in absolute terms but offers a richness of feeling that surfaces in inexplicable ways as one goes along: *solvitur ambulando.*

To move into this approach, we shall take a bird's eye view, in these last two chapters, of experience in the Diaspora. In the previous chapter, we established what was constant in Jewish experience. Now, we shall look at the varied situations that framed this constancy, discovering that the pattern was far from haphazard. As the center of Jewish life moved from one area to another, there was a progression of experience that was always, at the same time, hostile and creative. These polarized reactions arose most decisively in the setting of Germany; so while the Nazi determination to destroy the Jews reflected sentiments that had parallels everywhere, the character of the destruction there reflected the extreme intensity of attraction and repulsion which had characterized the German-Jewish relationship uniquely.

Death and Rebirth

I accept, then, in the grimness of hindsight, that there was always a diabolic theme working itself through in Diaspora existence toward some explosion that would make every other Jewish suffering look peripheral. In the same breath, I see the emergence of Israel as a miracle unpredictable until it happened and yet foreshadowed in every word and feeling expressed by Jews in the last two thousand years.

One cannot validate wide—or wild—generalizations of this kind in ordinary historical terms; and if they feel true, it is because one is drawing, in this mood, on the speculative attitude where one leaves facts behind and enters the realm of imagination and poetry. Those of us who are not mystical by nature have to stand in reluctant wonder, sometimes, at how vision-possessed men of the past—mystics, Kabbalists, Hasidim—found a framework for ideas about Jewish experience that was wildly divorced from facts as we know them and yet conveyed a meaning that was more logical than this reality. The most sophisticated expression of this attitude emerged in the Kabbalah system projected by Isaac Luria in sixteenth-century Safed. Among these Kabbalists, it was not enough to lament, as all Jews did, the loss of Jerusalem and the *galuth* which followed. Exile was not a political fact; it was a state of being, a disturbance of normality, an echo of a cosmic upset of the universe. How was it that God, whose existence fills the universe, had left a place for man who is not God? It is because God reduced Himself deliberately (this is called *ẓimẓum*), leaving space within His universe—a dark void. In this withdrawal, God exiled Himself, as Gershom Scholem puts it, "into the recesses of His being."[1] In this "exile" of God, the lower "spheres" of the Divine radiance were shattered; and though the husks *(klipot)* represent impurity and evil, they contain also Divine sparks which will ultimately be gathered together to yield the light of the redemption from exile. The Jews were given the Torah by God to be the means by which the primal Fall—God's own exile from Himself—will be reversed.

Leaving aside the minutiae of these ideas, expressed in the mysteries of numbers and (to some of us) endless obscurantist absurdity about man and the universe, one can see the framework as an imaginative paradigm of the agonizing perplexity of Jewish experience. In poetic terms, it magnifies but still lives with the two dominating preoccupations of Jewish experience—exile and Redemption. When Jerusalem fell to Roman attack in A.D. 70, Jews became abnormal in two respects: First, they were to become homeless, without the protection of a government; and second, they were to refuse forever to follow the religious faiths of the countries in which they lived. To be homeless and distinctive turned them into a world people whose exile was to have universal meaning, which is the basic premise of the Kabbalah. To a great extent, the ways Jews were treated could be seen as a living exemplification of the evil expressed in the shattered husks of God's radiance. When this rose to unimaginable heights of horror with the Nazis, it could still be seen, in cosmic terms, as the ultimate realization of the primeval Fall, when God "withdrew into Himself." The creation of the modern State of Israel lies half inside, and half outside, a cosmic plan of this kind. To the supremely orthodox, Redemption—the gathering of the sparks—will come only when the Jews are completely observant of the Torah. To most Jews, something miraculous, close to Redemption, has already happened with Israel. If the ultimate in horror was an overflow of Diaspora history, that history has been reversed—redeemed—by the existence, the status, and the achievements of this Jewish State.

In the Muslim World

With these ideas at the back of our minds, let us now look at Diaspora experience with the other—the matter-of-fact—attitude, following the progression of wanderings and settlings to see if there was some organic movement within the pattern that ultimately brought us to where we are. Even if this is not identifiable, I believe that we will feel a recurrent echo, a repetition of themes that might seem to be vanishing only to reappear on the scene with dramatic impact.

The most startling of these returning themes is the relation of Jews to the world of Islam. Because we normally think of the Diaspora in its Jewish-Christian aspect, we are likely to ignore the fact that it is only in recent centuries that the center of gravity of the Jewish people was in the Christian world. It is, of course, particularly relevant today to consider what was Jewish experience when, for many centuries, the great mass of Jews lived under one form or another of Muslim rule. How do we deal with the paradox that it was only in the twentieth century, when the Jewish people were finally finding what seemed like an assured place in the Christian world, they created the movement that was to make a Near Eastern land once again the center of their passion?

In tackling this question, it might seem enough to consider the position of Jews in the Near East setting after the rise of Islam at the beginning of the seventh century. But this experience was itself profoundly influenced by the fact that when Mohammed began to develop the new faith, Jews had long been established both in the cities of that ancient world and in the huge wastes of the Arabian peninsula.

It was in Babylonia, some thirteen hundred years before Mohammed, that the Jews first became a truly Diaspora people, lamenting their exile in poignant psalms, yet adapting themselves to it with considerable panache. When Jerusalem fell to Nebuchadnezzar in 586 B.C., Jews were already to be found in countries other than the Holy Land; but their expulsion and the resultant settlement "by the waters of Babylon" had a wholly different character. The Jews were largely congregated in their own area; and even if they absorbed a great deal from the new background, they were encouraged to live by and develop their own ancient traditions.

We have little direct knowledge of the large Jewish community in Babylon after Ezra and his followers left in the fifth century B.C. except that it is referred to by classical writers and Josephus as being very numerous. The social material appearing later in the Babylonian Talmud indicates that they were prominent in agriculture; and we know of their Torah studies. From the third century A.D., however, the story of the Jews there begins to float to the surface in the shadow of epoch-making changes in the government of these huge territories stretching from the Black Sea to India.

The Jews often appear this way as footnotes to the decline of one empire and the emergence of another; but these footnotes begin to be significant when they add up to a story of their own. To take a particular example, one looks in wonder at how Babylonian Jewry, which was initiated in the exile of

586 B.C., emerged eight hundred years later (c. A.D. 226) as a participant in the triumphs there of the new Persian Empire, grew in strength—numerically and culturally—for some four hundred years within this empire, and then, after its defeat by the Muslims, went on within the Muslim Empire for another three hundred years as leaders of world Jewry.

The assured position of the Jews had some links to their ancient origin in these lands. They had been established in the Arabian peninsula itself from biblical times and lived from the north to the south as farmers and artisans for the most part. The Arab conquests of the seventh century seem to have stimulated many Jews to move from the peninsula to more metropolitan parts of what had now become a huge empire; and the new conditions of prosperity were undoubtedly one factor in promoting a vast increase in the number of Jews under Muslim rule. The Holy Land, more or less barred to Jews under Christian rule, was now open to them. Egyptian Jewry also recovered and spread westward over North Africa. Arab armies were soon moving all over the eastern Mediterranean and westward into Spain.

It has been estimated that at the beginning of the eighth century, the huge Arab Empire contained more than 90 percent of the Jews of the world, though there is no way of establishing what this amounted to in absolute numbers. Apart from the very large communities of Jews in Babylonia itself, the most important would have been in Egypt and North Africa, Italy, Spain, and Constantinople. The famous Jewish traveler Benjamin of Tudela, who covered much of this ground in a journey of at least five years in the 1160s, gave figures for Jews in the places he visited amounting to more than 500,000. In the view of Salo Baron, arguing that Benjamin might have been able to check about half the population of Jews, the total could have been between 1 and 2 million Jews in the world in the twelfth century, the majority, of course, in Islam-dominated countries.[2] It was in the thirteenth century, he says, that the center of gravity of the Jewish people shifted to Western lands: "With the rest of the population, the Eastern Jewries declined sharply, to be revitalized only under the Ottoman Empire of the late fifteenth and sixteenth centuries."

If the Ottoman period was to give unique advantages to Jewish life, the earlier centuries of Muslim expansion brought their own rewards. In the transition to Muslim rule, it was relevant that the Jews had been numerous and well established, mainly as peasant farmers, throughout the Arabian peninsula. They seem to have been held in esteem, both for their enterprise (Baron adduces evidence that they pioneered new irrigation methods) and for the cultural pattern of their lives. If the Christians were more active in securing converts, Jewish laws, rituals, and ethics were widely respected; and Bible stories, embroidered with rabbinic tales from the Midrash, found a ready public. Mohammed drew on this for much in his new faith, with particular veneration for the Patriarch Abraham and Moses; and he was confident, at first, that this would make it natural for him to secure Jewish support.

One assumes, in fact, that as the faith and the empire spread, many Jews must have been absorbed; but in general there was a stubborn refusal to accept the new prophet. Under the Koran, infidels had to be converted or die; but as Jews and Christians were "people of the Book," which meant that they had holy scriptures which gave them a faith with some common ground with Islam, they were given a protected status, free to practice their religion and have their own leaders, provided they paid special personal and land taxes and accepted a whole range of demeaning social conditions—living in special areas and houses of low height, wearing special clothes, forbidden to carry weapons and to ride horses.

Though the Jews shared this belittling status and many other social and economic disadvantages with Christians, the role of Jews was always far more pervasive and significant. Mohammed had seen this and turned on the Jews with particular vehemence when his overtures were rejected. Like the early Christians, he argued that the Jews had been shown in their own Bible to be evil and that they misinterpreted Scripture. Though all the Bible prophets were important, the true tradition was founded by Abraham and Ishmael.*

Despite the careful definition of the protected and subservient status of Jews (and other scriptured infidels—Christians and Zoroastrians) in the Koran, the outcome was not too burdensome when the caliphate was spreading at an amazing pace through military conquest. As earlier empires had found, it was politic to grant a certain toleration and autonomy to subordinate groups. We are assured by the Arabist scholar S. D. Goitein that "the old legend of the diffusion of Islam by fire and sword has long been discarded";[3] and though "years of rule by a warrior caste" must have brought its terrors,

*He justified his return to what had been pagan worship at the Ka'ba stone in Mecca by claiming that it was founded by Abraham and Ishmael. The idea that the pure Abrahamic religion was superior to the Judaism and Christianity which followed is rather like the early Christian claim that true Christianity preceded Judaism. There has been much scholarly argument, discussed at length by Salo Baron in his *Social and Religious History of the Jews,* vol. 3 (New York: Columbia Univeristy Press, 1959), pp. 266–68 n. 15. on whether Mohammed was indebted more to Jewish or Christian teachings. Baron thinks that "it is next to impossible precisely to segregate the Jewish from the Christian elements in the formation of Islam." But he says that "E. Maintz is right in saying that familiar as Maimonides may have been with Christian teachings, he preferred to turn to Judaism in most matters."

difficulties were undoubtedly eased through migrations, sometimes forced transfers, in other cases voluntary, as when Jews moved from the peninsula to the large cities and also seized the chance to move westward to what became the relative safety of the Holy Land.

Despite the discriminations, the early years of the caliphate were undoubtedly a period of prosperity and expansion for Jews. If they were deemed to be inferior to primitive Arab tribesmen who were now buttressed in pride by conquest, war booty, distinctive dress, and wealth, those Jews who held on to their faith enjoyed equally a new flowering of culture. The heavy tax burden was collected through their own institutions, which enhanced their cohesion. In the migrations of these centuries, they found it natural and useful to play a role sometimes in welcoming or promoting military invasions, as in the Arab conquest of the Holy Land, the whole of North Africa, and ultimately (A.D. 711) of Spain.

At the center of the empire, the ancient community of Jews in Babylonia thronged to the new capital Baghdad after its foundation in A.D. 766. The court of the hereditary Jewish exilarch was maintained for centuries with royal flavor. In the lively air of Islam, in which Greek literature had been resurrected,* Jews were playing their part as translators, philosophers, and scientists. Above all, for the future of Jewish life in the ensuing centuries, the academies of Babylonia were alive with study, in close touch with the resurgence of Jewish study in the Holy Land and in the expanded areas of Jewish settlement in Asia Minor, Egypt, Tunisia, Morocco, and Spain. At the same time, the new stimulus to Jewish life in the Holy Land established and maintained contacts with Jews in the Eastern Mediterranean, Italy, and northward to the small communities of northwest Europe.

How free were Jews under Muslim rule? There is no way of generalizing for the whole of the vast empire, except that in personal relations with their Muslim neighbors there seems to have been little of the built-in hatred among Christians that reflected the stories of the rejection—and the killing—of their Savior. Nor was there, it seems, any of the imputation to Jews of devilish secret practices—the use of Christian blood, the desecration of the Host—that arose among Christians. Even where separateness encouraged hostility, it was not bolstered by the unhappy situation in the medieval Christian world which pushed the Jews heavily, for a long time, into the hated role of moneylenders.

*The translations into Aramaic of classical Greek writings were now translated into Arabic, as a step toward their later translation into Hebrew and Latin (see page 228).

If there were sporadic riots against Jews that could turn into a virtual pogrom (as in the massacre of Jews in Granada in 1066), the normal unruliness of those times posed no special threat to Jews, unlike the situation in the Christian world after the attacks of the First Crusade.

The test of Muslim rule came when their form of toleration gave way to fanaticism, and Jews who would not convert were exposed to a fury as deadly as that of the Crusaders or the Inquisition. An outstanding example of this was an invasion of fierce Berber tribes (Almoravides) into Moorish Spain around 1086, followed sixty years later by the arrival of a sect of ruthless unitarian tribes (Almohads) from the Atlas region. Calling on the "true" teaching of Mohammed, they decreed conversion or death to all infidels. Whatever the terror of the time, one sees this also, historically, in terms of the stimulus those fleeing from persecution could sometimes provide to their new homes. Most of the Jews in Moorish Spain moved north into the Christian areas, resenting the discomforts of refugee status but rising from this to play a fruitful and distinctive role for several centuries in the world around them. Among those who chose to pay a temporary subservience to Islam in order to secure escape southward to Morocco was the family of Maimonides, who was thirteen years old at the time and due to become the greatest Jewish scholar of the Middle Ages.

Inevitably, the records that have come down of Jewish life under Islam in these centuries deal with community leaders—among whom were rabbis, pietists, philosophers, doctors, and financiers—and those who served governments in the highest positions as officials, courtiers, and soldiers. The ordinary people go unrecorded for the most part. One knows only that in every country, life centered for Jews around the religious rituals of home and synagogue, that they pursued education (religious and secular) intensively, and that they lived by their own will close to each other, enjoying a great measure of local autonomy. Of people at the top, whose fame filtered down to the anonymous masses, there is a glittering and endless roll call, including bankers like the great Netira family of Baghdad (ninth to tenth centuries), political and military advisers to the Fatimid rulers of Egypt (tenth century), scholar-poets and soldiers in Moorish Spain, like the Vizier Hisdai ibn Shaprut (tenth century), and the even more powerful Samuel ibn Nagrela (eleventh century).

One marvelous echo of ordinary life surfaced only at the end of the nineteenth century with the discovery of a huge hoard of archives in a genizah (synagogue storeroom) in Old Cairo. From the family papers, scholars have been able to paint a vivid picture of the social and business life of Jews in

North Africa in the tenth century whose trading took them as far as India and China.[4] The archives are in Arabic, which had become for Jews a common language over a huge area, even though the scholars communicated on religious matters in a huge range of rabbinical responsa in Hebrew.

An iceberg tip like the Cairo Genizah reminds us poignantly how much we have lost through the lack of any serious historical writing among the Jews at this time. What we know of them when they were so heavily settled in the Arabic-speaking world arises to a great extent from local regulations or treaties with rulers everywhere, personal letters, and incidental references to contemporary life and politics in religious or philosophical writings. As one would expect, modern scholars have done much yeoman work even with this scanty material in bringing out details of Jewish life in various countries of this huge empire; but the most unusual raw material lies in the poetry that was written by Jews in marvelous Hebrew in Spain during the golden age, ending with the Almohades in 1172. In general, the passion and elegance of Hebrew poetry in many countries during the Diaspora is one element running counter to the false cliché that medieval Jewish life was merely rabbinic and sterile;[5] but nowhere is this more telling than in the chain of Hebrew poets in Spain, echoing Muslim philosophy and social life in skillful Arabic-style versifying, yet expressing at the same time a total involvement with Jewish tradition.

Perhaps we should not be surprised that a people who were originally molded by the poetry of the Bible should continue to express their deepest thoughts in this form, as became evident later in the Yiddish period of nineteenth-century Russia and in the voluminous Hebrew poetry of modern Israel. One theme that surfaced early in this poetry was an expression of the successive migrations and transplantings that characterized life in the Diaspora. In Moorish Spain, for example, we find a very robust and colorful Moses ibn Ezra, born in Granada around 1055, lamenting in verse the endless wanderings following the Almoravid persecutions that took him away from his beloved southland:

> O if indeed the Lord would restore me
> To beautiful Granada, my paths
> Would be "the paths of pleasantness";
> How sweet my life was in that land. . . .

To ibn Ezra, leaving Granada was like being "a prisoner in a jail, like one put away in a grave"; to another poet born a little later, Judah Halevi, one place of "exile" from the Holy Land was no better than another. In one of his many passionate lyrics on Zion, he says (if one may adapt an untranslatable play on words):

> How light in my eyes to leave the bounty of Spain;
> How bright in my eyes the dust of the Shrine again.

Between Two Worlds

Migration was never, of course, a clearly defined shift from one kind of life to something wholly disparate. For one thing, the Jews carried with them their own almost identical carapace of Jewish observance and found many parallels in attitude wherever they went. The interest of every new setting was that it offered Jews infinitely varied ways of adapting these common echoes of a firmly entrenched past.

It is absorbing to see how these adaptations worked themselves out as a continuing story of survival and fulfillment until, in the horror of our time, the pattern seemed to be shattered irredeemably into splinters—like the primeval "breaking of the vessels." The normal Diaspora pattern can be seen in the history of the Jews in Spain, when the golden Muslim age we have glanced at was clearly in decline. First, it renewed itself even more magnificently under Christian suzerainty; then, it was cruelly terminated in a massive governmental expulsion; but after that, it came to life again, bearing the richness of its traditions, both in Muslim and Christian settings.

This was not surprising, because the Spanish-Jewish experience took its form—unlike anywhere else—as a by-product of the long tension between the weakening Muslim and the expanding Christian kingdoms that ended with the driving out of the remaining Moors in 1492. For centuries before that, the Jews, finding themselves increasingly under Christian rule, had been playing an important part in the *Reconquista.*

They had been welcomed in the Christian kingdoms for the many scientific, cultural, political, and military skills that they had developed in the brilliant Muslim setting before it lost its pristine tolerance and power. In many ways, the Christians allowed the Jews to enjoy a new golden age; but it is sad that even when Christian Spain was a relatively open society, with Jews rising to the highest positions in diplomacy, finance, and the arts and with a high standard of living and autonomous government for the Jews as a whole, the underlying anti-Jewish tradition in Christian life began to express itself locally in persecution, riots, and slaughter. In a way that recalls Jewish experience with the fanatical Moors, it was in the passion to convert the obstinate infidel that the breakdown reached its height. Sporadic riots throughout the fourteenth century culiminated in a mass uprising against the Jews in Seville in 1391 after passionate denunciatory Easter sermons. The "pogroms" spread throughout the country with whole communities being slaughtered. The future was clearly bleak, but few could have foreseen its form.

During the century after 1391, riots and slaughter were frequent in a heightened campaign for conversion; and in this period, though many Jews were resolute, masses of their coreligionists did accept conversion, but very often, as was later learned, continuing as secret Jews (nicknamed perjoratively "Marranos") and rising as New Christians to the highest positions in Church and State. But the writing was on the wall for both these kinds of Jews. Those who stayed firm to their faith were finally expelled in 1492 when Spain was at last entirely in Christian hands. The faith of the New Christians began to be subjected, at about the same time, to the rigors of the Inquisition. As against many—perhaps most—who were sincere Christians and had been absorbed into Spanish life, others had indeed clung to some elements in their tradition. In the first session of the Inquisition, in 1481, six formerly Jewish men and women were burned at the stake; and in the years which followed, this number rose to thousands.

Yet large numbers of both these kinds of Jews survived to put down new roots. Those expelled as Jews—some 150,000 in all—suffered agonies of transportation but reestablished themselves to a great extent under Muslim suzerainty in conditions varying from the impoverished ghettoes of North Africa to the growing wealth of Ottoman Turkey, where the sultan thought them very useful settlers. The New Christians, if they survived the Inquisition, used their intelligence and financial connections to escape in large numbers to the Low Countries of Europe, where they lived freely as Jews and took part in the huge development from the sixteenth century on in trans-Atlantic and world trade. Their links with Spanish and Portuguese traders—pioneers in world trade—were as active as before, and to these were now added their family and other connections among the refugees in Italy and the Eastern Mediterranean and in the vastly expanding trade of Constantinople and Salonica.

Before considering the unique effect which these revived Jewish links with Muslim society had on the Jews, we should look briefly at how Jewish life had developed over the centuries in Christian Europe, and moved now into a new phase, helped by the arrival in northwestern Europe of the Jews from Spain and Portugal.

In Christian Settings

When Christianity first came to power under Roman aegis, there was enough bitterness in the situation to lead to much vilification and persecution of the Jews. This factor in the Christian-Jewish relationship was intensified as the centuries passed, though there was no consistency in the nature of discrimination or violence practiced against the Jews.

Christian authorities (popes and bishops) frequently tried to be temperate or judicious on theological grounds in the discriminatory regulations they issued; and many secular rulers (kings or dukes) who found the Jews useful offered them protection—often under charters—against local troublemakers. Too often this had little effect; yet it must be said that until the ferocious outbreak of hostility with the launching of the First Crusade in 1096, the Jews, who were beginning to spread to many parts of Europe, seem to have been able to lead peaceful lives, conducting their business (mostly as traders), practicing their faith, supporting traditional studies, and maintaining active links with fellow Jews in other lands, particularly in the heartland of Jewish religious authority in Babylonia.

In the Holy Land itself the line of hereditary patriarchs that had begun with Hillel and a succession of Gamaliels faded away soon after the beginning of the fifth century. Christian leadership there was hostile; and though the small surviving population began to revive in numbers after the Muslim takeover in the seventh century, the ravages of the First Crusade put an end to any reasonable life there for Jews until the community was revived in the sixteenth century.

In the virtual absence of any good historical records of Jewish life in Europe during the Dark Ages—starting with the fall of Rome to the vandals in A.D. 410—one has simply to assume uncoordinated migratory drives that ultimately gave Jews the position as merchants of which we begin to get clear signs in the ninth and tenth centuries. It is significant, for example, that the ruler of the land of the Khazars—a territory north of the Byzantine Empire between the Caucasus, the Volga, and the Don—converted to Judaism early in the eighth century. This argues for a population of Jews or half-Jews who used this as a base for expanding their trade northward and could thus have helped later to build up the huge Jewish population of Russia and Poland.* One may perhaps see a link to this in the fact that active Jewish trade in western Europe in the tenth century—market day at the great fair at Lyons was changed, because of the Jews, from Saturday to Wednesday—is said to have included the importation of slaves from "slav-land" (Russia).† One envisages traders moving northward up the great rivers of Europe, bringing merchandise from the East and settling quietly in all the growing cities of northern Europe.

As far as one knows, the longest unbroken settlement of Jews was in Italy. In Spain, too, the Jews had been resident from very early times. The harsh regulations against them promulgated in decisions of Church councils had not at first affected them there because the Visigoth Christians followed the creed of Arius, which was more monotheistic than the Trinitarian form established formally at the Council of Nicea in A.D. 325. Before the arrival of the Moors, however, the Visigoths had moved to Roman Christianity and now held doctrinally anti-Jewish views with the vehemence that was to become all too familiar among Church leaders.

An unexpectedly happy setting for Jews, again going back to early times, was in Provence. By the time we hear of them in written records, in the eleventh century, they are settled comfortably in all the old towns like Narbonne and Perpignan, deeply traditional in their passion for Hebrew studies, yet enjoying a comfortable coexistence with their neighbors. To Jews brought up in the sophisticated scholarship of Moorish and then Christian Spain, the Jews of Provence, who knew no Arabic, were woefully ignorant, unable to read the writings in that language on mathematics, science, philosophy, and philology. When a member of the Ibn Ezra family visited them in the middle of the twelfth century he noted this gap and also their passionate desire to be

*Arthur Koestler has indeed argued in *The Thirteenth Tribe* (New York: Random House, 1976) that the East European settlement was overwhelmingly from Khazars. As the Khazars were non-Semitic Aryans, this would make the Jewish people of today, who descend largely from Eastern Europe, Aryan! Scholars are convinced that the settlement was largely from the west, bringing Yiddish with them. See C. Raphael, "Chosen People" in *Times Literary Supplement* (London), June 11, 1976.

†The Jews referred to Eastern Europe, for this reason, as "Canaan," because the Bible had predicted, in patriarchal times, that Canaan would be a slave (Gen. 9:25–27).

introduced to this world of new learning. This was achieved, not long after, by the arrival in Provence of a number of scholars from Moorish Spain (fleeing from Almohad persecution) who set about translating basic works from Arabic to Hebrew. The Hebrew work of these translators (including the famed Ibn Tibbon family) was later translated further into Latin; and this was the channel through which Greek and Arabic literature was fed into European society. It is ironic that a by-product for the Jews of Provence was a series of fierce controversies between traditionalist scholars there and the rationalism revealed in a book like Maimonides' *Guide for the Perplexed,* now available to them.

But it was far to the north, in very different conditions, that influences were being fashioned at this time, which would have profound effects for the future of the Jewish people.

The dramas which were to transform them were taking place mainly in Germany. For several centuries before this, the Jews had begun to put down roots in central and northeastern France. They were active in trade, well housed, and even found as landowners despite repeated attempts by local bishops or secular rulers to enforce adverse social regulations of the Church councils. These tenth- and eleventh-century French Jews are famed particularly for the passion they applied to Jewish study, crowned by the emergence in eleventh-century Troyes of Rashi—acronym for the scholar Rabbi Shlomo ben Isaac (1040–1105)—whose brilliant teaching commentaries on the Bible and the Talmud became standard for the whole of the Jewish people and have remained so until today.

Trade had taken Jews from these areas into the growing markets of Rhineland towns, like Cologne, Mainz, Worms, and Speyer, which also attracted Jewish merchants making their way up the Danube and the Elbe. By the eleventh century they were to be found all over Rhineland and Bohemia in a settled and what one might call a religiously fulfilled life. As part of their acculturation, they were creating a new language, Yiddish, which was based on the language of the Rhineland area, to which they added words and phrases in the Hebrew and Aramaic they knew intimately from the Bible, the prayer book and the legal codes. Yiddish has often been called, pejoratively, a jargon; but to put this into historical perspective it has to be remembered that it emerged just at the time, around A.D. 1000, when a number of contemporary European languages (that is, French and English) were just beginning to take form as amalgams of different sources.[6] It must be said that the warmth of the Hebrew and Aramaic phrases within Yiddish gave the language a unique kind of history-laden intimacy. But the German base also had a great appeal; and it is significant for the early Jewish attachment to Germany that the Jews carried Yiddish with them, unchanged except for some Slav accretions, throughout all their subsequent migrations to East Europe.

It looked—wrongly—as if this rather hopeful putting down of roots might be setting a stable pattern for the future. Wherever there were new military adventures, the Jews were part of the scene, helping the new overlords in supplies and finance, in return for which they had a good deal of protection either within the city walls or in fortress areas outside. From their strong base in France some had gone to England after 1066 in the wake of William the Conqueror and were soon to be found in old towns throughout the country, as far as Lincoln or York. The historian Cecil Roth has said that "the settlement of the Jews in England was the culminating point in the movement which brought the mass of this people from East to West and converted them from Asiatics into Europeans."[7] As it happens, we have better records of the financial role of the Jews in England in the centuries which followed than anywhere else because "England was the most centralized and authoritarian of the West European kingdoms",[8] enforcing the registration of all financial records in documents called "Starrs" (the Hebrew word *shtarot,* means *deeds*) which have survived in large numbers.

A storm sweeping across the whole of Europe was due to break in on this scene, signalled by the slaughters of the First Crusade in 1096 and followed at intervals by a succession of horrors over the next two and a half centuries. That Germany was a main focus of these disasters reflected the very factor in German life—its enormous variety in rule—that had made Jewish settlement there increasingly attractive and successful.

With the collapse of the Roman Empire, the huge lands east of the Rhine had gradually become Christian in ways that held on to deep pagan memories, with local and tribal traditions persisting in government and emotion. If Jews, with their attraction as traders, could move easily between many growing cities all under individual rule, it was still evident that in these intensely Germanic settings they were imperishably identified as alien. In contrast to the position in Muslim and adjacent Christian societies where for centuries Jews had had a unified leadership (like the exilarchs or geonim) that was recognized as almost part of the state system, the government in northern Europe and eastward was, as it were, fractured, making for great flexibility in the early settlement period. Attempts in the north to offer Jews some kind of generalized rights, as set out, for example, in charters granted in A.D. 825 by Louis the Pious (son of Charlemagne and head of the Holy Roman Empire) could never be fully implemented. More typically, we see even in early times the safeguarding of Jewish rights through the emergence locally of prominent Jews who had access to the local authority (prince, duke, bishop) on an ad hoc basis, an obvious forerunner to the "court Jews" of later centuries.

The Jews who settled successfully in these lands in early centuries were not refugees from some specific persecution (a sad feature of Jewish life that was, however, soon to emerge) but rather colonizers with a sense of adventure. A gap had developed which only they could fill. The historian H. H. Ben-Sasson explains it in terms of the breakdown in trade and the distress of Western Europe following the Muslim conquests:

> The conquests of the Moslems and their control of the Mediterranean had cut off the long-standing commercial ties of the Germanic kingdoms in the West. Byzantine animosity to the Western Church and kingdoms, which was steadily increasing, served to complete the isolation. Jews became the international merchants of Western Europe, supplying the luxuries and spices it required and in return exporting the few commodities that were available in Europe to the wealthy territories of Islam. Some of these Jewish merchants settled in Christian lands, others remained in Islamic territory. The ties between them united these trade networks.[9]

Without formal chronicles covering this early phase, the growth and character of Jewish settlement in Germany has to be deduced from various kinds of indirect evidence. One hears of merchants coming together at all the great fairs—"three times a year at Cologne," for example. The intense religiosity of these Jews and their passion for study is reflected by the emergence in Mainz in the tenth century of a rabbi so famous in his authority as to be known as Rabbenu (our rabbi) Gershom, *Me'or Ha'Golah* (Light of the Exile). One knows of the existence of many other distinguished scholars there; but the respect accorded to Gershom was so great as to allow him to feel empowered to institute new *takkanot* (regulations) relevant to the surrounding circumstances, among which was his famous ban on polygamy.

But if the Jews of Germany were thus showing a strong individuality, they still felt themselves linked to the famous centers of Jewish life in far-off Babylonia. Max Weinreich, author of a classical study of Yiddish, points out that the Jews who founded this language and were to carry it across Europe always gave Jewish learning a high priority in their pioneering work as traders.

There were two main trading routes to Baghdad, home of the geonim: one led up the Rhine across the Alps to Byzantium, the other from the Main to Prague, East Galicia, and the Caspian. The Jews, he said, "didn't sit with folded hands, waiting for someone to present them with new means of communication." They were always exploring the possibility of new routes and always with Jewish study as a by-product. "The Jewish merchants carried with them not only furs, silks and spices, but also books and responsa." The drive to Baghdad was to the center of Jewish authority in "Babylon."[10]

No one would pretend that the situation in these areas offered Jews equality and security in modern liberal terms. Life as a whole was insecure; and Jews had a double measure in what might surface in an overflow of Christian animosity. But this had not yet become a dominant issue. Among other things, Jews had a whole range of occupations and had not yet been pushed mainly into moneylending and the merchandising connected with it. All the greater, then, was the shock when violence erupted on a massive scale with the First Crusade.

Martyrdom and Migration

The impetus for the sermon by Pope Urban II on November 26, 1095, which summoned Christendom to rescue Jerusalem came from reports of sacrilege of the Holy Places by Muslims; but when the call was answered, it was the Jews of Europe—and then of Jerusalem—who were to suffer.

It was a decisive moment in Jewish history, painful to follow in detail, but clear in its mounting effect on the position of Jews within Europe for centuries to come. In Christian ideology, the attacks on Jews—offering baptism or extermination—as the Crusaders set out through Europe could be presented as part of the battle for the Faith; in practical terms, it also served as a chance for looting on a grand scale. Within Jewish life, the courage to suffer martyrdom rather than abjure belief was manifested in one city after another as the mobs moved on, preceding or following the Crusaders. And when the immediate dangers had finally subsided, many of the survivors began to migrate toward the east and southeast to find places where life might be more secure. Ultimately, this was part of the drive which took Jews increasingly into Poland in the thirteenth century, laying the foundation there for the building up of what became the heartland of the Jewish people.

Sadly, the formal writing of history begins to emerge soon after this in chronicles recording slaughter or self-immolation in city after city in Germany and Bohemia, and even in Salonica, en route to Jerusalem, where all Jews who could be found were driven by the Crusaders into a synagogue which was then set on fire.

In the story given by the chronicles, we read of fighting resistance by the Jews everywhere before they are overwhelmed; but in the deaths, recorded in many thousands, the emphasis is always on *kiddush hashem* ("sanctification of God's Name"), the belief that the Torah is fulfilled by unwavering courage even to death. Somehow or other, the survivors were trying to find a meaning that could redeem or transform tragedy on this scale. They found it in pride as well as lamentation. Memorial prayers linked the martyrs to Akiba and the other rabbis of the second century A.D. who had defined Roman persecution in the same way. But in its true form, the lament linked itself to the ultimate sadness, the exile of God (as Kabbalists thought) embodied in the primeval Fall. Thus it is not surprising that the sorrows of this time led to the emergence in Germany of a movement known as *Hasidei Ashkenaz* ("the pietists of Germany") whose writings reached out in mystical terms, influenced to some extent by Christian mysticism, toward a view of life that transcends ordinary reason.[11]

The pattern of riots and murders was repeated in successive Crusades launched in 1146 and 1189. In between these outbreaks, life reestablished itself in old or new settlements going further from the Rhineland; but the twelfth century as a whole saw anti-Jewish feeling take root in insidious forms throughout Christian Europe.

Historians have noted that the mob violence of the First Crusade reflected an increasing Christian fanaticism among the masses, stimulated by monkist orders. It was also the time when Jews began to bear the brunt of intense dislike as moneylenders. Jews had lost out to Christians to some extent in international trade; and the encouragement by Christians of a growing trade with the Muslim world had reduced the cash available for internal uses—the clearance of forests, the needs of the woolen trade, building, court and military expenses, and consumer goods. This became an area open to Jews, who had no natural position in feudal society and who were less affected than Christians by the Church's ban on interest. Moneylending led the Jews into profitable (if demeaning) trade in the valuable chattels (owned or stolen) which they took as pledges. In various countries Jews were regarded as agents (virtually the property) of rulers, acting for them in tax-collecting and due at any time to transfer to them the title to debts.

In England, this process, which led to great wealth being owned by a few Jews, began to gather strength in the twelfth century; and it was part of the background which persuaded the rulers to seize their wealth and expel all Jews in 1290. In some ways this was only a culmination of growing Jew-hatred, which had led to the emergence in 1144 of the blood libel and a series of violent attacks.* Something similar was happening in France, where, after sporadic persecution, Jews were finally expelled by edict—first in 1306 and finally in 1394—from the whole area around Paris under royal control. In Germany, because Jewish occupations were more varied, moneylending did not become dominant until the thirteenth century, and there was never any general expulsion. The Jews had great freedom to find new homes in different cities under different rulers; and this flexibility, with its great potential for good living over the vast area known as "Ashkenaz" (the name of a biblical people mentioned in Genesis 10 which Jews had come to apply to Germany) was partly why German life had a strong hold on Jews for centuries to come.

This is not to ignore the religious and social tensions—rising frequently to riots and slaughter—to which the Jews were subjected in German-speaking lands in the thirteenth century. The Church itself was playing an aggressive role as part of its war against heresies within and outside its own ranks. Among the regulations of the Fourth Lateran Council of 1215 was the institution of a special distinguishing mark for all Jews (it became a yellow badge) to maintain apartheid. Jews were denounced not just for usury but for their devotion to the Talmud, which was held to be immoral and blasphemous. Side by side with the mainstream loyalty of Jews to their faith, there must have been also in this situation a great mass of converts to Christianity. In the public disputations on the Talmud to which Jews in a number of countries were summoned—the first was in 1240—the expert witnesses against it were inevitably apostate Jews; and after the forseeable verdict, the Talmud would be burned.

Yet it would be wrong to ignore the desire to protect the Jews offered by

*The body of a Norwich boy, William, was found there on Easter Eve, 1144, and the story spread that he had been killed by Jews so that they could use his blood for Passover rituals. The riots which followed were repeated in many countries when this monstrous libel took hold. In England, a bitter memory was left from the drama of York in March 1190. During riots, the Jews had taken refuge in the royal castle but decided, after what must have been intolerable pressure, on mass suicide, a horrible but passionately held expression of *kiddush hashem*.

the Church in many situations. The most dramatic effort was in the aftermath of the Black Death, in 1348–49. For fifty years before this, the anti-Jewish actions had been mounting in force. When the plague began to rage through the whole of Europe, wiping out towns and villages on an unprecedented scale, the Jews were picked out as the scapegoat. It was said that they had been poisoning wells in order to wipe out the whole of Christendom. Pope Clement VI spoke out vehemently against this, pointing out that the plague raged where no Jews existed and that where they were to be found, it struck down Jew and Christian alike. This rational argument had no effect; but it is typical of the mixed attitude to the Jews that has characterized all history, with intelligence and goodwill forced to fight—usually in vain—against deeply ingrained superstition and hate.

11

The Dynamics of Jewish History

New Horizons, East and West

T MIGHT have seemed at this stage in Jewish life that much of its creative spirit was being stifled, with little hope for the future. In northern Europe, expulsions and persecution were driving many Jews toward unknown lands eastward; in southern Europe, conversion and a major expulsion in 1492 were already casting a baleful shadow. Yet by the end of the fifteenth century, the Jews were launched toward an intensification and expansion of their life in positive terms that would have been unimaginable earlier.

The drive eastward had taken Jews to Poland from the thirteenth century. In the wake of Tartar invasions, unsuccessful but devastatingly destructive, there were huge territories for settlement and colonization. German merchants and craftsmen were invited in warmly by Polish rulers; and Jews, also included, had their rights guaranteed by a charter of 1264, reaffirmed and extended by Casimir the Great in 1354. Inevitably, many Church-stimulated accusations and persecutions followed; but Jews were soon settling in rapidly increasing numbers in cities throughout Poland and Lithuania, where they lived by choice in their own quarters as merchants, craftsmen, and financiers. They lived also in villages or concentrated Jewish settlements which their descendants came to know as *shtetls*.

From the beginning, Jewish life in Poland and Lithuania produced a self-sustaining cultural independence that had not been seen in this form before. In the golden ages of Babylonia and Spain, Jewish culture had flowered with a considerable relationship to the non-Jewish world. In Poland, for three or four centuries at least, the rapidly growing communities forged ahead in their own terms. They spoke their own language, Yiddish; and although they had a lively business relationship with the non-Jewish world as traders, craftsmen, innkeepers, credit merchants and sometimes as tax agents, their whole ethos was Jewish. Their religious and social life was all-absorbing. They showed a passion for Jewish studies—particularly the Talmud—without reference to the cannons of scholarship and science that had been displayed by Jewish culture under Muslim rule. Their communities, which were self-governing, soon developed representative councils covering the country. It all seems inward-looking; yet this culture was due to be transmuted with an explosive cosmopolitan character that was to be a hallmark of Jewish life in later centuries.

A special feature of the new life in Poland was the role of some Jews as administrators of the large estates of noble landowners, and in particular of the vast empty areas of the Ukrainian steppes that fell firmly under Polish rule in the sixteenth century. Following the pacification of the area, the peasantry had to be put to work in new settlements on cultivation and forestry; and the large-scale financing required for this came from the Jews. In the same way, the forests to the north were being administered by Jewish experts to produce a flow of timber to western Europe. The nobleman tended to concentrate on his military and social roles, with Jews left in sole authority (sometimes as financial partners) to administer the vast complexes of small towns, villages, and estates.

While this led to the creation of sizable wealth and in some cases great fortunes for enterprising Jewish administrators, it was also liable to stimulate Jew-hatred among the serfs, especially as the Jews were also entrusted very often with unpopular duties as collectors of taxes. Jews considered the pros and cons of these new developments at meetings of their councils; but they clearly brought much economic benefit. With great significance for the future, Jews handling the export of agricultural produce on a very large scale to the West found themselves dealing often, in Germany, with Jewish importers, agents of the enormous variety of princelings of that land. These contacts must have helped to lay a base for the pull that cultured and prosperous Germany was to exercise later on many Jews of Eastern Europe.

There would always be tension between these two worlds; the East European Jews, powerful in numbers and vitality, yet shut off to a great extent in a medieval world; and the German Jews in a world of increasing sophistication and modernity. But if there was tension, there was also a constant cross-fertilization. Many ardent Jews of Germany saw the rapidly burgeoning Jewish centers of Eastern Europe as the locus of infrangible Jewish authority; to the Jews in Eastern Europe, Germany was to emerge as dangerous for the faith but at the same time a lodestar.

New Life in the Near East

The dynamics of Jewish life were at work in a different way in the Near East, with the Ottoman Empire as the locus of a new kind of regeneration.

To some extent, there was a parallel to what had happened when Jews, moving from central Europe toward Poland in the thirteenth century, had put to good use skills and cultural confidence nurtured originally in Germany. The same was to happen, but in a more sophisticated way, when the Jews who had been expelled from Spain and Portugal were able to settle in large numbers in the Ottoman Empire at the end of the fifteenth century.

When Constantinople fell to the Turks in 1453, the new masters of the vast Byzantine lands saw a need to welcome outsiders like the Jews to help them make the most of their new empire. The Turks had been brilliant in the military field but needed Jews, Greeks, and Armenians to develop the new trade potentials that would transform the economics of medieval life. They also needed men with professional skills—scientists, inventors, financiers, scholars, doctors, and administrators, all to be found in considerable number among Jews who had filled these roles for some centuries under the aegis of the Moors and Christians of Spain and Portugal.

In the first phase, the Jews who fitted into this stirring society were those who had remained staunch to their faith and had to make their way toward the Bosphorus under desperate conditions after the expulsions from Spain (1492) and Portugal (1497). Soon after, they were joined—and overtaken in power and style—by Marranos who arrived by diverse routes determined to return openly to Judaism. If differences had existed in the past between these two kinds of Jews, they were at one now not just in skills but in their undying —if ironic—attachment to their lands of origin. There was soon a great proliferation of communities, with Jews active in the huge trade now developing (Salonica, bursting at the seams, was to all effects a Jewish city) and in industry, medicine, and diplomacy. But if the new arrivals were immensely innovative, everything they did carried a continuing echo of life in the old lands. It was a style which they imposed automatically, with effortless self-confidence, on all the other Jews of the area. They were an elite, full of lamentation at what they had lost but emerging in the new situation with a bravura that was in fact more creative than the life they had left behind.

They had always been known as Sephardi Jews: Sepharad was the name of a region in the Bible (Obadiah) which had somehow been applied to Spain, as Ashkenaz had to Germany. Wherever they were now, they held on passionately to the Sephardi ethos, expressing it in language, dress, songs, folktales, religious rituals, and family connections. In some ways, their truly Spanish pride was too rigorous and antiquarian; but it sustained them with its discipline and carried them forward into new developments.

One immediate consequence of their new situation was a greatly increased interest in the Holy Land, now so close to them physically and within the rule of the empire in which they lived. The relatively few Jews living there had fallen into low estate, but now immigration was stimulated and practical schemes launched, including a highly imaginative project undertaken by Joseph Nasi, the most prominent Jew in the Ottoman Empire. In the spirit centuries later of Baron Rothschild of Paris and Sir Moses Montefiore of London, he concentrated on a practical idea: the rebuilding of Tiberias on the shores of Lake Galilee and the founding there of a silk and textile industry to provide an economic base for newly arriving immigrants. It is typical of the efflorescence of Jewish life in this setting that Joseph, whose family had been rich and distinguished in Spain and Portugal, with huge international banking connections in the Low Countries and elsewhere, was able to harness support for his Tiberias plans from communities in Italy and indeed all over the Mediterranean.*

The intense attention that was being given to practical developments in the Holy Land was only one aspect of the impact on Jewish life of the newly invigorated Sephardi communities of Turkey and the eastern Mediterranean. An even more important consequence for the future—and very moving in how it came about—was a spiritual movement that suddenly emerged in messianic and mystical forms in the Galilean hill town of Safed.

This story shows how deeply embedded the messianic idea was—and perhaps still is—among Jews.[1] The fall of Constantinople in 1453, in which Byzantine government had been overthrown, had seemed to some Jews to carry supernatural overtones, perhaps heralding the Messiah. Far more direct in its influence was the Jews' expulsion from Spain and Portugal. An upheaval on this scale surely indicated the birthpangs of the Messianic Age. A number of eloquent chronicles written by children of the refugees—notably *Consolations for the Tribulations of Israel* by Samuel Usque and *The Vale of Weeping* by Joseph ha-Cohen—reveal the intensity of the feeling. Don Isaac Abrabanel, a powerful financier who was also a profound Hebrew scholar, was more explicit in trying to persuade Sephardi Jews in a number of his books that the arrival of the Messiah must now be imminent. In one interpretation of Daniel, he gave the date of arrival as 1503!†

These messianic ideas took two interrelated forms. At the simplest level, one awaited a marvelous man who would appear and lead the Jews—and the world—to salvation. More profoundly, one had to commit oneself to a spiritual

*Joseph, who was created Duke of Naxos, had almost a royal status. His family, Miguez, had fled from Spain to Portugal and been forcibly converted to Christianity in 1497. His aunt (and mother-in-law to be), Beatrice de Luna, had married into the Mendes family, famed as international bankers and dealers in gems. Joseph took part in major international political affairs, both as adviser to the sultan and in his private role, negotiating with the Netherlands and Venice and doing everything he could throughout Europe to help Jewish communities in trouble with local rulers.

†Samuel Usque was a Hebrew and classical scholar whose family fled from Spain in 1492. His *Consolations,* written in Portuguese and published in 1552, takes the form of a pastoral dialogue discussing the great events of Jewish history, including the expulsion from Spain. His aim was to persuade Marranos everywhere to return to Judaism. Joseph ha-Cohen, whose parents fled from Spain to Avignon and thence to Genoa, included in his book *Emek Ha-bachah* (written in Hebrew and published in 1558) an account of Joseph Nasi's rebuilding of Tiberias. Don Isaac Abrabanel (1437–1508) was one of the most remarkable of the leaders of Spanish-Portuguese Jewry. As scholar, philosopher, statesman, and financial adviser to King Alfonso V of Portugal, he tried desperately to get the expulsions stopped. After he failed, he traveled through Europe in great status but finally gave all his attention to his Hebrew books, believing that earthly power must give way to the Messiah. His works contributed to the powerful messianic movement among Jews in the sixteenth and seventeenth centuries.

process of the most extreme piety that would bring about the restoration of the universe in cosmic terms. It was this second approach that started in Safed in the middle of the sixteenth century by the arrival there of a visionary called Isaac Luria. He had been born in Jerusalem (of Ashkenazi extraction) in 1534 and had absorbed the kabbalistic ideas that had developed in Spain around a work called The *Zohar.** After an early life as a hermit (and also a poet), he moved to Safed, where bands of disciples gathered around him, responding to the extraordinary power of his visions and the detailed kabbalistic ideas that surfaced through him. This was not a rejection of Talmud legalism; within a few years there were eighteen yeshivot (Talmud colleges) in this tiny town; but in a wholly different approach his followers also sought, through kabbalistic interpretations of the Bible and of life itself, to reach a higher level of existence in mystical communion with the Creator. When a self-proclaimed messiah called Sabbatai Zevi appeared—and won wide support—more than a hundred years later, it was within the context of the Lurianic teachings that had spread over the whole of the eastern Mediterranean.†

The centers of Jewish life seemed to be moving eastward, and with a strong interconnection; for the swiftly expanding Jewish community of Poland began to send pilgrims and settlers to the Holy Land, and the Polish rabbis, for all their passion for Talmud, were also profoundly interested in Kabbalah. Yet side by side with this eastward movement, a move westward had also been launched, which would in time envelop and transform the whole Jewish people.

It is easily memorable that 1492, the year of expulsion from Spain, was the year in which Columbus discovered America. Within a short time, Cortes had conquered Mexico (1520) and the new empires of Spain and Portugal were launched, with the strong interest, certainly, of some Jewish or Marrano sailors, traders, and financiers. More significantly, the refugees from Spain and Portugal had been establishing themselves during this time in the Netherlands, where they were free to resume Judaism. By the end of the sixteenth century, Jews were part of an active network of trade stretching from the ports and business centers of northwest Europe to Italy, Salonica, and further afield. These trade connections were due to become important when the Dutch and

*The *Zohar* was a mystical work supposed to have been written by a second-century rabbi called R. Simeon b. Yochai but is now thought by scholars to have been composed by a thirteenth-century Spanish mystic called Moses de Leon. It had made its way from Germany via the Jews of Provence.

†Gershom Scholem's great work *Sabbatai Sevi: The Mystical Messiah 1626–76* (London: Routledge and Kegan Paul, 1973) gives an unforgettable picture of the whole background.

British became active in the western hemisphere. The Jews were first heard of in South America and the West Indies, but in 1660 they set foot in New York City (then New Amsterdam), and the door to the West was clearly open.

Though this early incursion was small, it confirmed the pattern that had already been emerging, in which the Jews of the Diaspora showed that as part of a living and expanding world, they were always to make the most of their experience, unless some malign force set out to destroy them. And even when this happened, the vitalizing principle would still display itself at work.

The Paradoxes of Emancipation

In this bird's eye view of how the Jews changed their main centers of settlement in recent centuries, we are not offering any detailed picture of the cultural content of their lives in the various areas in which they lived. The common factor everywhere was the practice of Judaism. Beyond this, the variety of living was enormous.

As two extremes, one might think of sixteenth-century Poland, where a rapidly increasing population lived wholly Jewish lives, and Renaissance Italy, where Jews absorbed and contributed to every aspect of the culture around them. Polish Jews were renowned, above everything, for their great talmudic skills; Italian Jews were famed in medicine, active in social life, and included philosophers, musicians, dancing masters, poets, actors, and playwrights.

No contrast was, in fact, as black and white as this. The Jews of Italy had many outstanding Talmudists. In Poland, the rabbis were never content to be excluded from philosophic argument. Students of the rationalist Rabbi Moses Isserles (1520–70) were accused by an unbending traditionalist, Solomon Luria, of "using the prayers of Aristotle." Isserles' disciple Abraham Horowitz (d. 1615) argued for wider studies in order to create better understanding in the world around them: "If we know no more than the Talmud we shall not be able to explain the ideas and methods of the Talmud in a way that Gentiles will like."

Nor did Poland offer a wholly poor and dangerous life compared with the light and grace of Italy. There was to be a turning point for Poland in 1648;

but until then, Jews were engaged in every occupation, breeding horses and cattle, busy in agriculture, mining, and finance, and active in large-scale trade internationally, with land routes between Christian Europe and the Ottoman Empire. It was usually at the great trade fairs that they held meetings of their autonomous land councils. Above all, it is significant that by 1648 this community, future heartland of Jewry, had grown to around 300,000.

The turning point of 1648 began with the massacre of Jews in the Cossack uprising led by Bogdan Chmielnicki, followed by a series of Polish wars for thirty years with Tartars, Swedes, and Russians. Superficially, a kind of inertia seemed to set in. Many Jews lost heart and began a trek westward. Yet one sees with hindsight that the Polish-Lithuanian heartland was gaining much more than it lost. Within little more than a century, the population had grown to 750,000. This was now much the most populous center of Jewish life, "seething with excitement and movement," to quote one historian,[2] as it worked its way in the eighteenth century toward the challenges that would come with "modernity." Before this stage was reached, there were great issues to be dealt with as legacies of the past. The messianic ferment aroused by Sabbatai Zevi in the 1660s left an abiding mark on later generations, with wild neo-Sabbateans of the Frankist movement attacked by heresy-hunters. In the same primitive area of Podolia in southern Poland, in the first half of the eighteenth century, the simple pietist Baal Shem Tov began to attract a rapidly growing following of Hasidim, through which many thousands of Jews came to reshape their lives in total obedience to, and love of, their chosen "masters." In fierce opposition to this, the Gaon of Vilna—a great Talmudist called Rabbi Elijah b. Solomon Zalman (1720–97)—urged the importance of rational study and responsible judgment through which we reach the full potential of our human existence.[3] This argument between Hasidim and mitnaggedim (opponents) was perpetuated by family loyalties, but in a deeper way it foreshadowed issues that were to be pursued in many forms in succeeding centuries—the gap in approach between the rational and the mystical, expressed sometimes in the conflict between the religious and the secular view of Jewish life. In turn, it was to be straddled by the crucial argument that developed—all from this cradle of Jewish existence in Eastern Europe—between those who saw political emancipation as a road to a free life as citizens of Diaspora countries and those who believed that freedom for Jews would emerge only in terms of a new free life in the ancient Jewish homeland.

If the year 1492 signaled both the end of the great Spanish era and the first faint hint, in the voyage of Columbus, that Fate (or Providence) would one day offer a locale to replace this, the death of the Gaon of Vilna (1797) in the first decade of the French Revolution was equally symbolic for the new life that might now start for Jews in the context of general emancipation. In more immediate terms, it was the beginning of the era in which Napoleon's armies, achieving momentous victories in Italy and Austria, were, for a time, to express the political liberation of the masses of Europe.

By this time, the great Jewish community of Poland-Lithuania had fallen into new hands. By the three Partitions of Poland, starting in 1772, the Jewish area was now mostly part of czarist Russia, while the other areas containing Jews were part of Prussia or Austria. It is typical of the irony of Jewish life that Jews were among the most fervent supporters of Polish nationalistic revolt, a reflection of the ardent nationalism that was to be the outstanding feature of nineteenth-century Europe.

For Jews themselves, it was to signal, in the birth of an official Zionist movement toward the end of the century, a form of nationalism that would transform them forever. But before and after this happened, the Jews were also caught up by the appeal of patriotic nationalism in every country in which they lived.

In many ways, this was to produce a richly rewarding life combining security with adventure. After an initial retreat in some countries from Napoleonic liberalism, political emancipation for Jews began to gather force everywhere, with even some glimmerings in czarist Russia. But a dark force lay in wait as a product of the same exciting nationalism. The more Jews were given equal political and economic rights and went on from this to identify with the nationalism of the countries that had now opened the way to freedom and prosperity, the more opposition they encountered from those who found the Jews ineradicably alien. There was no common pattern for this. It could be detected everywhere, but was particularly virulent, of course, in Germany, where it was to end in unexampled tragedy.

The reason was that in this setting, attraction and repulsion operated with extreme power. From the early Middle Ages, the Jews settled in Germany had found it deeply appealing despite the many painful experiences that befell them. When life in Eastern Europe lost much of its security after 1648, many Jews drifted back toward Germany; and their numbers increased when Jews were absorbed in Prussia and Austria after the Partitions of Poland. In the nineteenth century, Germany took a leadership in science, scholarship, industry, and literature that Jews found almost irresistibly attractive. Socially, they were kept firmly at a distance, and many thousands of Jews tried in this situation to bridge the gap through baptism and total acculturation.

By the end of the nineteenth century, the appeal of all things German to emancipated German Jews had a unique power. Gershom Scholem, the great Jewish scholar who had himself been born in Berlin in 1897, said of the German language that "it bestowed the gift of unforgettable experiences: it defined and gave expression to the landscape of our youth." He saw that there were good historical reasons for the hold that Germany had on Jewish feeling. When emancipation began, he wrote,

> It was German culture the Jews first encountered in their road to the West. Moreover—and this is decisive—the encounter occurred precisely at the moment when that culture had reached one of its most fruitful turning points. It was the zenith of Germany's bourgeois era. One can say that it was a happy hour when the newly awakened creativity of the Jews . . . impinged precisely on the zenith of a great creative period of the German people, a period producing an image of things German that, up to 1940, and among very broad classes of people, was to remain unshaken, even by many bitter—and, later, most bitter—experiences."[4]

It is clear that it was the very strength of this attachment that was intolerable to Germans who decided that it was grafting a horribly alien quality onto a racial purity going back to pagan times. Pagan was the key word; for looking back one cannot help seeing everything that happened as a rejection of civilized life in order to worship at the primitive shrines of this paganism. Anti-Jewish feelings had surfaced repeatedly for centuries; but when it was finally molded into government policy by the Nazis, it was expressed with the passion that had once led primitive peoples to exult in slaughter. Yet even this does not cover what happened; for whereas the exultant slaughters of ancient times were conducted in the heat of battle, man to man, the Holocaust was carried out with the cold precision of an industrial process, in which objects are handled by machinery. And whereas the old battles led to the deaths of enemy soldiers numbered in thousands, here the human beings to be destroyed by direct and deliberate action were men, women, and children numbered in millions.

The Forces of Regeneration

A Jew contemplating this tragedy can find no words to describe the weight of its impact. But in thoughts that rise to the surface, one stands amazed at the power in Jewish life that generated new vitality even when these horrors had taken place. Moreover, one sees that what emerged followed a pattern that has already been demonstrated in this story, with every successive center of Jewish life creating a potential of enterprise, imagination, and idealism that arises in new forms when a new balance emerges in Jewish life.

One sees this demonstrated in the immense shift from the position in the nineteenth century, when there were two major centers of Jewish life. The first, obviously, was in Eastern Europe. At the end of the century where were some 5.2 million Jews in Russia, despite emigration. If one adds in Rumania, the total was nearly 5.5 million. Eastern Europe was a unique center of Jewish life, with its own language, Yiddish, and a whole culture centered around it.

The other area that has to be considered as basic to Jewish life, though in a very different way, was Germany, with the very large Jewish population of Austria-Hungary spanning the two. There were some 520,000 Jews in Germany in 1900. Austria-Hungary had more than 2 million, a large part Yiddish-speaking Hungarian Jews. Together, there were clearly more than 6 million Yiddish-speaking Jews in Eastern Europe at the end of the nineteenth century, and perhaps 1 million German-speaking Jews in Germany and Austria.

At this time, there were 1 million Jews in the United States. Today it has become the largest center, with some 6 million Jews. If one talks of the Americas as a whole, the total is about 7 million, with half a million in Argentina and some 300,000 in Canada.

The other main center of Jewish life today is, obviously, Israel, which now has a population of nearly 3 million Jews. In numerical terms, the USSR is close to this, with some 2.6 million registered as Jews in the system they use, but Russia cannot be considered a center of Jewish life in the sense we are using here.

There are, of course, important communities of Jews in other countries, all with features of great interest. The leadership of the British community, which now numbers something over 400,000, reflected at the beginning of the century much of the prestige (and stuffiness) of Victorian England, and it probably still has something of this character. In size it has been overtaken since World War II by French Jewry, partly because of the immigration into France of many North African Jews, who had full French citizenship under the old French colonial system. The number of Jews in France has grown from 260,000 in the mid-1930s to 535,000 (the 1967 figures), and there has been a notable resurgence of Orthodoxy there.

Holland had a unique role in Jewish history in the seventeenth and eighteenth centuries as a channel through which a number of leading Jewish families (many of them Marranos) played an important part in opening worldwide trade and finance. It was helped in this by the proximity of Hamburg and other active Jewish centers. Today, the Jews in Holland are a very small community, having shrunk in size from 112,000 in 1930 to about 30,000. Numbers alone do not always signalize, of course, the value of inner activity. One does not hear much, in the ordinary way, of the half million Jews in Argentina, except for their active concern with Israel. There are some 115,000 Jews in South Africa and 70,000 in Australia; but more significant than all these, perhaps because of their strong links with the United States, are the Jews of Canada, who number today nearly 300,000. This brings us back to the main point: that for the Jews in the Western world, the center of Jewish life has now shifted from Europe to the United States and Israel.

How did this enormous change in the balance of the Jewish people come about, and in what sense, particularly, can it be seen as generated organically by the character of life in the earlier centers, which we have characterized here as Eastern Europe and Germany (or German-speaking Europe) respectively?

It is in relation to building a major community in the United States that we have to consider, first, the influence of German Jewry. Early in the nineteenth century, the qualities from what Scholem called "the zenith of Germany's bourgeois era" began to be transmitted to America by a wave of German-Jewish immigrants. If they were mostly poor, they usually came with some cash; but more important, they came with pride and confidence, and they seem to have had a good basic education. Those who were enterprising enough to find a part to play in the opening up of America and thus became the founders of legendary fortunes remained loyal in their own way to the formal, rather stiff Judaism they had been taught in childhood. By the 1880s, when hordes of immigrants began to pour in from Russia, America's German-Jews shuddered a little but rallied with wealth and responsibility to take the lead in the sustenance and education of these strange fellow Jews. In the hundred years since then they have not simply grown enormously in wealth and social acceptability, but continued to present, rather dully but virtuously, the uprightness and solidity which was their hallmark from the beginning. In a major way they have transmitted the best side of German bourgeois culture to the United States and its Jewish community.

Very different has been the contribution of the immigrants from Eastern Europe, whose descendants constitute far and away the largest element in American Jewry. The signal for the first waves of these immigrants was given by pogroms which broke out in Russia in 1881, sending a feeling of horror through the Jewish world. But if this signal was in the forefront, beneath the surface the stimulus was to escape from poverty, which was endemic in Eastern Europe and a pointed contrast to the chances open in the "golden land" of America. Though the United States was the main target, other western countries (including South America) also received large numbers of Jews. The scale can be seen in the astonishing fact that between 1890 and 1914, some 30 percent of all East European Jews changed their residence to some overseas country.

Between 1880 and the end of open immigration to the United States in 1925, some 2.4 million Jews had arrived. In this period, the total Jewish population of the country grew from 280,000 to 4.5 million.* Jewish life had undergone a revolution in the process. In this new huge homeland, first-generation immigrants from Eastern Europe developed what was virtually a new Yiddish culture. The second and third generations have drawn from this and from their now native American sources an amalgam of enterprise and culture that reflects the flavor of Jewish loyalty and tradition to an intense degree even if it is, at the same time, wholly typical of the open, mobile civilization of America.

What is magical in this move of Jewish life to America is that it drew on and validated the native intelligence, the originality, and the idealism which had battled for expression in Eastern Europe but was never able to find the forms for full realization. It has come to us in recent years—perhaps as an aftermath of the Holocaust—how vibrant life was in *der heim,* the old homeland. In no sense must it be idealized, for in experience it was, for most of the six million Jews of Eastern Europe, a life of extreme hardship. But it had unique qualities that now, at this distance, we feel called on to admire. Most particularly, it is immensely revealing to see how much of the astonishing

*Salo Baron, "Population," *Encyclopedia Judaica,* vol. 13, cols. 866–903. He points out, however, that in many countries, including the United States in that period, the figures on Jews could never be accurate because of census difficulties and Jewish ambivalence sometimes in answering questions on whether one was Jewish.

achievement of American Jewry had its roots in the strange culture of the Jews of Russia. Much of this world has been relayed to us in a flow of absorbing books. It is a living tradition that still sends us its echoes directly through translations of Yiddish stories and poetry and in a more transfused way through the writings of Isaac Bashevis Singer.

Irving Howe, who said, in his classic *World of Our Fathers,* that the Jews of Eastern Europe were a nation without recognized nationhood, evokes brilliantly the mixed elements in their life: "they were bound together by firm spiritual ties, by a common language, and by a sense of destiny that often meant a sharing of martyrdom."[5] The drive to emigrate intensified at a time when the old rabbinical authority had given way, to a great extent, to a full participation in political ideas and contemporary literature. Until then, subservience to the authority of the past had given them a great sense of security from the problems of the external world. Howe quotes Isaiah Berlin on this: "Poor, down-trodden and oppressed as they might be, and clinging to each other by warmth and shelter, they put all their faith in God, and concentrated all their hope either upon individual salvation—immortality in the sight of God—or upon the coming of the Messiah."[6] But by the last third of the nineteenth century, pietist safety had been replaced by a ferment of political and cultural movements, expressed in Yiddish but looking out through translation to a passionate involvement with the politics and culture of the whole world.

One can note in passing how different their pull to modernity was from that of the Jews of Germany. German Jews responded passionately to Schiller and Goethe, as they responded to Wagner, because they felt that it enabled them to share the German soul. The Yiddish-speaking Jews of Eastern Europe read, overwhelmingly in translation, everything that was great in Russian literature in the same spirit in which they also read Dickens, Balzac, and Zola. They were not interested in the Russian soul but in the soul of humanity.

Inevitably they were positivist in sentiment, with August Comte and H. G. Wells their idols; but even when religious authority had lost its hold, they were still at home in the religious traditions which they had absorbed in childhood through synagogue and home rituals. As Maurice Samuel said in his uniquely evocative book *The World of Sholem Aleichem,* "the Bible was a daily newspaper." Yet if Yiddishkeit—an indefinable term expressing Jewish moral attitudes—contained much that was religious in origin, a dominant mark of this new life was its secular quality. Socialism and the brotherhood of man were what mattered. Science, in all its ramifications, would bring mankind to the messianic age.

It was in this spirit that a large part of the growing Jewish proletariat of Russia in the latter part of the nineteenth century rejected the quasi religious element in Zionism and opted for the Bund, a movement of workers who wanted to build a free life in the land they lived in, drawing on their cultural Yiddish traditions instead of artificially re-creating the Hebrew of their ancestors. The populist historian Simon Dubnow wrote his magnificent *World History of the Jewish People* with this model in mind, drawing on community records in a highly original way and expressing in everything he wrote both a love for his people and a longing for the triumph of reason. One notes with a particular bitterness that at the age of 81, Dubnow, living quietly at Riga, was deported to a death camp and shot by a Nazi on December 8, 1941, in an act of supremely gratuitous evil.

It is not difficult to see how the idealism, the historical imagination, the love of scholarship and science, and all the other questing virtues of Jewish life in Eastern Europe were fed into the emerging Jewish life in America to culminate triumphantly in the originality and experimentalism which has become a mark of that land. For centuries Jews had struggled with the Talmud and turned outward, when they had a chance, to explore worlds unrealized. Now that their descendants are free to pursue everything with the same intellectual and emotional vigor, they are, inevitably, not as Jewish as they once were, and the value of their achievements in business, science, politics, music, literature, and the theater has to be judged by different standards. One wonders what form the Jewish element will take in this new free civilization; but there is no doubt that it will still be strong.

The Springs of Israel's Life

The double source potent at the beginning in American Jewry is visible equally in the opening up of a wholly new Jewish civilization in Israel. But as the country has developed, a third force has entered the field, which is almost like Jewish history coming full circle.

When Zionism was at its formative stage in the latter part of the nineteenth century, the impetus came from the power of Jewish feeling in the great community of Eastern Europe. The German source was potent too. What few expected, however, was that in this revolutionary development in Jewish life the Jewries of Muslim countries, so important to Jews in earlier centuries, would now come back powerfully into the Jewish historical picture.

Before this was to happen, the build up of a new life in the Holy Land reflected the same polarization of Eastern Europe and Germany in relation to American Jewry. With East European Jews, the drive for Zionism had vitality and color, even if it was unruly and inchoate. The abnormality of Jewish life in Russia had stimulated a passion to win a free homeland so that Jews could have their own government and be as normal as other people. The vision was fed also by the labor ideology which had led the Jewish masses of Eastern Europe to work for a socialist brotherhood. But there were religious strains even among the secularists. The passion to give reality to the age-old longing "next year in Jerusalem" had an inner religious intensity; surely the brotherhood of Jews in their own land would be religious in its new, true meaning.

It was, then, the Zionist passion of the Jewish masses, expressed first by those in Eastern Europe itself and then by their descendants in the United States, that gave the building of the homeland an inexpressible fervor; but the generating force also included the solid practicality—the bourgeois virtues—that had been expressed historically by German-speaking Jewry. Theodor Herzl, the prophet of Zionism, emerged from Vienna. The organization established at the first Zionist Congress, which was held in Basel in 1897, had its headquarters in Berlin. To authentic Jews from Eastern Europe, these confident and somewhat bossy coreligionists from Germany seemed—like the later refugees from Germany—hardly recognizable as Jews. This was not simply because of their Germanic pronunciation of Hebrew and their endless devotion to Goethe and Wagner; it had to do, also, with their organized thoroughness and their never-failing display of superiority. But this was Jewish history working itself through. The long centuries spent by Jews in the German background had left their mark and to good effect, even if the vitalizing spark today, in Israel as well as in the United States, reflects the dynamism of Eastern Europe.

There is an apt parallel in the cultural field to this interaction of the two elements in Jewish life, Yiddishkeit and Germanism. One cannot but be struck by the fact that much that was original and vital in the culture of Eastern Europe was given lasting form only through the work of German Jews, two in particular: Martin Buber and Gershom Scholem. Martin Buber (1878–

1965) personalized our understanding of Hasidism—the most remarkable development in Jewish life since the creation of the Talmud—through his collections of Hasidic folktales. Though born in Vienna, he had spent his childhood with a scholar grandfather in the Polish town of Lemberg, where he could study Hasidism at first hand. Unlike his philosophic writing in German, which often seems un-Jewish, his tales reflect the poetry of his Jewish background. By contrast, Gershom Scholem (1897–1982) was born in Berlin of a thoroughly assimilated German-Jewish family, so that his researches into the hitherto unexplored world of Jewish mysticism were entirely the product of his brilliance and application, qualities that one associates automatically with German scholarship. Yet taking these two men together, it is clear that they were illuminating—and germanicizing—a world with its own magic, waiting to be uncovered.

This is a familiar picture to a Jew brought up in the European scene. Even knowing that in the most recent picture of Israeli life one has to take account of influences outside this pattern, one must always give pride of place to the contribution of Eastern Europe. It was the Jewish youth of Russia—only a few of them but highly significant—who in 1882 organized the first aliyah (immigration) to the Holy Land, with the battle-cry "BILU," initials of a verse from Isaiah (5:2): "O House of Jacob, come, let us go!" The second aliyah (1904–14), which also came mainly from Russia, was carried out by some 40,000 Jews inspired by a labor ideology and willing to suffer the greatest physical hardships in pursuing their ideals. David Ben-Gurion, the future prime minister of Israel, was a member of this group, leaving Poland for the Holy Land in 1906. The third aliyah, which followed the Balfour Declaration of 1917, and the fourth, mainly in 1924–25, were also heavily from Eastern Europe. It was not until the immigration drives of the 1930s that many settlers began to come from Germany.

More significant than mere numbers, it was the training of young Jews, undertaken in many Jewish centers in Eastern Europe, that provided the agricultural and technical skills, and a defiant courage to go with them, on which, starting in the 1920s, the leaders were able to build a fully organized community, ready to take over in every field—military, as well as political and economic—when statehood was declared in 1948. It is a supreme tragedy of the Holocaust that many thousands of well-trained pioneers in Eastern Europe who, by British policy, had not been granted immigration permits, were caught in the Nazi trap. Before their death, they played a valiant part in the Resistance. The historian Martin Gilbert, biographer of Winston Churchill, has pointed out in his writings on the Holocaust that the scale of this resistance goes unacknowledged in most quarters: "There was armed resistance in dozens of ghettoes, tens of thousands of acts of individual resistance, courage in the face of overwhelming odds, the heroism of the starving and the unarmed against the military might of victorious armies and armed thugs."[7] It can be taken for granted that of those who escaped death and finally battled their way to Israel, many played an equally valiant part in the war of the Jews for independence.

All this is the history one would expect. What is one to make, then, of the irruption into Israel's life of many thousands of Jews from Asia and Africa, and the effect that this is having on Israel's development?

In loose parlance, Jews of this origin are called "oriental," as distinct from "western" which includes Europe, the Americas, and Jewish communities of the British Commonwealth. In some respects, this nomenclature overlaps with a more traditional division of Jews into Sephardi and Ashkenazi; but in social terms, the oriental and western distinction is more useful.

One could hardly find a better example than this to illustrate the dynamics of Jewish history. For centuries, while Jewish creativity was being fostered in Eastern Europe, Western Europe and the United States, the Jews living in the Muslim countries of Iraq, Iran, Yemen, Syria, Egypt, Algeria, Tunisia, and Morocco had ceased to be prominent on the world scene. In all these countries, the Jews of the Middle Ages had a dignified story to their credit. They were largely artisans, devoted to Judaism; and every country included men who had risen to high estate in trade, finance, the professions and government. Usually, there were a few very wealthy Jews and impoverished masses; but by the nineteenth century there was often an active middle class. If their way of life was not familiar to most European Jews, there were many contacts at the trade, personal, and scholarly levels. One of the most fruitful points of contact was the setting up by Jewish organizations in France and England of schools for Jewish children, the most famous of which were the French "Alliance" schools throughout the Middle East.

Before World War I, Jews from these countries had settled in small numbers in the Holy Land, side by side with Sephardi Jews deeply rooted in the land and a growing number of Ashkenazi settlers. In the Palestine of the British Mandate, 1922 to 1948, these numbers grew somewhat; but when the State of Israel was founded in 1948, immigration of "oriental" Jews was unprecedented in scale and highly significant for the future.

There were two major factors in play. The first was the idealism generated by the founding of the state and the excited demand for a mass of immigrants. The second was the hostility of Arab or Islamic governments to the Jews living among them, as a result of the foundation of Israel. The two factors worked together to transfer to Israel, in a few short years, a very large part—in some cases virtually all—of the Jewish populations of these countries.

This aliyah equaled the aliyah from Europe. Between May 1948 and December 1951, there was an immigration of 304,000 Jews from Eastern Europe and 25,000 from the rest of Europe, 329,000 in all. In the same period, 330,000 Jews were brought in from Asia and Africa, of which 237,000 came from Asian countries (the largest coming from Iraq and Yemen) and 93,000 from North African countries.

At the beginning, it was the task of the western Jews, whose base had already been established, to take care of the oriental immigrants in every possible way. At this stage, the oriental Jews, thoroughly bewildered by the change, were a minority of the population. By 1969, partly due to a high fertility rate, Jews of Asian and African origin constituted 52 percent of those whose origin was known, while for those of European and American origin the figure was 48 percent.

For these twenty years, this vast change in the constitution of Israel's population generated social problems of great severity. In very broad terms, the large gap in income, education, professional skills, and political power between westerners and orientals had the sharpness of a class differentiation. Studies showed that it manifested itself, also, in crime involvement. Not that this was a uniform pattern. It was a striking fact that the Jews of Iraq and Yemen, who had come from a settled Jewish background, tended to be stable in the new situation, while half-assimilated Jews from the French colonies of Algeria and Morocco were disturbed and aggressive.

In line with what has been discussed in this chapter, one would like to know how far the sources of Jewish life that flowed in these oriental countries will affect the new pattern of life in Israel. In trying to answer thus, one cannot identify and then add in some of the old aspects of Jewish life in these countries. Israel is itself evolving rapidly in ways that affect all old habits and loyalties. One has therefore to consider the social pattern that is developing in Israel as a whole, in which these immigrant and Israel-born orientals play a natural part.

The sociologist Geoffrey Wigoder, director of the Institute for Contemporary Jewry at the Hebrew University of Jerusalem, has put the development graphically by identifying four generations that have been exemplified in

Israeli culture, especially in literature and painting, but which illustrate at the same time developments in the social and political fields.

In general, all four generations have had to weigh the pull, on the one hand, of Jewish tradition, and on the other, of relating to the world scene. At first, the particularist tendencies were dominant; later, the emphasis was more on universalism and less on introspection:

> The first generation was firmly based on its European roots; the second generation was rooted in its experience in Eretz Israel, especially those connected with *aliyah* and the kibbutz movement; the third generation, emerging around the 1948 War of Independence, was dominated by the sabra with his newly found self-confidence; while the fourth generation (or the second sabra generation) has been the most universalistic and outward looking, seeing Israel culture as one expression of contemporary world culture.[8]

It is clear that in this formulation oriental Jews, now increasingly native born and integrated fully through education, army service, and politics, are likely to make a strong contribution to the fourth generation. In more specific terms, Israeli life has been opened up by the stimulating liveliness that emerges in the enjoyment of the great variety of ethnic origins among the population. It is seen very clearly in music, the dance, and poetry. In another realm, the most direct influence of the orientals, now in a majority, has come in politics. Until a decade ago, the Ashkenazi Europeans dominated politics; it is significant today that the President of Israel is a Sephardi, a member of the old and highly respected community established in the Holy Land long before the idealists of Eastern Europe came to settle there.

The New Balance in Jewish Life

In wholly different ways, the United States and Israel are now the two dominating centers of Jewish life. The most significant of the figures which illustrate this are given in table 2 which is based on the researches of the foremost expert on this subject, Jacob Lestchinsky.*

*Salo Baron, "Population," *Encyclopedia Judaica,* vol. 13, cols. 866–903, provides these figures which he says are largely cited from the work of Lestchinsky. On the loss of the six million, he points out that by ordinary population growth, the 1939 figures of 16.7 million for world Jewry would have risen in twenty years to 19 or 20 million, and was, in fact, no more than 12.8 million in 1960, demonstrating in another way the loss of the six million.

Is it possible to identify qualities in these two societies that will make them significant for the future of Jewish existence?

Taking Israel first, it is a focus of Jewish loyalty and faith in ways that represent a triumph of will and courage unimaginable in the past. In some ways, Israel has unique living links with its ancient origins; in others, it is a whole-hearted realization of the spirit of the modern world. Two aspects of Israel call for mention in even the briefest of summaries.

The first relates to what has been said about the influx of Jews from Muslim countries. The transformation that this has brought into the lives of many thousands of hitherto underprivileged men and women may prove to have startling effects. History shows that Jews have been most enterprising and creative at the margin, while still under pressure. Oriental Jews may demonstrate this in the Israel context; and their successes in business, science, and the arts may well have a special flavor that reflects their distinctive origin.

The second point is that Israel as a whole has become a center of learning and self-awareness that opens up for all of us a new understanding of what the Jewish story has been about. The word *Jew* itself is being redefined.

The Jews of the United States are more difficult to categorize; and it is therefore hard to know what is meant when we see the main center of gravity of the Jewish people now in that land as, in a numerical sense, we must. Certainly, the Jews of America have risen to their full responsibility in exercis-

TABLE 2
Jews in Various Countries, 1939–67
(in thousands)

Country	1939	1948	1967
Eastern Europe			
USSR (including Latvia, Lithuanias, Estonia)	2,825	2,000	2,650
Poland (including Galicia, Posen, etc.)	3,250	88	21
Rumania	850	380	100
Austria	191	31	12
Czechoslovakia	367	42	15
Hungary	445	174	80
Germany	504 (1933)	153	30
Israel	475	750	2,436
U.S.A.	4,975	5,000	5,870
Canada	156	180	280
World Totals (including other countries)	16,724	11,373	13,837

SOURCE: Salo Baron, "Population," *Encyclopedea Judaica*, vol. 13, cols. 866–903.

ing their huge resources for the benefit of Israel; and it is notable, too, that in the Jewish field they have carried forward on an intense scale the forms of study and communal organization that characterized the earlier places—Babylonia, Spain, Eastern Europe—which were central to Jewish life in their time. But having said this, one feels wary of carrying parallels too far. Everything in American civilization strikes a new note; and though American Jews are deeply attached to Jewish traditions in some basic ways, the great majority seem, like the people of Israel, to be a new kind of Jew.

No one can say how the pattern of Jewish migration and settling might change in the future. All one knows is that it is in the shadow of the two new centers of Jewish life—United States and Israel—that the Jews of the world are drawn to a reevaluation of their own position.

But if detailed experience is different in every country, there are moments when all Jews are still motivated in the same way. In this sense, the security of Israel is now far and away the most potent link for all. But there are instances, also, at the religious and folk level. One thinks of the feeling that surfaces throughout the whole Jewish world at the Seder ceremonies on Passover Eve. There are absolutes in the Jewish story; and one feels something about them sitting round the table that night, listening to the Four Questions, eating matzah, and drinking the four cups of wine.

Appendix

Appendix

Feasts and Fasts of the Jewish Year

The Festivals

THE THREE MAJOR FESTIVALS are *Pesach,* Passover, in spring, *Shavuouth,* Pentecost, in early summer, and *Succoth,* Tabernacles, in autumn. In Temple times they were pilgrim festivals with Jews coming to Jerusalem from all over the Holy Land and beyond.

PASSOVER celebrates the Exodus from Egypt. It begins on the fifteenth of Nisan, usually in April, and is prescribed in the Bible to last for seven days, the first and last being holy festival days, and the intervening five workaday. (In the Diaspora, the festival was lengthened to eight days to ensure that the correct period according to the times of the new moon in the Holy Land was being covered. With eight days, the first two and the last two are holy, and the intervening four workaday.)

The special feature of Passover is the eating of *matzah,* unleavened bread. The Bible tells that in the haste of the Exodus, there was no time to allow the bread to rise: In memory, matzah, not bread, is therefore eaten during the whole of the festival. In

Jewish tradition the entire household had to be purified before Passover, with different dishes used to ensure that no trace of leaven was carried over.

Passover is introduced with great drama (and fun) at the *Seder* ceremony at home on the eve of the first day(s). The *haggadah* (tale), is read, telling the story, embellished with prayers and songs. A feature of the Seder is the recital of Four Questions about matzah and other Seder ceremonies, in reply to which the father expounds the Exodus story, with its emphasis on freedom.

The Seder is a home ceremony of universal appeal. By bringing scattered families together, with children, grandchildren, and guests, it has probably done more than any single celebration to perpetuate the attachments that have kept Jews together.

SHAVUOTH, the Feast of Seven Weeks, Pentecost, is celebrated on the sixth of Sivan (and the seventh in the Diaspora), which is usually in May or June, seven weeks after Passover. It originally marked the end of the barley harvest and the beginning of the wheat harvest. But in rabbinic times, it came to be regarded also as the anniversary of the giving of the Torah on Sinai and has retained this special significance. In folk terms, it is a summer festival, enjoyed with flowers and dairy foods.

SUCCOTH, booths or tabernacles, is ordained for seven days (eight in the Diaspora), starting on the fifteenth of Tishri, usually late September, with the first (and in the Diaspora also the second) days holy, the remainder workaday. A day which then follows is called *shemini atzereth* (eighth day of convocation).

In the Bible, Succoth is a harvest festival, celebrated by taking four types of plants (citron, myrtle, palms, and willows) in hand while praying. It is ordained, also, to live in booths for the festival, "because I made the children of Israel to live in booths when I brought them out of the land of Egypt" (Lev. 23:42). These and other agricultural echoes always give a special flavor to Succoth. An additional feature of great, even boisterous, joy is that the last day of the festival is known as *Simhath Torah,* Rejoicing of the Torah, because the annual reading-cycle of the Torah is completed on this day, followed immediately by a reading of a first section of Genesis, to avoid any break. Simhath Torah as a special day is not specified in the Bible and was not known in talmudic times, though the Bible reading cycle was completed on this day, the last day of Succoth. The special celebration of Simhath Torah began in geonic times. The custom of restarting the Bible cycle on the same day is said to have begun after the ninth century A.D.

The festive year also includes two other festivals, Hanukkah and Purim. Though minor in comparison with the great pilgrim festivals, they have always been occasions of great folk joy.

HANUKKAH, Feast of Dedication, is an eight-day festival beginning on the twenty-fifth of Kislev, usually in December, and celebrates the rededication of the Temple after the victory of the Maccabees in 166 B.C. over the Syrians who had desecrated it as part of their campaign against traditional Judaism. In the rededication service, the Temple lamp was lit with a little oil that was found; but by a miracle this oil lasted for eight days, leading to the current ritual in which a menorah, caudelabrum, is lit for Hanukkah, with one candle on the first night, increasing daily to eight on the last night. The memory of military triumph and Temple dedication, symbolized in the candles for eight days, has made Hanukkah a great national festival.

PURIM, Feast of Lots, is a one-day festival on the fourteenth of Adar, one month before Passover and usually in March, celebrating the delivery of the Jews of Shushan (Persia) from the massacre planned by the wicked Haman, as described in the Book of Esther.* Esther is read in the synagogue from a special scroll; and the whole occasion is treated as a carnival, with plays, special food and every kind of jollity.

In the Near East, autumn is the time in which nature is renewed after the months of fierce summer heat and drought. The Hebrew New Year begins then, and the first ten days are set aside for spiritual resolution, which includes repentance for past sins and prayers to God for peace and strength in the year ahead. This period begins and ends with two solemn holy days, Rosh Hashanah and Yom Kippur, known as the Days of Awe.

The Days of Awe

ROSH HASHANAH is ordained for one day (two in the Diaspora), the first of Tishri, usually in September. In the Bible, it is "a day of memorial, proclaimed with the trumpet's blast." This has made the blowing of the *shofar*—an ancient ram's horn trumpet—a peak moment in the festival's celebrations. The sense of memorial permeates the religious services: Our shortcomings in the past year have been recorded on high, with repentance the only way to achieve forgiveness. It is our fate trembling in the balance that gives this period the name *yamim nora'im,* days of awe; but as New Year, Rosh Hashanah also evokes celebration in many happy folk customs.

YOM KIPPUR (more correctly Yom Ha'kippurim, Day of Atonement) is a twenty-four hour fast, ordained for the tenth of Tishri, the whole period from Rosh Hashanah to Yom Kippur being designated as the Ten Days of Repentance. The fast is total, without even a drink of water, beginning at dusk on the evening before and ending at dusk on the day itself. As a fast and the climax of the repentance period, it has immense solemnity in Jewish life. The service on the eve before is called *Kol Nidre,* the first words of an unusual and moving prayer referring to vows unfulfilled during

*The massacre day was chosen by lot, hence the name, according to the Book of Esther.

the year just ended. On the day itself, services are continuous in synagogue, ending with a final service, as dusk is falling, called *Ne'ilah,* after which the blowing of the shofar releases the tension. Without doubt, *Yom Kippur* has a hold on Jewish religious feeling which is unique in its power.

Other Fasts and Feasts

There are other fast days in the Jewish year, one a twenty-four-hour fast in memory of the destruction of the Temple on the ninth of Ab, usually in July, while shorter fasts —from sunrise to sunset—are prescribed for a variety of reasons.

There are also days for joyous celebration other than the major ones mentioned above. Various historical deliverances established a memorial day, often called a special Purim. There is a remarkable list in *Encyclopedia Judaica* (vol. 13, cols. 1395–1400) of a hundred special Purims of this kind, ranging from a Purim of Algiers established in 1540 to a Purim of Vidin (Bulgaria) established in 1878. The article also lists eleven family Purims, ranging from one established in Spain in 1038 by the family of the great leader Samuel ha-Nagid, to the Purim of the Danzig family of Vilna, established in 1804.

There are also a number of other minor holidays associated with seasons in the natural or agricultural calendar; and every new moon is greeted with special rules and blessings.

List of Abbreviations

Against Apion — Josephus, *Against Apion,* trans. H. St. John Thackeray, Loeb Classics (Cambridge: Harvard University Press, 1942).

Ant. — Josephus, *Antiquities of the Jews,* trans. H. St. John Thackeray, Loeb Classics (New York: G. F. Putnam's Sons, 1927).

Jewish War — Josephus, *Jewish War,* trans. H. St. John Thackeray, Loeb Classics (New York: G. F. Putnam's Sons, 1926).

Notes

Introduction

1. Yigael Yadin, *Bar Kokhba* (London: Weidenfeld and Nicolson, 1961), p. 133.

Chapter 1

1. John Bright, *A History of Israel,* 2nd ed. (Philadelphia: Westminster Press, 1972), p. 130.

Chapter 2

1. On this whole subject see Martin Noth, *The History of Israel,* 2nd ed. (New York: Harper and Row, 1960).
2. Joshua Gutmann in *Encyclopaedia Judaica,* vol. 2, cols. 961-6.
3. Elias Bickerman, "The Historical Foundations of Postbiblical Judaism" in Louis

Finkelstein, ed., *The Jews: Their History, Culture and Religion,* 4th ed., 3 vols. (New York: Schocken Books, 1970), vol. 1, p. 75.

Chapter 3

1. Elias Bickerman, "The Historical Foundations of Postbiblical Judaism" in Louis Finkelstein, ed., *The Jews,: Their History Culture and Religion,* 4th ed. (New York: Schocken Books, 1970), vol. 1, p. 77.
2. Martin Hengel, *Judaism and Hellenism,* vol. 1 (Philadelphia: Fortress Press, 1974), p. 12.
3. Ibid., p. 18.
4. Ibid., pp. 66–67.
5. Ibid., p. 140.
6. See a full account in C. Rabin, *The Zadokite Documents* (Oxford: Oxford Univ. Press, 1958).
7. Gershom Scholem, *Major Trends in Jewish Mysticism,* 3rd ed. (New York: Schocken Books, 1954), p. 42.
8. See p. 147. For a discussion of Akiba and Bar Kokhba, see C. Raphael, *Encounters with the Jewish People* (New York: Behrman House, 1980), pp. 190–98.
9. For this and other stories on the same subject, see C. Raphael, *The Walls of Jerusalem* (New York: Knopf, 1968), pp. 180–82.
10. See "The New Covenant" in *The Dead Sea Scriptures* by Theodore H. Gaster (New York: Doubleday, 1964), p. 331.
11. Scholem, *Jewish Mysticism,* p. 359, n. 24.
12. Geza Vermes, *Jesus the Jew,* (London: Collins, 1973), pp. 58–69.
13. Ibid., p. 83.
14. Hengel, *Judaism,* p. 198.
15. M. P. Nüllson, *Geschichte der Griechischen Religion,* 2nd. ed., vol 2, p. 558, as quoted in Martin Hengel, *Judaism and Hellenism*, vol. 2, p. 135, n. 609.
16. *Daily Prayer Book,* ed. S. Singer, (London: Eyre and Spottiswoode, 1935), p. 5.

Chapter 4

1. See "A Clash on Ideologies" in A. Toynbee, ed., *The Crucible of Christianity* (New York: Thames and Hudson, 1969), p. 74.
2. See L. Finkelstein, "Pre-Rabbinic Ideals and Teachings in the Passover Hag-

gadah" in *Harvard Theological Review,* vol. 31, 1938; vol. 35, 1942; and; vol. 36, 1943. (Summarized in C. Raphael, *A Feast of History,* 2nd ed. [New York: Behrman House, 1981], pp. 129–33).

3. See Bernard Lewis, *History: Remembered, Recovered, Invented* (Princeton: Princeton Univ. Press, 1976).

4. *Ant.* 15:4:2

5. Explaining this view in *The Crucible of Christianity* (New York: Thames and Hudson, 1969), p. 73, Schalit refers to a forthcoming book on the subject called *König Herodes*.

6. Emil Schürer, *The History of the Jewish People in the Age of Jesus Christ,* vol. 1, rev. by G. Vermes and P. Miller (Edinburgh: T. and T. Clark, 1973), p. 316.

7. Ibid., pp. 428–41.

Chapter 5

1. Salo W. Baron: *A Social and Religious History of the Jews,* 2nd ed. (New York: Columbia University Press, 1952–76), vol. 2, p. 184.

2. Emil Schürer, *The History of the Jewish People in the Age of Jesus Christ,* vol. 1, rev. by G. Vermes and P. Miller (Edinburgh: T. and T. Clark, 1973), p. 455.

3. Ibid, p. 460.

4. Tacitus, *Histories,* trans. W. Hamilton Fyfe (Oxford: Oxford University Press, 1912), vol. 2, v. 9.

5. For details of the rabbinic story and a discussion of the parallel, see C. Raphael, *The Walls of Jerusalem* (New York: Knopf, 1968), pp. 20–21.

6. For details see Raphael, *Walls,* p. 24.

7. Ibid., p. 26, n. 7.

8. Schürer, *History,* p. 510, n. 133, and voluminous references there.

Chapter 6

1. See, for example, J. Neusner, *A Life of Yohanan ben Zakkai* (Leiden: E. J. Brill, 1970), and *Rabbi Eliezer ben Hyrcanus* (Leiden: E. J. Brill, 1975), 3 vols.

2. The Midrash on Lamentations is the theme of C. Raphael's *The Walls of Jerusalem* (New York: Knopf, 1968). The relation of the weekly synagogue sermons to the text of the Midrash is discussed there in a section called "The Writings," pp. 53–83.

3. Eusebius, *Ecclesiastical History*, Book IV, para. 2.

4. Seder Olam Zuta in A. Neubauer, *Medieval Jewish Chronicles,* reprint (1967), p. 66.

5. For details see Raphael, *The Walls of Jerusalem,* p. 39.

6. Ibid.

7. A Jewish Alexandrian poet, writing as the Jewish Sibyl, speaks with exultation of his accession, see Heinrich Graetz, *History of the Jews* (London: Myers and Co., 1901), vol. 1, p. 415: "A happy man . . . within whose hands a sceptre given by God/ and over all he rules with glory. . . ."

8. See W. D. Gray, "The Founding of Aelia Capitolina," in *American Journal of Semitic Languages and Literature,* vol. 39 (July 1923); 248–56.

9. R. Joshua made use of Aesop's fable of the Wolf and the Crane (*Gen. Rabbah* 64), but told it as the Lion and the Crane. See Jacobs, *Jewish Encyclopedia* (1906–7), vol. 1, p. 221.

10. The papyrus is quoted by Gray in "Aelia Capitolina." On the travels of the rabbis, see C. Raphael, *Encounters with the Jewish People* (New York: Behrman House, 1980), pp. 192–94, where it is argued that the travels of Rabbi Akiba were to advise Jewish communities on the correct calendar.

11. Cf. his many conversations with the aged R. Joshua b. Hannaniah; for example, a series of questions upon the manner of the angels (Midrash on Lamentations, 3:8); the resurrection of the body (*Gen.Rabb.* 28); his mocking question about the smell of Sabbath food (Tal.*Shab.* 119a). Joshua was once called upon to debate with a *Min* (Judaeo-Christian) in the emperor's palace (Tal. *Hagigah* 5b). See Raphael *The Walls of Jerusalem*, pp. 41 ff.

12. Doubts are summarized in Raphael, *Walls* p. 45, n. 6. But Emil Schürer, *The History of the Jewish People in the Age of Jesus Christ,* vol. 1, rev. by G. Vermes and P. Miller (Edinburgh: T. and T. Clark, 1973), p. 545, is firm: Bar Kokhba "certainly occupied Jerusalem"; see argument there.

13. Jozef T. Milik, et al. *Les Grottes de Muraba'at,* Discoveries in the Judaean Desert, vol. 2 (Oxford: Oxford University Press, 1966).

14. Yigael Yadin, *Bar Kokhba* (London: Weidenfeld and Nicolson, 1961), p. 133.

15. Ibid., p. 15.

16. Raphael, *The Walls of Jerusalem,* pp. 192–94, and references there.

17. Schürer, *History,* pp. 553–57, and references there.

18. Dio, *Roman History* (Loeb Classics) 8.451.

19. Raphael, *The Walls of Jerusalem,* p. 203.

20. Roth, *Short History of the Jews,* rev. ed. (London: East and West Library, 1969), p. 113; Margolis and Marx, *A History of the Jewish People* (Philadelphia: Jewish Publication Society, 1927), p. 213; S. W. Baron, *Social and Religious History of the Jews* (New York: Columbia University Press, 1952), vol. 2, p. 98.

21. Chaim Potok, *Wanderings* (New York: Knopf, 1978), p. 227.

22. For examples see Raphael, *The Walls of Jerusalem,* pp. 187–88.

23. Yadin, *Bar Kokhba*, pp. 124–39.

24. Yaacov Herzog, *A People That Dwells Alone* (London: Weidenfeld and Nicolson, 1975), p. 170.

Chapter 7

1. H. D. Mantel *World History of the Jewish People* (London: Allen, 1977) vol. 8, p. 43. On this view, he sees the origin of the name Pharisee ("separated") as "separate from the authority of the High Priest" (p. 327, n. 32).

2. See Ibid, pp. 59–64, for a full discussion of "What is halakhah?" which draws on a study in comparative law by N. Isaacs, "The Law and 'the Law of Change,' " in *University of Pennsylvania Law Review* 65 (1917), pp. 659–79, 748–63.

3. S. Safrai, "The Synagogue and Its Worship," in *World History pp. 67–70.*

4. *Social and Religious History of the Jews* (New York: Columbia University Press, 1952), vol. 1, pp. 226–27.

5. See Geza Vermes, *Jesus the Jew* (London: Collins, 1973), *passim.*

6. Haim Cohen, *The Trial and Death of Jesus* (London: Weidenfeld and Nicolson, 1972)

7. Vermes, *Jesus the Jew,* p. 140.

8. Ibid., p. 143.

9. Ibid., p. 144.

10. Ibid., p. 149.

11. Hyam Maccoby, *Revolution in Judaea: Jesus and the Jewish Resistance* (New York: Taplinger, 1980).

12. Vermes, *Jesus the Jew,* p. 49.

13. Ibid., pp. 154–56.

14. James Parkes, *The Conflict of Church and Synagogue* (London: Soncino, 1934), p. 69.

Chapter 8

1. James Parkes, *The Conflict of Church and Synagogue* (London: Soncino, 1934) p. 79.

2. S. W. Baron, *Social and Religious History of the Jews* (New York: Columbia University Press, 1952), vol. 2, p. 87.

3. Ibid., p. 87.

4. Ibid., p. 216.

5. Ibid., p. 151.
6. Parkes, *Conflict* p. 96.
7. Justin Martyr, *Dialogue with Trypho,* trans. A. L. Williams (New York: Macmillan Co., 1930), pp. 32–33.
8. Parkes, *Conflict,* pp. 99–100.
9. Eusebius, *Ecclesiastical History* 1:4:20:76, as quoted in Parkes, *Conflict,* p. 100.
10. Parkes, *Conflict,* p. 118.
11. Ibid., p. 125.
12. Ibid., p. 128.
13. Ibid., p. 148.
14. Ibid., p. 150.
15. Henry Chadwick, *The Early Church* (London: Penguin Books, 1967), p. 125.
16. Parkes, *Conflict,* pp. 158 ff.
17. Ibid., p. 163.
18. Ibid., p. 165.

Chapter 9

1. See his enormously influential book, *Major Trends in Jewish Mysticism* (New York: Schocken Books, 1961). For some reservations, see C. Raphael, *Encounters with the Jewish People* (New York: Behrman House, 1980), pp. 78–82.
2. "Reform Judaism and the Bible" in *Commentary* (February 1982), pp. 31–35. In this essay Alter documents very clearly the ways in which the rigidity of early Reform Judaism has given way in recent years to a welcoming attitude to tradition.
3. Louis Jacobs, *Principles of the Jewish Faith* (London: Vallentine, Mitchell, 1964), pp. 216–301.
4. In annotated edition of *Daily Prayer Book,* ed. S. Singer (London: Eyre and Spottiswoode, 1935), p. civ.
5. On this subject in general, see, Rabbi Hayim Halevy Donin, *To Be a Jew: A Guide to Jewish Observance* (New York: Basic Books, 1972).
6. Mishnah, *Ethics of the Fathers* ch. 2, xiii.

Chapter 10

1. *Sabbatai Ṣevi: The Mystical Messiah, 1626–1676* (London: Routledge and Kegan Paul, 1973), Chap. 1, which presents a clear account of Lurianic Kabbalah. There is a much longer account in Scholem's article "Kabbalah" in *Encyclopedia*

Judaica, vol. 10, cols. 489–653, certainly the fullest and most authoritative study of the subject.

2. See his classic article, "Population," in *Encyclopedia Judaica,* vol. 13, cols. 866–903.

3. United Nations, Economic and Social Council, *Jewish Society Through the Ages,* "Jewish Society and Institutions Under Islam," p. 171.; also (London: Vallentine, Mitchell, 1970).

4. See the thrilling account given by S. D. Goitein in *A Mediterranean Society,* 3 vols. (Berkeley: University of California Press, 1967–78).

5. See a splendid volume, *The Penguin Book of Hebrew Verse,* trans. and ed. by T. Carmi (London: Penguin, 1981).

6. The subject can be studied in a massive volume: Max Weinreich, *History of the Yiddish Language* (Chicago: University of Chicago Press, 1980).

7. Cecil Roth, *Short History of the Jewish People,* rev. ed. (London: East and West Library, 1969), p. 169.

8. H. H. Ben-Sasson, *A History of the Jewish People* (Cambridge: Harvard University Press, 1976), p. 463.

9. Ibid., p. 397.

10. Weinreich, *History of the Yiddish Language* (Chicago: University of Chicago Press, 1980), pp. 49–50.

11. See Gershom Scholem, *Major Trends in Jewish Mysticism,* "Hasidism in Medieval Germany" (New York: Schocken Books, 1961), pp. 80–118.

Chapter 11

1. For a discussion of the modern aspect of this theme, see J. Katz, "Israel and the Messiah" in *Commentary* Jan. 1982, pp. 34–41.

2. H. H. Ben-Sasson (Polish-born) in his major article on "Poland" in *Encyclopedia Judaica,* vol. 13, cols. 709–89; the phrase is in col. 732.

3. See "The Gaon of Vilna" in C. Raphael, *Encounters with the Jewish People* (New York: Behrman House, 1980), pp. 72–88.

4. Gershom Scholem, *On Jews and Judaism in Crisis* (New York: Schocken Books, 1976), p. 78.

5. Irving Howe, *World of Our Fathers* (New York: Harcourt Brace Jovanovich, 1976), p. 7.

6. Isaiah Berlin, *Chaim Weizmann* (London: Weidenfeld and Nicolson, 1958), p. 17. It is included in *Personal Impressions* (London: Chatto and Windus, 1980), pp. 32–62.

7. From an article in *The Times* (London), March 6, 1982. See also his study of one aspect of the Holocaust, *Auschwitz and the Allies* (New York: Holt, Rinehart and Winston, 1981).

8. *Encyclopedia Judaica,* vol. 9, col. 997. On the same theme see Amos Elon, *The Israelis: Founders and Sons* (New York: Holt, Rinehart and Winston, 1971).

Books for Further Reading

A. General

Encyclopaedia Judaica. 16 vols. Jerusalem: Keter Publishing Co., 1972, is uneven in the scale of its articles, but on some subjects the articles are classical in treatment and remarkably up-to-date. The earlier *Jewish Encyclopaedia,* 12 vols. (New York: Funk and Wagnall, 1902–6) is thoroughly readable and very informative for its time.

Baron, Salo W. *A Social and Religious History of the Jews,* 2nd ed. 16 vols. New York: Columbia University Press, 1952–76.

Ben-Sasson, H.H., ed. *A History of the Jewish People.* Cambridge: Harvard University Press, 1976.

Finkelstein, Louis, ed. *The Jews: Their History, Culture and Religion.* 3 vols. 1960. New York: Schocken Books, 1970.

Roth, Cecil. *A Short History of the Jewish People.* Revised edition. London: East and West Library, 1969.

Seltzer, Robert M. *Jewish People, Jewish Thought.* New York: Macmillan, 1980.

Silver, Daniel J. and Martin, Bernard. *A History of Judaism.* 2 vols. New York: Basic Books, 1974.

Waxman, Meyer. *A History of Jewish Literature.* 2nd ed. 5 vols. New York: Thomas Yoseloff, 1960.

B. A Short List on Various Themes of This Book

1. Bible period (Old Testament)

Albright, William F. *Yahweh and the Gods of Canaan.* New York: Doubleday, 1968.
Alter, Robert. *The Art of Biblical Narrative.* New York: Basic Books, 1981.
Bright, John. *A History of Israel.* 2nd ed. Philadelphia: Westminster Press, 1972.
Eissefeldt, Otto. *The Old Testament.* Translated by P. R. Ackroyd. New York: Harper and Row, 1965.
Noth, Martin. *The History of Israel.* 2nd ed. Translated by P. R. Ackroyd. New York: Harper and Row, 1960.
Pearlman, Moshe. *Digging up the Bible.* London, Weidenfeld and Nicolson, 1980.
Thomas, D. Winton, ed. *Archaeology and Old Testament Study.* Oxford: Clarendon Press, 1967.

2. Early Postbiblical Period

Brandon, S. G. F. *Jesus and the Zealots.* New York: Scribners, 1967.
Cohen, A. *Everyman's Talmud.* New York: Schocken Books. 1975.
Ginzberg, Louis. *The Legends of the Jews.* 7 vols. Philadelphia: Jewish Publication Society of America, 1909–38.
Hengel, Martin. *Judaism and Hellenism.* 2 vols. Philadelphia: Fortress Press, 1974.
Lieberman, Saul. *Greek in Jewish Palestine.* New York: Feldheim, 1965.
———, *Hellenism in Jewish Palestine.* New York: Ktav Publishing House, 1962.
Montefiore, C. G. and Loewe, H. eds. *A Rabbinic Anthology.* 1938. New York: Schocken Books, 1974.
Neusner, Jacob. *From Politics to Piety: The Emergence of Pharisaic Judaism.* Englewood, N.J.: Prentice-Hall, 1973.
Parkes, James. *The Conflict of the Church and the Synagogue.* 1934. New York: Meridian Books, 1961.
Schürer, Emil. *The History of the Jewish People in the Age of Jesus Christ.* Revised by G. Vermes and F. Miller. Edinburgh: T. and T. Clark, 1973.
Vermes, Geza, ed. *The Dead Sea Scrolls in English.* 2nd ed. Baltimore, Md.: Penguin Books, 1975.
———. *Jesus the Jew.* London Collins, 1973.
Yadin, Yigael. *Masada.* New York: Random House, 1966.
———. *Bar Kokhba.* New York: Random House, 1971.

3. Middle Period

Abrahams, Israel. *Jewish Life in the Middle Ages.* New York: Athaneum, 1969.

Baer, Yitzchak. *A History of the Jews of Christian Spain.* 2 vols. Philadelphia: Jewish Publication Socety of America, 1961.

Finkelstein, Louis. *Jewish Self-government in the Middle Ages.* New York: Feldheim, 1964.

Glückel of Hameln. *The Memoirs of Glückel of Hameln,* 1654–1724. Translated by Marvin Lowenthal. New York: Schocken Books, 1977.

Goitein, S. D. *Jews and Arabs: Their Contacts Through the Ages.* New York: Schocken Books, 1984.

———. *A Mediterranean Society: The Jewish Communities of the Arab World as Portrayed in the Documents of the Cairo Genizah.* 3 vols. Berkeley and Los Angeles: University of California Press, 1976–78.

Kobler, Franz. *Letters of Jews Through the Ages.* 2 vols. London: Ararat and East and West Library, 1952.

Marcus, Jacob R., ed. *The Jews in the Mediaeval World: A Source Book: 351–1791.* New York: Harper Torchbooks, Harper & Row, 1965.

Newman, Abraham. *The Jews in Spain.* 2 vols. Philadelphia: Jewish Publication Society of America, 1942.

Twersky, Isidore, ed. *A Maimonides Reader.* New York: Behrman House, 1972.

4. Later History and Literature

Baron, Salo W. *The Russian Jews under Tsar and Soviets.* 2nd ed. New York: Macmillan, 1975.

Buber, Martin. *The Origin and Meaning of Hasidism.* New York: Harper & Row, 1966.

Carmi, T., ed. *The Penguin Book of Hebrew Verse.* London: Penguin Books, 1981.

Cohn, Norman. *Warrant for Genocide: The Myth of the Jewish World Conspiracy.* New York: Harper & Row, 1966.

Dawidowicz, Lucy, ed. *The Golden Tradition.* New York: Holt, Rinehart and Winston, 1966.

———. *The War Against the Jews 1933–45.* New York: Holt, Rinehart and Winston, 1975.

———. *A Holocaust Reader.* New York: Behrman House, 1976.

Gay, Peter. *Freud, Jews and Other Germans.* New York: Oxford University Press, 1978.

Greenberg, Louis. *The Jews in Russia.* New York: Schocken Books, 1976.

Books For Further Reading

Grunfeld, Frederic V. *Prophets Without Honour: Background to Freud, Kafka, Ein stein and Their World.* London: Hutchinson, 1979.

Herzberg, Arthur. *The French Enlightenment and the Jews.* New York: Columbia University Press, 1968.

Hilberg, Raul. *The Destruction of the European Jews.* New York: Quadrangle, 1961.

Howe, Irving. *World of Our Fathers.* New York: Simon and Schuster, 1976.

Katz, Jacob. *Exclusiveness and Tolerance.* New York: Schocken Books, 1962.

———. *Tradition and Crisis: Jewish Society at the End of the Middle Ages.* New York: The Free Press, 1970.

———. *Out of the Ghetto: The Social Background of Jewish Emancipation 1770–1870.* Cambridge: Harvard University Press, 1973.

Kochan, Lionel, ed. *Jews in Soviet Russia Since 1917.* London: Oxford University Press, 1978.

Marrus, Michael. *The Politics of Assimilation (in France at the Time of the Dreyfus Affair).* London: Oxford University Press, 1971.

Mosse, George L. *Germans and Jews.* New York: Grosset and Dunlap, 1970.

Netanyahu, B. *The Marranos of Spain.* New York: American Academy for Jewish Research, 1967.

Parkes, James. *Antisemitism: A Concise World History.* New York: Quadrangle, 1964.

Poliakov, Leon. *The History of Antisemitism.* 3 vols. Translated by Richard Howard. New York: Vanguard Press, 1965–66.

Roth, Cecil. *A History of the Jews in England.* London: Oxford University Press, 1949.

———. *The Jews in the Renaissance.* Philadelphia: Jewish Publication Society of America, 1950.

Samuel, Maurice. *The World of Scholom Aleichem.* New York: Schocken Books, 1954.

Scholem, Gershom. *Sabbatai Sevi: The Mystical Messiah 1626–76.* Translated by R. J. Z. Werblowsky. Princeton, N.J.: Princeton University Press, 1973.

Schwartz, Howard and Rudolf, Anthony eds. *Voices Within the Ark: Jewish Poets in the 20th Century.* New York: Avon, 1980.

Schwarz, Leo W., ed. *Memoirs of My People: Self-portraits from the 11th to the 20th Century.* New York: Schocken Books, 1963.

Sklare, Marshall. *America's Jews.* New York: Random House, 1971.

Werblowsky, R. J. Z. *Joseph Karo: Lawyer and Mystic.* Philadelphia: Jewish Publication Society of America, 1977.

Weinryb, Bernard D. *The Jews of Poland.* Philadelphia: Jewish Publication Society of America, 1973.

Wistrich, Robert S. *Revolutionary Jews: from Marx to Trotsky.* London: Harrap, 1976.

5. Zionism and Israel

Elon, Amos. *The Israelis: Founders and Sons.* New York: Holt, Rinehart and Winston, 1971.

———. *Herzl.* New York: Holt, Rinehart and Winston, 1975.

Frankel, William. *Israel Observed: An Anatomy of the State.* New York: Thames & Hudson, 1981.

Halkin, Simon. *Modern Hebrew Literature.* New York: Schocken Books, 1950.

Herzberg, Arthur. *The Zionist Idea.* New York: Doubleday, 1959.

Laqueur, Walter. *A History of Zionism.* New York: Schocken Books, 1976.

Spiegel, Shalom. *Hebrew Reborn.* Cleveland, Ohio: William Collins and World Publishing Co., 1962.

Vital, David. *The Origins of Zionism.* London: Oxford University Press, 1975.

Weizmann, Chaim. *Trial and Error.* New York: Harper and Row, 1949.

6. Judaism

Agus, Jacob B. *Modern Philosophies of Judaism.* New York: Behrman House, 1941.

Baeck, Leo. *The Essence of Judaism.* New York: Schocken Books, 1948.

Blau, Joseph L. *Judaism in America.* Chicago: University of Chicago Press, 1976.

Buber, Martin. *I and Thou.* New York: Scribners, 1970.

Glazer, Nathan. *American Judaism.* Chicago: University of Chicago Press, 1972.

Guttmann, Julius. *Philosophies of Judaism.* New York: Holt, Rinehart and Winston, 1964.

Herberg, Will, ed. *The Writings of Martin Buber.* New York: Meridian, 1956.

Hirsch, Samson R. *The Nineteen Letters on Judaism.* Translated by Bernhard Drachman. New York: Feldheim, 1960.

Jacobs, Louis. *A Jewish Theology.* London: Darton, Longman and Todd, 1973.

Kaplan, Mordecai M. *Judaism as a Civilization.* New York: Yoseloff, 1957.

Kaufman, William E. *Contemporary Jewish Philosophies.* New York: Behrman House, 1976.

Rosenzweig, Franz. *The Star of Redemption.* Translated by William H. Hallo. New York: Holt, Rinehart and Winston, 1970.

Rotenstreich, Nathan. *Jewish Philosophy in Modern Times.* New York: Holt, Rinehart and Winston, 1968.

Scholem, Gershom. *Major Trends in Jewish Mysticism.* New York: Schocken Books, 1954.

Index

Aaron, 43
Abba Arika (rabbi), 176
Aboth (Mishnah), 63
Abrabanel, Isaac, 239, 239*n*
Abraham (patriarch) 20, 26, 28, 30, 67, 204, 219
Abrahams, Israel, 171*n*, 200
Acre, 88, 138*n*
Actium, battle of, 100
Acts of the Apostles, 106, 165, 168, 179, 181, 184
Africa: North, 136, 219, 221, 225, 246; South, 246
Agrippa I (Herodian king), 112–15, 117, 124
Agrippa II (Herodian king), 113, 115, 117–19
Ahiram, 47
Ahura Mazda, 47
Ai (biblical town), 31
Akiba (rabbi), 90, 101, 134, 145, 146, 195, 199; on free will, 63; views on Messiah, 72, 73, 146–50, 232
Albo, Joseph (philosopher), 200
Albright, William F., 30*n*
Alcimus (high priest), 89
Alexander the Great, 35, 50, 52, 54, 58, 60, 83
Alexander Jannai, 93, 94, 96, 159
Alexandria, 63, 97, 114, 118–19, 121, 123, 127
Algeria, 252
Alibus (procurator), 118
Aliyah (immigration to Israel), 251, 253
Almohads, 222, 228
Almoravides, 222
Alter, Robert, 195, 196
Ammonites, 87
Ananus (high priest), 109, 118, 120, 122
Andrew (apostle), 164
Angels, 47–49, 68–69, 70, 72, 76, 78, 174
Angra Mainyu, 48
Antioch, 84, 93, 121, 138*n*, 189–90

Index

Antiochus III (Syrian king), 84–85
Antiochus IV (Syrian king), 85, 87; and Hellenization of Jews, 56; as satirized in *Daniel*, 68–69
Antipas, *see* Herod Antipas
Antipater, 96, 97, 98
Antiquities (Josephus), 109, 110
Anti-semitism, 74
Antonia (Temple tower) 118–19, 125
Apion, 114
Apocalypse: and apocalyptic literature, 40, 47–49, 54, 68–69, 84, 134; and chaos before Messiah, 74, 107
Apocrypha, 40–41, 59–60, 67, 77
Appian (historian), 135
Arabs: 13, 49, 87, 96, 219, 221, 253; fighting for Romans against Jews, 103, 126; Pangar as leader of, 126
Aramaic, 46, 58, 69–70, 71*n*, 129, 133, 142, 174, 228
Archelaus (son of Herod), 103, 107
Arch of Titus, 127–28
Argentina, 246
Arianism, 186–7
Aristeas, *see Letter of Aristeas*
Aristobulus (Egyptian-Jewish philosopher), 57, 63
Aristobulus (high-priest), 95–96, 99
Aristotle, 13
Arius, creed of, 227
Armenians, 96, 237
Artaxerxes (Persian kings), 43
Ascension of Isaiah (visionary book), 70*n*
Ashdod, 88
Ashkenazi, 233, 252, 254
Asia Minor, 53, 85, 221
Assumption of Moses (visionary book), 70 *n*, 107
Astrology, 76
Athanasius, 186
Athens, 58*n*, 60
Augustus, 98, 100–2
Australia, 246
Austria, 243
Ba'al: Canaanite god, 23, 29; epic, 30
Ba'al Shem Tov (Hasidic leader), 242
Babata (family archive), 133, 143
Babel, Tower of, 47
Babylonia, 10, 18, 20, 27, 29, 33, 34–50; and influences on Jews, 45–48, 50, 75–76, 78; Jewish community in, 172, 176, 218–19, 221, 226, 230, 236
Baghdad, 221–22, 231
Balaam, 26
Balfour Declaration, 194
Barabbas, 11
Bar Kokhba, 10, 16, 28, 82, 133, 135, 136–38, 142, 144–45, 147, 149; and relation to Rabbi Akiba, 72, 140, 146; *see also* Bar Kokhba letters; Bar Kokhba rebellion
Bar Kokhba letters, 132, 140–44; *see also* Bar Kokhba
Bar Kokhba rebellion, 139, 140, 152, 159; *see also* Bar Kokhba
Bar Kosiba, Simon, *see* Bar Kokhba
Bar mitzvah, 23
Baron, Salo W., 6, 148, 171, 172, 178, 219, 220*n*, 247*n*, 266*n*1, 267*n*20, 268 *n*4
Baruch (apocalyptic book), 135
Belisarius, 127
Ben Dosa, Hanina (rabbi), 77
Ben Galgula, Joshua, 142–43
Ben Gorion, Joseph (Defender of Jerusalem), 120, 122
Ben-Gurion, David (prime minister), 14, 86, 144, 251
Ben Hananiah, Joshua (rabbi), 134, 138
Ben Hyrcanus, Eliezer (rabbi), 134
Ben Matthias, Joseph, *see* Josephus
Ben Sasson, H. H., *History of the Jewish People, A*, 46*n*, 230, 270*n*8
Ben Simon, Eleazar (rebel leader), 122
Ben Sira, *Wisdom of Ben Sira*, 40, 59–63, 72, 165
Ben Torta, Jonathan (rabbi), 147–48
Ben Ya'ir, Eleazar (leader of Masada), 127–29

Index

Ben Zaccai, Johanan, 121–24, 126, 134
Ben Zvi, Izhak (President of Israel), 144
Berenice (princess), 118
Berlin, Isaiah, 248
Bethar (fortress), 173
Beth Din, the Great, 105, 116
Beth-Horon, 120
Bethlehem, 99
Beth-Zechariah, 88
Bible: and archaeology, 27–29; completion of, 37, 46; critical theories and, 28–30; in Jewish life, 4, 12, 14–15, 18, 20–33, 199, 207; study of, 22–23, 34, 39, 41, 44–45, 52, 72, 90, 95, 100, 155, 204; *see also* Torah, Written and Oral
Bickerman, Elias, 49, 52, 58, 265*n*4
Black Death, 234
Bohemia, 228, 232
Book of Adam and Eve (visionary book), 70*n*
Bright, John, *History of Israel, A* 46*n*, 264*n*1
Buber, Martin, 250–51

Caesarea, 103, 118, 123, 127
Caesarea Philippi, 163
Cairo, genizah in, 60, 71, 222–23
Caligula, 114
Canaan, 20, 29
Canada, 246
Carmi, T., 270*n*5
Casimir the Great, 236
Certius Gallus (Syrian governor), 119–21
Chadwick, Henry, *Early Church, The,* 187, 269*n*15
Challah, 30
Charlemagne, 230
China, 223
Chmielnicki, Bogdan, 242
Christianity: and early relationship to Jews, 111, 115, 118, 159, 165–66, 168, 173, 175, 179–82; and classical world, 11, 35, 53, 63, 64*n*, 81, 83, 172, 174, 176, 178–79, 181, 188, 191; and false allegations of persecution by Jews, 184–85; and hostility toward Jews, 11, 74, 153, 176, 181–83, 185–90, 226; institutions of, 158, 179, 186–88, 202; and Old Testament anti-Jewish testimony, 74, 155, 159, 164, 166, 168–69, 173, 180–83, 188–89; schisms in, 186–88; and trial and death of Jesus, 105–6, 108–12; visionary ideas of, 65–69, 71–72, 74, 106, 146; *see also* Jesus
Chrysostom, Saint John, 189–90
Cilicia, 63
Circumcision, 45
Claudius, 114, 117
Clement VI (pope), 234
Cleopatra, 81, 100
Cohen, Haim, 268*n*6
Coins, 52
Cologne, 228, 230
Columbus, Christopher, 240, 243
Community Rule (Dead Sea Scroll), 75
Conflict of Church and Synagogue (Parkes), 183, 184, 185, 188, 268*n*1, 269*n*8
Constantine, 176, 179, 187, 188
Constantinople, 127, 219, 225, 237
Corinth, 168
Cortes, Hernando, 240
Cossacks, 242
Crassus (proconsul), 96
Crescas, Hasdai ibn (philosopher), 200
Crucifixion, 111, 168, 171, 180
Crusades, 27, 222, 226, 229, 231–32
Cumanus (procurator), 117
Cuspius Fadus (procurator), 116
Cyprus, 136–37
Cyrenaica, 97, 136
Cyrus, 35, 39, 42, 45, 68

Index

Damascus, 116, 180
Damascus Document (sectarian book), 71
Daniel, 38, 45, 48, 78, 86; messianic ideas in, 66, 68–70, 73–74, 106
Darius, 35, 39, 42, 68, 91
David (king), 21, 23, 32, 42, 59, 86, 181
Dead Sea Scrolls, 48, 54, 58, 60, 66–67, 70–71, 75, 78, 84, 140, 141, 180
Destruction (of Temple): and legend of Messiah, 73; by Nebuchadnezzar, 25, 33, 35, 42, 46*n*; by Titus, 11, 35, 37, 44, 91, 99, 124–26, 145
Deuteronomy, 22, 42
Diaspora, 6, 8, 14, 19, 26, 41, 45–46, 49–50, 90, 176, 192, 224; in Hellenistic and Roman times, 10, 37, 55, 57, 63, 82–83, 136, 172; in Holy Land, 14–17, 175–76
Domitian (brother of Titus), 127, 139
Donin, Hayim Halevy, 269*n*5
Dio Cassius (historian), 135–36, 145, 147*n*
Diocletian, 185–86
Dionysus, 74
Drusilla (princess), 117
Dualism, 75
Dubnow, Simon, 249
Elijah, 23, 147
Elon, Amos, 270*n*8
Elysian Fields, 78
En-Gedi, 16, 140, 143
England, 229, 233, 245
Enoch, 47–48
Enoch, 69–70, 70*n*, 72, 74, 76, 78
Epicurus, 62
Epistle of Barnabas, 138*n*
Esau, *see* Idumea
Essenes, 66, 78
Esther, 21, 23, 24, 209; *see also* Purim
Ethiopic translations of early books, 66, 69
Eucharist, 180
Euripides, 57
Europe, Eastern, 237, 245, 247–52, 256
Eusebius, 130, 135–36, 147*n*, 189, 269*n*9
Exilarch (in Babylonia), 176, 221
Exodus, 30–1, 53, 57
Ezekiel, 48, 68, 72
Ezekiel (Egyptian-Jewish poet), 57
Ezra, 38–42, 44, 52–53, 55, 64, 78, 90, 95, 154, 155
Ezra, 20, 27, 53
Ezra, IV (apocalyptic), 107, 135

Early Church, The (Chadwick), 187, 269*n*15
Ecclesiastes, 24, 57, 59–62
Edom, *see* Idumea
Egypt, 21, 27, 30–31, 52, 54, 63*n*, 83–84, 92, 99, 100, 119; Jewish community of, 57, 63, 97, 114, 136, 139, 172, 219, 221, 252
Eighteen Benedictions, 155, 170, 206
Eleazar b. Simon (rebel leader), 122
Eleazar Macabee, *see* Macabee, Eleazar
Eliezer ben Hyrcanus (rabbi), 134
Felix (procurator), 117, 118
Festus (procurator), 118
Finkelstein, Louis, 265*n*2
Flaccus (prefect), 114
Flavius Silva (general), 127
Florus (procurator), 118
IV Ezra (apocalyptic), 107, 135
France, 228, 233, 243, 246; and Alliance schools, 252
Frankists, 242
Free will: Ben Sira on, 62; rabbinic views of, 63
Freud, Sigmund, 13

Index

Galba (emperor), 123
Galicia, 231
Galilee, 88, 98, 100, 114, 142, 161; rebellions in, 98, 102–3, 112, 117, 147; Roman-Jewish War, 120–22
Galuth (exile), 18, 27, 29, 35, 37, 45
Gamala, town of, 122
Gamaliel family, 104, 106, 115, 116, 161, 165; Simon ben, 122, 175; *see also* Judah Ha-Nasi
Gaon of Vilna, 242–3
Genesis, 47, 69
Genizah, in Cairo, 60, 71
Germany: early period in, 193, 228–30, 232–34, 237, 243; nineteenth and twentieth centuries, 200–1, 244, 246, 248, 250–51; under Nazis, 7, 214–16
Gerousia (Jewish council), 58
Gershom (rabbi), 230
Gilbert, Martin, 251–52
Ginzburg, H. L., 69*n*
Gish-Halav, Johanan of (rebel), 121–22, 126, 127
Gnosticism, 74, 76, 186
Goitein, S. D., 220, 270*n*4
Golan, 122
Gospels, 55, 72, 76–77, 102–4, 161; and Pharisees, 64, 91, 95, 111, 160
Graetz, Heinrich, *History of the Jews,* 138 *n,* 267*n*7
Granada, 222–23
Gray, W. D., 267*n*8
Greece: closeness and conflicts, 51–52, 58, 63; and Egyptian Jews, 57, 59; influences on Jews, 18, 49, 52–53, 57, 60, 74–75, 80
Greek cities, 87, 96, 100
Gutmann, Joseph, 265*n*3

Hades, 74
Hadrian, 82, 135, 137, 138, 139; edicts against Judaism by, 144, 159; and rebuilding of Temple, 138, 139, 145
Haftarah, 23
Haggadah for Passover, 73, 209, 260
Haggai, 45
Halakah (law), 73, 105, 154, 185, 201
Halevi, Judah, 223–24
Haman, 24, 209
Hananiah (rabbi), 145
Ha-Nasi, Judah, *see* Gamaliel family
Hanina ben Dosa (rabbi), 77
Hanukkah, 27, 41, 87, 137, 209, 260–61
Harnack, Adolf van, 184, 185
Hasidei Ashkenaz, 232
Hasidim, in Maccabean times, 56, 61, 64, 66–67, 78, 89, 91
Hasidism, 27, 195, 205, 216–17, 242, 251
Hasmoneans, 35, 37, 44, 53, 56, 82, 90–93, 96, 99, 114
Hazor, 32
Hebron, 31, 88
Hell, 79; *see also* She'ol, Hades
Hellenism, 35, 38, 50–79 passim, 80, 85
Hengel, Martin, 54, 55, 62, 78, 265*n*2
Herod, 82, 90, 92–93, 97–102, 106–7, 114, 128
Herod Antipas (son of Herod), 103, 108, 111
Herodian Dynasty, 103, 119, 158, 172
Herodium (fortress), 127, 142
Herzl, Theodor, 250
Herzog, Yaacov, 150, 267*n*24
Hezekiah (rebel), 98, 102, 107
Hillel (rabbi), 71, 90, 100, 122, 132, 175–76, 212
History of Israel (Bright), 46*n,* 264*n*
History of Israel (Noth), 46*n*
History of the Jews (Graetz), 138*n*
Hitler, 194, 214
Holocaust, 7, 27, 244, 247, 251
Honi (the circle drawer), 77
Horowitz, Abraham (rabbi), 241
Howe, Irving, *World of Our Fathers,* 248
Hungary, 245
Hyrcanus (Hasmonean prince), 95–99, 159

Hyrcanus, John (the Hasmonean), 92–93
Hyrcanus (of Tobiah family), 84

Ibn Crescas, Hasdai (philosopher), 200
Ibn Ezra, Moses, 223
Ibn Nagrela, Samuel, 222
Ibn Shaprut, Hisdai, 222
Ibn Tibbon family, 228
Idumea, Edom and Esau, 31, 49, 53, 82, 87–88, 92, 96, 103, 120, 122, 179
Immortality, 79
India, 223
Inquisition, 27, 222, 225
Iran, 27, 252
Iraq, 252
Isaac (patriarch), 229
Isaiah, 4, 23, 45, 53
Ishmael (rabbi), 134
Ishmael (son of Abraham), 219
Israel: ancient state of, 29–33, 42; modern state of, 8, 14–16, 27, 49*n,* 54*n,* 88, 141–42, 144, 149, 194, 245–46, 249, 251–56; relation to Diaspora, 14–17, 255–56
Isserles, Moses (rabbi), 241
Italy, 99, 219, 240–41
Iyyar, 46

Jacob (patriarch), 30
Jacobs, Louis, 157*n,* 159–60, 269*n*3
Jaffa, 97–98
James (brother of Jesus), 109
Jamnia, 119, 121, 123, 134, 169
Jason (high priest), 84–85
Jason, *Maccabees,* 57
Jeremiah, 21, 23, 25
Jericho, 28, 31, 100
Jerome, 147*n*
Jerusalem: destruction by Nebuchadnezzar, 25, 33, 35, 42, 68, 74, 218; destruction of, by Titus, 11, 35, 37, 44, 66, 79, 82, 124–27, 134, 169; dream of restoration, 10–11, 13, 125, 134, 146, 193; importance of, to Jews, 6, 28, 42, 53, 55–56, 65, 81; Roman involvement in, 37, 96–97, 117, 119–20; under Ptolemies and Seleucids, 37, 49, 55–56, 85–88
Jesus, 18, 35, 55, 76–77, 99, 108, 160–61, 166, 180–81; attitude of, to 'the Law,' 108, 154, 159; as Messiah, 102, 106, 109, 162–65, 183; as political rebel, 108, 111, 164; relationship of, to Pharisees, 95, 172; trial and death of, 82, 88, 101, 103–10, 149, 161; *see also* Christianity
Jesus the Jew (Vermes), 162–64, 265*n*12
Jethro, 26
Jews: attitude toward Jesus and Church, 12, 146, 151, 182, 185; distinctiveness of, 3–5, 9–13, 37, 83, 213–14, 228; history and kinship of, 6–10, 17, 34, 37, 83, 136, 193–94, 202, 213–16; in Holy Land and Diaspora, 15, 33, 37, 53, 55; in Muslim world, 12–13, 199, 218–24, 236, 250; population figures for, 242, 245–47, 251, 254–56; as world people, 11, 14–15, 19
Jezebel, 23
Job, 19, 21, 23, 26, 48
Johanan ben Zaccai, 121–24, 126, 134
John, 111, 161, 163, 166, 168, 180, 182
John the Baptist, 74, 108–9, 111, 147, 162
John Hyrcanus (Hasmonean), 92–93
Jonathan (high priest), 118
Jonathan Maccabee, 88–89, 92
Jonathan ben Torta (rabbi), 147–48
Jordan, and Trans-Jordan, 31, 55, 87
Joseph ben Gorion (Defender of Jerusalem, 120, 122
Joseph ben Matthias, *see* Josephus

Index

Josephus, 35, 41, 43, 66, 72, 78, 86, 93, 97, 99, 101, 103–4, 107–10, 112–3, 114, 117, 119, 123, 125, 126, 128–30, 135, 166, 218; *Book of Jossipon,* 41; on Jesus, 109–110; on martyrdom, 158–9; Roman-Jewish War, 120–22, 124, 129–30
Joshua, 14, 23, 30–31, 32, 46, 86
Joshua ben Galgula, 142–43
Joshua ben Hananiah (rabbi), 134, 138
Josiah (king), 42
Jossipon (Josephus), 99
Jotapata (fortress), 121–22
Jubilees, book of, 48, 70*n,* 107
Judah, ancient kingdom of, 31–32, 42
Judah (b. Simon) Ha-Nasi, 175–76, 198; *see also* Gamaliel family
Judah of Galilee (rebel against Rome), 102–3, 107, 116, 117
Judah Halevi, 223–24
Judaism: attitude toward Christian dogma, 151–53, 156, 161, 166–68, 173, 179–80, 183, 185, 197; Covenant with God, 21, 32–38, 61, 69, 79, 134, 169, 196–98; credos, 9, 18, 196–201, 205; dietary laws in, 210–11; and intimacy with God, 203–4, 206; and Jewish-Christian conflicts, 152, 168, 170, 173–74, 176; the 'Law' and prayer, 65, 73, 77, 83, 174, 206–7; Messiah, and role in, 49, 71, 146, 201, 239–40; and proselytism, 172–73; and rabbinic Judaism after the 'Destruction,' 38, 69, 123, 131, 134, 144, 146, 157, 174, 178; and reform movement, 194, 200–1; rituals, festivals, and fasts in, 18, 192–212; secularism in, 194, 249, 250; worship at Jerusalem Temple, 37, 42–44, 56, 169, 206; *see also* Pharisees; *Torah*
Judah Maccabee, 86, 89–93
Judea (Roman province), 43, 49, 87, 103, 114, 119, 138
Judges, 23, 31
Julius Caesar, 96–98
Julius Severus (general), 140
Justin Martyr, 171*n,* 183, 184
Juvenal, 130

Kabbalah (mystical teachings), 67, 195, 216–17, 232, 240
Kaddish, 174, 202, 207
Katz, Jacob, 270*n* 1
Kennizites, 31
Kibbutz, 16
Kiddush, on wine, 207–8
Kiddush hashem (martyrdom), 232
Kings, 46, 46*n*
King's College, Cambridge, 202
Kol Nidre, 202, 261
Kosher, *see* Judaism, dietary laws in
Krauss, Samuel, 138*n*

Lamentations, 21, 24–25, 214; Midrash on, 135, 137, 143, 145
Lateran Councils, 188, 233–34
Law, The, 134, 155, 157, 159–60, 178, 181
Lebanon, 114
Lemberg, 251
Lestchinsky, Jacob, 254–5
Letter of Aristeas, 57
Levites, 43, 45
Leviticus, 53
Lewis, Bernard, 90, 266*n*
Lilianus (rebel), 137
Lincoln, 229
Lithuania, 236–37, 242
Logos, role in Christianity, 64*n,* 167–68
Lord's Prayer, 155
Lucius Quietus (general), 136–37
Luke, 112
Luria, Isaac (mystic), 216, 240
Luria, Solomon, 241

Index

Ma'ase merkabah (mystic ideas), 68, 70
Maccabee, Eleazar, 88
Maccabee, Jonathan, 88–89, 92
Maccabee, Judah, 86, 89–93
Maccabee, Simon, 88, 92
Maccabees, 27, 37, 40, 45, 51, 54, 56, 60–61, 63, 69, 86–89, 91–92, 159, 166, 172, 209, 260–61; *Books of the Maccabees,* 57, 86; and dependence on Rome, 82, 88, 92–93; origin of name, 87*n*
Maccabees (Jason), 57
Maccoby, Hyam, 268*n*11
Macedonians, 52, 54
Machaerus (fortress), 127
Magi, 48
Magic, 49, 76
Magnesia, bottle of, 85
Maimonides, 13, 198–203, 212, 222, 228
Mainz, 228
Mantel, H. D., 268*n*1
Manual of Discipline (Dead Sea Scroll), 71
Marcion, 186
Margolis, Max, 148
Mark, 77, 105, 106, 180
Mark Anthony, 98, 100, 102
Marranos, 225, 238, 240, 246
Martyrdom, 86, 124, 145, 158, 231, 232; and Christian martyrs, 159, 184, 186
Marx, Alexander, 148
Mary, 99, 167–68
Masada, 27, 28, 41, 61, 98–99, 125, 127–30, 135
Mattathias (Maccabee leader), 87
Mattathias Antigonus (Hasmonean), 98
Matthew, 99, 111, 171–72
Matzah, 209, 259
Mazda, 47–48
Megiddo, 28
Mendelssohn, Moses, 200
Mendes family, 239*n*
Menelaus (high priest), 85
Menorah (lamp), 209
Messiah, 46, 49, 67, 70–74, 101–2, 146–47, 166, 199, 239; and rebels in Galilee, 72, 107; Sabbatai Zevi, 25, 27, 240, 242; warlike, 74, 106–7
Mexico, 240
Mezuzah (on doorpost), 211
Midian, 31
Midrash, 66, 73, 135, 148; on Bar Kokhba war, 139, 145–49; on Roman-Jewish war, 123, 128
Milik, Josef, T. (Father), *Les Grottes de Muraba'at,* 141, 143, 267*n*13
Minerva, 52
Miriam (wife of Herod), 98
Mishnah, 132, 142, 153, 175, 206
Mithridates, 96
Mitnaggedim (opponents), 242
Mitzvah (moral duty), 211
Moab, 24, 29, 53
Mohammed, 218, 219, 219*n*, 222
Money lending, 222, 232–33
Montefiore, Moses, 238
Morocco, 221, 222, 252
Moses, 21–2, 26, 28–30, 38, 63, 67, 70*n*, 90, 219
Muslim world, 177, 191, 218, 224, 250
Mysticism, 65–67, 71, 74, 205, 232

Nabatean, 133, 172
Nahal Hever (Dead Sea area), 141
Napolean, 243
Nasi, Joseph, 238–39, 239*n*
Nazism, 194, 214–17, 251
Nebuchadnezzar, 20, 33, 39, 50, 68, 74, 218
Nehemiah, 38, 39; as leader, 20, 41, 45, 55
Nero, 121, 123
Netherlands, 240, 246
Netira family, 222
Neubauer, Adolf, 266*n*4
Neusner, Jacob, 266*n*, 268*n*
New York, 241

Index

Nicanor, 89
Nicean Council, 186–87
Ninth of Ab, 25, 124–5, 137, 209
Nippur, 45
Nissan, 46
Noah, 70
North Africa, 136, 219, 221, 225, 246
Noth, Martin, *History of Israel, The*, 46 *n*, 264*n*

Octavian, *see* Augustus
Omar, 49
Onias (high priests), 84
Oriental Jewry, 252–53, 255
Orpheus (Orphic mysteries), 48, 74–75, 78
Ottoman Empire, 214, 219, 225, 237–40, 242

Pangar (Arab leader), 126
Pappus (rebel), 137
Parixes, and James Parkes's *Conflict of Church and Synagogue, The*, 183, 184, 185, 188, 268*n*1, 269*n*10
Parthians, 87, 96, 137, 176
Pascal, Blaise, 81
Passover, 25, 53, 208–9, 259–60; Seder for, 25, 196, 207, 256; and trial of Jesus, 103–4
Patriarchs, 29
Paul, 104, 116, 118, 159, 161, 166–68, 178, 180 1, 191
Pella (Trans-Jordan), 169
Pentecost, 24
Perea (Trans-Jordan), 103, 107
Persepolis, 91
Persians, 35, 75, 80, 91; and encouraged return from exile, 39, 43, 49; Zoroastrianism, 47–48
Peter (apostle), 106, 163
Pharisees: attitude toward Jesus, 106, 111, 160–61, 168; and attitude toward rebellion, 107, 119–20; and attitude toward Rome, 81, 114; and early rabbinism, 52–53, 57, 59, 61, 63–64, 67–68, 71, 79, 82–83, 89–91, 94–95, 100; and observance of Torah, 64–65, 91, 95, 106, 132, 154, 159–72; origin of name, 91; political influence on, 91, 93–94, 98, 100, 114; and role in Sanhedrin, 101, 104–5, 116
Phazael, 98, 126
Philip (son of Herod), 103
Philippi, battle of, 98
Philistines, 88
Philo of Alexandria, 57, 63, 112–4, 117, 166–7
Phoenicians, 52, 55, 63*n*
Pilate (procurator), 106, 109–12, 117, 161
Plato, 63, 78
Pliny, 130
Plutarch, 130
Podolia, Poland, 242
Pogroms, 27, 214, 225, 247
Poland, 58, 231, 235–7, 240–1, 242
Pompey, 37, 82, 96–97, 103
Portugal, 214
Potok, Chaim, 148
Prague, 231
Priestly document, 46
Priests: interest of, in Hellenization, 85; and social class, 44, 46, 60, 71, 83–85, 134
Prophets, 46*n*, 71, 73
Proselytes, 53, 172–73
Provence, 228
Proverbs, 21, 25, 26, 57, 59, 61, 208
Psalms, 21, 23–24, 29, 30, 45, 71
Pseudepigrapha, 67
Ptolemy, dynasty of, 35, 54, 60, 83, 84
Publicani: tax-farmers, 60, 103; *see also* Tobiah family
Publius Marcellus (governor), 140

Purim, 24, 209, 261
Pythagoras, 63, 78

Quirinius (Roman prefect), 107
Qumran (site of Dead Sea sect), 71

Rabbinism, *see* Pharisees, and early rabbinism; Judaism, rabbinic Judaism
Rabbis: attitude of, toward mystical ideas, 49, 66, 72, 162; emergence of, 44, 64, 95, 100, 132–34, 159–60; and rabbinic Judaism, 18, 33, 38, 152–53, 157
Rabin, C., 265*n*6
Raphael, *see* Angels
Rashi, 228
Resurrection: of Jesus, 164, 168, 180; Jewish ideas on, 78–79, 199, 201
Revelation, 21, 199–201
Rhineland, 228
Rhodes, 100
Rome, 18, 35, 37, 80–82, 99, 101, 111, 115; and destruction of Jerusalem, 9, 99; law and economic development under, 82–83, 87–88, 104; revolts against, by Jews, 10, 27, 43, 53, 98, 107, 110, 135, 138; Roman-Jewish War, 41, 81, 90, 100, 103, 113–30
Rosh Hashanah (New Year), 198, 209, 261
Roth, Cecil, 148, 229, 267*n*20, 270*n*7
Rothschild family, 238
Russia, Jews in, 58, 214, 245
Ruth, 23, 24

Sabbatai Zevi, 27, 75, 240, 242
Sabbath, 43, 45, 63, 85; observance of, 25, 26, 73, 142, 160, 207–8
Sadducees, 79, 94, 154; role in Sanhedrin, 104, 109, 111, 116, 134
Safed, 216, 239
Safrai, S., 268*n*3
Salome Alexandra, 93–95
Salonica, 225, 232, 238, 240
Samaria, 103, 114, 117, 138, 172
Samuel, 23
Samuel, Maurice, 248
Sanhedrin, 95, 98–101, 104–6, 116, 120, 132, 134, 161
Sassanids (Persian dynasty), 176
Satan, 48
Saul, 23
Scapegoat, 167*n*
Schalit, Abraham, 81, 88, 101, 266*n*5
Schechter, Solomon, 71, 193
Scholem, Gershom, 67–68, 72, 75, 195, 205, 216, 244, 246, 250–51, 265*n*7, 269*n*1, 270*n*11
Schürer, Emil, 102, 109, 110, 115, 117, 266*n*6, 267*n*12
Seder, *see* Passover
Seleucid, dynasty of, 37, 43, 54, 83, 84
Seleucus, 85
Self-government, 84, 100, 103–4, 174–76
Sephardi, 238, 252, 254
Sephoris (town in Galilee), 121
Septuagint, 57, 173
Seven, role of, as number, 63*n*, 64*n*
Seventeenth of Tammuz (fast), 124
Seville, 225
Shamai (rabbi), 100
Shavuot (Pentecost), 208–9, 259–60
Shechem, 32
She'ol (post-death underworld), 78
Sh'ma, 145, 155, 197–98, 206, 211
Sicarii, 118, 123, 127, 130
Siddur (prayer book), 67
Simhath Torah, *see* Tabernacles
Simeon Bar Giora (rebel leader), 122, 126–27
Simon (rebel against Herod), 107
Simon Maccabee, 88, 92
Simon Peter (apostle), 164

Sinai, revelation at, 21, 30, 38, 70*n*
Singer, Isaac Bashevis, 248
Slavonic translation of *Enoch*, 70*n*
Socrates, and ideas credited to Moses, 63
Sodom and Gomorrah, 204
Solomon (king), 24, 25, 32, 42, 59, 92, 116
Song of Songs, 24–25
Soul, ideas on, 75, 78–79
South Africa, 246
South America, 241, 247
Spain, 199, 214, 219, 221; expulsion from, 225–26, 238, 243; golden age, 27, 223–5, 236
Speyer, 228
Starrs, 229
Stephen (apostle), 165, 168
Stoics, and Jewish thought, 49, 60, 78
Succoth, 24
Svetonius, 130
Synagogue, origins of, 45, 52, 72, 95, 154
Syria, 29, 37, 43, 55, 83–84, 87, 89, 91–93, 96–98, 102–3, 127, 139, 172, 252

Tabernacles (festive), 94, 143, 149, 159, 208–9, 259–60
Tabur (fortress), 122
Tacitus, 117, 130, 266*n*4
Talmud, 40, 66, 72, 79, 86, 133; influence and, 132, 153, 165–66, 176–77, 195
Tarfon (rabbi), 101, 134
Tarsus, 116
Tefillin (phylacteries), 211
Tekoa, 143
Temple: desecration by Antiochus IV, 86, 91; organization and meaning of, 56, 65, 134, 154; reestablishment of, under Ezra, 39, 42–3, 46*n*, 55–56; treasures of, plundered by Romans, 27, 103, 110, 112, 116, 118; *see also* Destruction (of Temple)
Tertullian, 184
Testaments of the Twelve Patriarchs, 48, 70*n*
Theudas (rebel), 116
Tiberias, 238
Tiberius (Roman emperor), 113
Tiberius Alexander (procurator), 117, 119
Tigranes, 96
Tineius Rufus (general), 139–40
Tithes, 44, 65
Titus, 37, 121, 124–29; Arch of, 127–28
Tobiad, Tobiah family, 55, 84
Torah: study of, 64, 154 (*see also* rabbinic Judaism); Written and Oral, 18, 22, 30, 32, 37, 41, 43–44, 49, 52, 57, 59, 64, 72–73, 79, 83, 90, 94–95, 131–32, 154, 186, 199, 205, 211; *see also* Bible
Toynbee, Arnold, *Crucible of Christianity, The*, 265*n*1
Trajan, 135–37
Tudela, Benjamin of (traveler), 219
Tunisia, 221, 252

Ugarit, 29
United States, 49*n*, 88, 245–47, 250, 254–56; Reform Judaism in, 193, 201
Usha (town in Galilee), 175
Usque, Samuel, 239, 239*n*

Varus (Governor of Syria), 103, 107, 136
Vermes, Geza, *Jesus the Jew*, 162–64, 265*n*12, 268*n*5
Vespasian, 103, 121, 123, 126–27, 133, 136, 145
Vienna, 13, 251
Vilna, Gaon of, 242–43
Vitellius (general), 123

Wadi Murabba'at (Dead Sea), 140
Weinreich, Max, 230–31, 270*n* 10
Wellhausen, Julius, 29
Wigoder, Geoffrey, 253–54
Winter, Paul, "Josephus on Jesus and James," 109–10
World of Our Fathers (Howe), 248
Worms, 228

Yadin, Yigael, 61, 128–29, 132, 141, 141 *n,* 143–44, 264*n* 1, 267*n* 14
Yellow badge, 233
Yemen, 252
Yiddish, 55, 223, 228–30, 245, 247–49; revival of, in Israel, 17
Yigdal, 199
Yom Kippur, 198, 209, 211, 261–62
York, 229

Zadok (high priest), 43, 94
Zadok (Pharisee, supporter of Judah's rebellion), 107
Zealots, 106, 108, 117, 122, 123, 128, 130, 135
Zechariah, 45, 48
Zeno, 60
Zeus, 78
Ziggurats, 47
Zionism, 14–16, 243, 249–50
Zohar (mystical work), 67
Zoroaster, 47–48, 220